Remembering

THE GOOD WAR

THOMAS SAYLOR

Remembering
THE GOOD WAR

MINNESOTA'S

GREATEST GENERATION

MINNESOTA HISTORICAL SOCIETY PRESS

Publication of this book was supported by a generous grant from PCL Construction Services, Inc.

www.mhspress.org

The Minnesota Historical Society Press is a member of the Association of American University Presses.

Manufactured in the United States of America

10 9 8 7 6 5 4 3 2 1

∞ The paper used in this publication meets the minimum requirements of the American National Standard for Information Sciences—Permanence for Printed Library Materials, ANSI Z39.48–1984.

International Standard Book Number 0-87351-525-0 (cloth)

Library of Congress Cataloging-in-Publication Data

Remembering the Good War : Minnesota's greatest generation / Thomas Saylor.

p. cm.

Includes bibliographical references and index.

ISBN 0-87351-525-0 (casebound : alk. paper)

1. World War, 1939–1945—Minnesota. 2. World War, 1939–1945—Personal narratives, American. 3. Minnesota—Biography. 4. Minnesota—History—1858–
5. Oral history. I. Saylor, Thomas, 1958–

D769.85.M6R74 2005
940.54'81776—dc22

2004028200

Maps on pages xxii and xxiii by Matt Kania, Map Hero, Inc.

Images on pages 6, 90, 100, 114, 118, 173, 233, 236, and 284 are from Minnesota Historical Society collections. Unless otherwise noted, all other illustrations are from private collections.

Permission to use poem on pages 215–16 granted by Ken Firnstahl

Book design and composition by Diane Gleba Hall

Contents

Preface

WORLD WAR II—which began in Asia in 1937, spread to Europe by 1939, and ended in 1945—was arguably the transforming event of the twentieth century, fundamentally altering power structures and unleashing forces few foresaw when the war began. This book paints a representative picture of the different ways women and men were themselves transformed by this cataclysmic experience, focusing in particular on how the war affected the individual lives of people in Minnesota and the Upper Midwest. The perspectives are endless; the range of emotional responses equally so: no one, it seems, emerged from the 1941–46 period unchanged. For some it was an exhilarating time they have since been unable to equal; for others these were years of stress and uncertainty; for yet others this was a tragic period that has left deep scars.

Over the past several decades, multitudes of books documenting U.S. experiences during World War II have appeared, reflecting a long-standing interest in the period. With *Remembering the Good War*, yet another title is added to the list. Why now? First, I believe we have a societal responsibility to create for future generations a permanent firsthand record, as complete as possible, of the men and women who formed—and were formed by—this era. In order to learn from the past, to employ history as a decision-making tool, we must assemble the historical record. Second, on a more practical level, is the fact that this generation of Americans is rapidly dying off. Indeed, an eighteen-year-old GI or Home Front high school senior of the war's final year, 1945, is nearing eighty years of age. We do not have the luxury of waiting another decade before compiling works such as this.

This book contributes to the existing literature in these two respects, but it also goes several steps further. Many oral history books have covered different aspects of the military conflict; others have focused on the Home Front: relatively few have sought to synthesize the two, to document the war's broad range as it affected civilians and soldiers alike, to compare and contrast their experiences in the same volume, to see World War II as one conflict experienced in many ways. This book meets this challenge in five ways. First, it records the experiences of women and men who spent the war years outside the military—farmers, homemakers, workers, students, teachers, military spouses, and others—and in the process emphasizes the many and varied contributions made by women and adds their voices to the record.

Second, this volume documents the experiences of veterans in different service branches and theaters of operation and in a broad representation of occupations—pilots and paratroopers, but also army privates and chaplains, submarine crewmen and navy WAVES, mechanics and nurses. Some went through intense combat; others neither saw the enemy nor fired a gun.

Third, and importantly, this collection aims to increase awareness of and make more accessible the experiences and contributions of people of color in Minnesota during the early 1940s, when the state had a level of diversity often overlooked. In these pages are the memories of African Americans, Japanese Americans, and Mexican Americans from different walks of life.

World War II has been memorialized in the United States as "the Good War," the noble cause. Indeed, in many ways it was: European society was delivered from the horror of National Socialist Germany, and Asia was spared Japan's economic and military control. Many proud stories have been recounted, and in the collective national memory 1941–45 has advanced to icon status. In this self-congratulatory rush, many darker sides of the war have been pushed aside or ignored. These recollections and experiences, sometimes unpleasant, need to be included in our historical consciousness, and they form a fundamental part of this volume. So, amid the good and the positive—and there is much of both—we confront hate and racism, cowardice and depression, self-doubt and loss of faith, mental breakdowns and nightmares. World War II was all of these things, too.

Finally, *Remembering the Good War* is structured to maintain a focus on both civilians and veterans and to encourage the reader to see as a single conflict the challenges these two populations faced under distinct circumstances, their vastly different experiences always interlocked, like the strands of a spider's web. Thus, an initial chapter presents memories of and reactions to Japan's December 1941 attack on Pearl Harbor, the speakers ranging from those on active duty to high school students. The narrative then leads readers in separate yet parallel directions, with chapters two and four devoted to the military experience of men and women stateside, in Europe, and in the Pacific and chapter three detailing the varied undertakings of civilians at their jobs, on the farm, or as homemakers and mothers. Three final chapters, which again blend the memories of civilians and veterans, explore several human dimensions of the war, consider various perspectives on the year 1945, and allow men and women to reflect on that period from a twenty-first-century vantage point. Although introductions and some context are provided, these authorial interventions have been kept to a minimum so that the focus can remain squarely on the words of the participants.

But this modest book has its limits, and those should be addressed here, too. Although the initial goal was to make this study as inclusive as its pages would allow, interviews with people from all walks of life soon made clear that it would simply not be possible to adequately deal with certain categories of experience. Specifically, the experiences of Native Americans demand a separate volume. More than three years with this project have just begun to teach me what enormous burdens and challenges these Americans still face; whatever could be included in these pages would perform an injustice. Additionally, prisoners of war, especially those held by the

Japanese, endured a form of psychological and physical torment unrelated to that of any other civilian or veteran. Their experiences cannot be adequately conveyed in the few pages of this book.

FROM THE BEGINNING, the goals of this project were clear: to collect, evaluate, and permanently preserve the experiences and memories of Minnesotans during the World War II years of 1941 through 1946. For the purposes of this project, "Minnesotan" was broadly defined to include those who were born and/or raised in the state, who relocated here during the war years, or, in a few cases, who have resided here for a meaningful period of time; the term was interpreted to be inclusive, not exclusive. Interviewees were born in Minnesota but also in the upper midwestern states of North and South Dakota, Wisconsin, and Iowa and in the Canadian province of Saskatchewan; several are from more distant locations.

The geographic constraint imposed on this volume may yield a distinctly Minnesotan—or even upper midwestern—World War II experience. Certainly there are features that differentiate the state's war experience from that of other regions. In the aftermath of the 1941 attack on Pearl Harbor, there was no panic as in California, no fear of a possible Japanese invasion. After all, the Midwest was more than a thousand miles from the Pacific Coast. And with rare exceptions during the immediate post–Pearl Harbor period, when the extent of the potential danger was still unknown, Minnesotans endured almost no emergency blackouts or air raid drills. In addition, without a Japanese American population to speak of in 1941, Minnesota witnessed no deportations or incarcerations of American citizens of Japanese descent. Just the opposite, actually: in 1942 the U.S. Army established at Camp Savage, south of the Twin Cities, a facility to train Japanese linguists, for which Japanese American servicemen, like one interviewed for this book, were *brought to* Minnesota.

Additional issues of ethnicity and race mark differences between the Upper Midwest and other regions. In the early 1940s, Minnesota's population contained more people of German heritage than of any other ethnic or national group. While Nazi sympathies were minimal or kept to oneself and represented no threat to the war effort, more than one woman among those interviewed recalled German grandparents being upset about America fighting the land of their birth. In contrast, one Minnesota woman described her German-born father, then in his early forties, trying desperately to join the U.S. military to prove his loyalty to his adopted land. He failed in the endeavor but pressured her to enlist, which she eventually did.

Racism directed against blacks and, to a lesser extent, those of Mexican heritage is another notable difference. With many military training facilities located in the South, young men from Minnesota were exposed to locations, people, and cultures they had not encountered previously. African Americans and Mexican Americans suffered racial discrimination in Minnesota, but the overt nature—and the extent of it—in the South was new to most. Blacks, of course, served in a still-segregated military that limited them to specific jobs (navy) or kept them in separate units (army). Many African Americans interviewed for this book were taken aback and enraged by racism in the South, but their reactions varied—from internalizing the anger, to trying to get even, to acceptance that things were not going to change right then, much as they might like them to. Of the Mexican Americans whose stories are included here, most claimed that they expected to endure discrimination in the South but found conditions on the whole to be acceptable; the causes behind their experiences and the reasons for their reactions are varied and complex.

White men and women in the service also noticed this discrimination and commented on it for this book. Here, too, reactions varied—a few admit to their own racist tendencies, some chose to ignore it, others realized they were rather powerless, a few remember making their opinions known. Several who spoke out recall southerners telling them bluntly to mind their own affairs. The responses and range of emotions from people of different racial and ethnic groups are not markedly different from what we know about how people in other regions reacted to similar situations during this time, but their distinct memories—of specific incidents that have stayed with them for more than fifty years—suggest that encountering institutionalized racism had a lasting impact.

In many other ways the World War II experience in Minnesota resembled larger national trends. The economy boomed as industrial firms retooled for war production—Minneapolis Moline and

International Harvester are just two of many companies that quickly shifted to supplying products for the military. Jobs were plentiful, too, and the unemployment of the 1930s soon became merely a memory as, for example, Iron Range mining firms worked around the clock producing iron ore. Numerous Mexican Americans in St. Paul benefited from higher rates of employment as well as from access to better-paying jobs. Women, many employed in industry for the first time, joined Minnesota's factories and workshops in record numbers. Quite a few of those interviewed for this project recall their mothers taking a job outside the home—and causing seismic shifts in household patterns. Finally, mirroring a national trend that saw African Americans moving by the millions to northern industrial centers, the Twin Cities registered an increase in its black population. Several interviewees came to the state during the war for jobs—and stayed.

The economic upswing had other benefits, too. Employment opportunities on the West Coast—in shipyards, aircraft factories, and military bases—worked like a magnet and drew the state's young people away. In this book are recollections of young women who left home for California and Washington, and for Georgia and the East Coast, and realized that the world is bigger than North Minneapolis or rural Palisade.

But above all it was the military that provided the opportunity for tens of thousands of young men and women to leave small towns, farms, and cities for points previously unknown. Not all left willingly, to be sure, but once in the service they saw much of the globe. Among the sample of people whose stories are told in these pages, there were duty stations from the Aleutian Islands to rural China, from the hills of Okinawa to the skies over Italy, from the bombed-out cities of Germany to the jungles of the Philippines, from a hospital in France to a battleship in Tokyo Bay. The experiences were in more than a few cases life altering, and although many returned to places like Chisholm, Moorhead, International Falls, and St. Paul, they were changed in ways that sometimes took years to decipher.

Finally, there is the human side that links Minnesota's World War II experience to the national story. Leaving home for the first time, worrying about loved ones in the military, being a working mother, landing on a beach during a Pacific Island invasion, treating wounded in a military hospital—these parts of the war were shared with millions of others across the country and are a major reason this conflict represents the unifying experience spoken of by veterans and civilians alike.

THE STORIES collected in this book are based on hundreds of hours of interviews. The interview process was sometimes easy and at other times challenging. Initial contact with an interviewee was usually a telephone conversation, during which I described the themes I wished to cover during the interview. With some personal information, I was often able to do background reading that provided a framework for our time together.

All interviews were conducted in person, one-on-one, and usually in the individual's home or apartment or my office at Concordia University—but also in a hotel lobby in Duluth, a corporate conference room in New Brighton, the private library of former Minnesota governor Elmer L. Andersen, a senior center in Hibbing, several nursing homes or long-term care facilities around the state, and a handful of restaurants. Only follow-up information or corrections were submitted by mail or e-mail or collected by telephone. These parameters required substantial amounts of travel around Minnesota and parts of the Upper Midwest, but the advantage was personal contact with each woman or man. The ability to sit across a table from someone, to share a cup of coffee or lunch, or to glance through scrapbooks of photographs or news clippings individualized each interview, helped build a level of trust, and increased the quality of our time together. On the personal side, it also permitted the establishment of several ongoing friendships.

Once we got together for the interview—and the most productive sessions were more like conversations than interviews—some themes were the same for everyone, whether civilian or veteran: memories of and reactions to the attack on Pearl Harbor, for example, and the opportunities and challenges of the postwar world. Of course there were different themes, too, depending on whether one spent time on a farm, in a bomber over Germany, as a homemaker, in a factory, or ducking bullets on a Pacific island.

During the interview itself, the list of themes provided a starting point, a guidepost really, but even so, no two interviews were ever the same—some women and men had a lot to say on some subjects, while others did not. Some conversations lasted one hour, most were around two, and several went more than three. In general the interviews with combat veterans proved the most complicated, as emotional recollections and the memories of terrible situations or comrades killed or wounded made for the occasional difficult moment. Initially, many of these men were somewhat reluctant to participate, but when they saw a typical transcript or spoke with a friend or veteran who already had been interviewed, almost all were willing to speak with me. Indeed, of nearly ninety veterans approached about participation, only three declined to be interviewed.

Difficult as these interviews may have been, after the session was over many combat veterans stated (or wrote to me later) that they were glad they had decided to share their memories, recollections, and experiences. One, an army infantryman who fought in Europe, said he feels a responsibility to tell his story because society seems to be forgetting what his generation contributed; another, a former POW of the Germans, finds talking about his prison camp time therapeutic; and a former Pacific theater medic wrote that during his interview he finally shared memories that had been bottled up since the war's end—an experience he called cathartic.

For Home Front civilians, interviews generally presented fewer difficulties. Many felt the impact of war—brothers or relatives in the service, worrying parents, deaths of loved ones, rationing, relocation across the continent to take a new job or join a military spouse—but talking about these aspects of their lives came much more easily.

IN SELECTING EXCERPTS for this book, I endeavored to verify information provided by interviewees. For those in the military, discharge papers confirm dates of service, awards, duty stations, and more; unit histories and reference works can supply the larger picture; and other interviewees can corroborate some recollections. For Home Front civilians, there is no single document that contains so much information, but sources such as high school and college yearbooks, local papers, other interviewees, family members, neighbors, and letters are useful. Ultimately, though, it is simply not possible to confirm everything shared in the course of nearly 140 interviews. Thus, errors, intentional or unintentional, are almost certainly contained in the pages of this book.

But this book is oral history, not an academic monograph or a traditional piece of historical research. It is conceived primarily as a memory book, a book of recollections. And memory through its very nature presents its own difficulties. Noted scholar Samuel Hynes, author of *The Soldiers' Tale: Bearing Witness to Modern War,* writes that "though memory is the muse and source of memoirs it is untrustworthy, not only as a source of history but as a story of self. It selects and colors the shapes and feelings of the past that it offers us" (23). The eminent oral historian Studs Terkel once put it more simply: memory is fallible. Yet the man or woman who was there, Hynes correctly asserts, adds his or her own relative truth, and it is by considering the aggregate of these recollections that we are able to arrive at "the sum of witnesses, the collective tale" (25). The collective tale of *Remembering the Good War* will by necessity constitute an imperfect record, but as we are unable to question every actor on that far-away stage, now more than fifty years distant, it is the best we are able to compile.

In talking with people on this subject for more than two years, I followed the approach of the collective tale. The goal: assemble a representative mosaic of the World War II years based on people's perceptions of what was happening around them, their reactions to events large and small, their feelings about particular situations, their emotional responses—all elements of oral history and part of its enduring power. I don't pretend to put forth a definitive picture of these years; I also don't think it's possible to have just one picture.

Taken together, these interviews provide a tapestry of Americans and American life during an important period in history. The whole is made up of the perspectives and memories of many individuals: the reader is challenged to visualize her or his own image of that era, to draw his or her own conclusions about how the war changed various aspects of American society. There was no single World War II experience, but thousands of different ones that depended on a multitude of factors. People who had similar experiences may remember them—and emerge from them—in quite different ways.

One challenge as I assembled this manuscript was deciding whose stories would be told. I talked with far more people and collected far more information than I could possibly include in a single volume. In all, these interviews generated almost 300 hours of tape and 5,500 pages of transcript—of which less than ten percent appears in the pages of this book. Broad representation being the objective, if several people had similar experiences, not all could be included; instead, one or two examples were selected. With these facts in mind, I wish to thank everyone who participated in the Oral History Project of the World War II Years, especially those whom I have had to exclude from this volume for lack of space. Your contributions are very much appreciated.

The excerpts presented in this book are the interviewees' own words. To make the excerpts read smoothly and transition clearly from one thought to the next, some necessary editing has been done. All *uhs, ahs,* and repetitions of words have been eliminated, unless the latter changed the flavor of what was said. While a theme may have been discussed more than once in the course of a conversation, yielding some shorter pieces of several sentences that could stand alone, I generally selected those pieces that dealt with a single topic and wove them together into a single longer narrative. My questions and responses have been removed to further provide an uninterrupted piece of text. Despite these caveats, every attempt has been made to preserve the original style of the interviewee, that person's particular way of speaking. Anything added for context stands in block parentheses.

THIS RESEARCH PROJECT has easily been the most rewarding of any I have undertaken. I will long remember the wonderful people who opened both their homes for me and their memories for this project; today I count many among my friends. Some experiences especially stand out. Former schoolteacher Vivian McMorrow and I had a heartwarming conversation in which she talked about losing her husband, Ralph Gland, in the invasion of France in 1944 and how for decades, after she remarried and had a family, she kept photos and a scrapbook hidden away in a small box. After we finished talking, she got out the box and for more than half an hour we sat quietly and looked through their last photos together, the telegram informing her of Ralph's death, and other memories. Army veteran Earl Nolte humbly discussed serious injuries he suffered in a 1944 Pacific island invasion but spent little time on his actions that fateful day in the Philippines. Only later, in documents supplied by his family, did I learn how he had saved lives, been awarded the Silver Star for bravery, and in 1945 was nominated for the Congressional Medal of Honor. He inspired through humility and selflessness.

A final word, if I may: take time to have a conversation with a member of this generation. They are your friends, neighbors, and family members. Simply ask what they did during the early 1940s, during the war. Perhaps the words will start slowly, or they will tell you, "Oh, I didn't do much." But wait. And listen. The result can be a most rewarding experience for all involved.

Acknowledgments

D URING THE INTERVIEWING and research for and writing of this book, I received invaluable assistance from a number of people and organizations. I am pleased to have this opportunity to thank them.

Major financial contributions that made this work possible were provided by the Minnesota Historical Society; the Archie D. and Bertha H. Walker Foundation; the Elizabeth C. Quinlan Foundation; the Archibald Bush Foundation (Student Learning Grant program); Marjorie and Leonard Johnson; and Alicia Winget. The faculty development committee of Concordia University, St. Paul, twice provided generous grants to support the interviewing and research associated with this book. Thank you to all committee members and to Vice President for Academic Affairs Carl Schoenbeck. I am also grateful to the many people who provided smaller financial gifts.

Individuals throughout the state were instrumental in establishing contacts with both civilians and veterans. A word of thanks is due to many, but I wish to identify some who went above and beyond the call of duty. My friend Al Muller of Maple Lake supplied the names of nearly twenty veterans interviewed for this book and often made the initial contact with these men. Gilbert Delao and Ray Rangel, both of St. Paul, helped me meet veterans in that city's Mexican American community. Cheryl Chatman and Mary Kay Boyd, both of St. Paul, guided me to African American senior citizen groups at the city's Hallie Q. Brown Center and Pilgrim Baptist Church; Martin O. Weddington of Roseville led me to African American veterans across the Twin Cities metro region.

Numerous civilian and military interviews in northern Minnesota's Carlton and St. Louis counties are thanks to the hard work of Velda Beck of Cloquet and Katryna Johnson of Minneapolis. The stories of Iron Range women and men included in this book are largely due to the efforts of Chisholm residents Steve Breitbarth, Don Marinkovich, Veda Ponikvar, and Nick and Dessie Zobenica. The Hibbing senior citizens center and Aaron Brown of the Hibbing *Tribune* also provided assistance. Interviews with farm residents in western and southern Minnesota were set up with the help of Dan Borkenhagen (White Bear Lake) and David Mennicke (St. Paul). In the Twin Cities metro area, I benefited from the extra efforts of Ardice Brower (St. Louis Park), Lawrence Brown (Minneapolis), Michael Dorner (Minneapolis), Jim Gerber (Cottage Grove), Eleanor Heginbotham (Washington, DC), Paul Hillmer (Burnsville), Robert Holst (St. Paul), John Jensvold (Burnsville), and Tom Ries (Burnsville).

Transcribing of audio interviews is one of the most important aspects of any oral history project. This project benefited greatly from the work of Linda Gerber, who demonstrated careful attention to detail and always produced top quality results—ahead of schedule. Further transcribing assistance was provided by Kimberly Johnson and Shannon Smith.

AN INDIVIDUAL word of thanks is also due to the following people:
Greg Britton of the Minnesota Historical Society Press, for the encouragement I needed to take this project forward and see it as a book. Sally Rubinstein and Shannon Pennefeather, whose careful editorial work greatly increased the quality of the final product. Dan Borkenhagen (Concordia University '02), who was part of the project from its inception in spring 2001 through summer 2002. He served for more

than a year as project manager, scheduling, interviewing, and transcribing. The Concordia University students of my spring 2001 class on the second world war—where this all started. Thanks for your enthusiasm and for some great interview work. You taught me a lot. Clarke Chambers, history professor emeritus at the University of Minnesota, for ideas and editorial assistance. Deb Miller of the Minnesota Historical Society, for help with a grant application. Bill Johnston of the Department of Applied Linguistics at Indiana University and Kimberly Johnson of Second Languages and Cultures Education at the University of Minnesota, for help with questions concerning linguistics and interviewing techniques. And Trevor Saylor, for the author photograph on the book jacket.

And to my family, for living more than three years with the Oral History Project of the World War II Years.

ABOVE ALL, thanks to the more than 130 women and men across the region who were generous with both their time and their memories. Without them there would be no project, and no book.

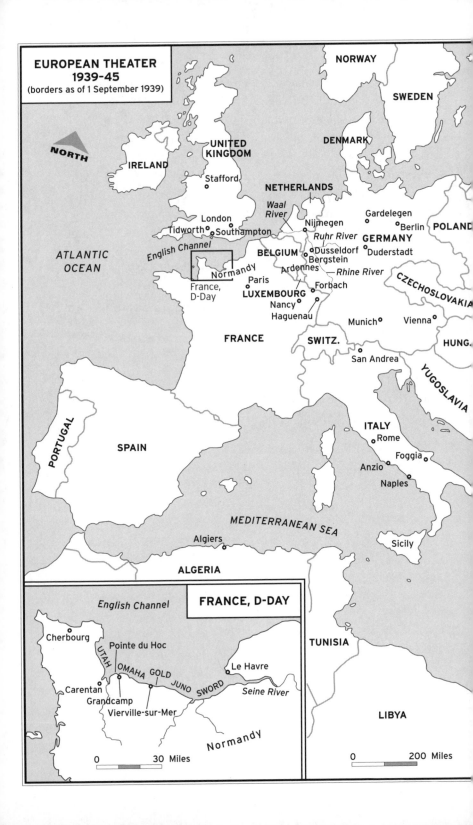

EUROPEAN THEATER 1939-45
(borders as of 1 September 1939)

NORTH

NORWAY

SWEDEN

DENMARK

UNITED KINGDOM

IRELAND

Stafford

NETHERLANDS

Waal River

Gardelegen

Berlin

POLAND

London

Tidworth Southampton

Nijmegen

Ruhr River

GERMANY

English Channel

BELGIUM

Dusseldorf
Bergstein

Duderstadt

ATLANTIC OCEAN

Normandy

Ardennes

Rhine River

CZECHOSLOVAKIA

France, D-Day

Paris

Forbach

LUXEMBOURG

Nancy

Haguenau

Munich

Vienna

HUNG.

FRANCE

SWITZ.

San Andrea

YUGOSLAVIA

PORTUGAL

SPAIN

ITALY

Rome

Foggia

Anzio

Naples

MEDITERRANEAN SEA

Sicily

Algiers

ALGERIA

FRANCE, D-DAY

English Channel

Cherbourg

Pointe du Hoc

UTAH

OMAHA GOLD JUNO SWORD

Le Havre

Seine River

Carentan
Grandcamp
Vierville-sur-Mer

Normandy

TUNISIA

LIBYA

0   30 Miles

0   200 Miles

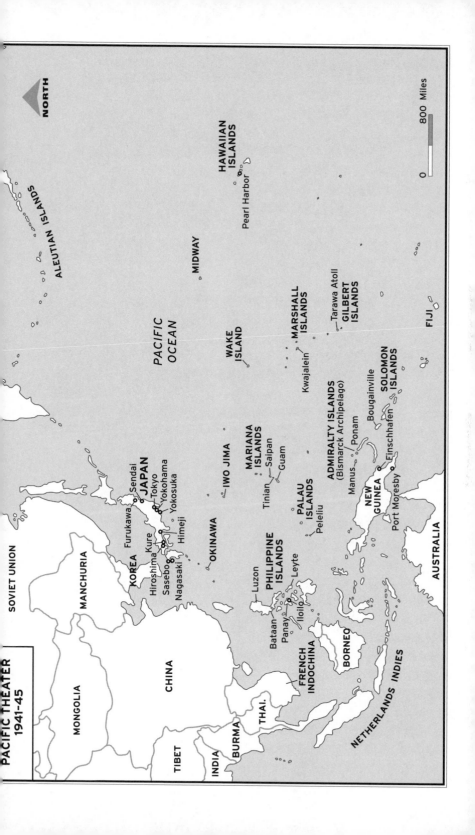

PACIFIC THEATER
1941-45

NORTH

0 ——— 800 Miles

SOVIET UNION

MONGOLIA

MANCHURIA

ALEUTIAN ISLANDS

KOREA
Furukawa
Sendai
Kure
JAPAN
Tokyo
Hiroshima
Yokohama
Sasebo
Yokosuka
Nagasaki
Himeji

OKINAWA

IWO JIMA

PACIFIC
OCEAN

WAKE
ISLAND

MIDWAY

HAWAIIAN
ISLANDS

Pearl Harbor

CHINA

TIBET

INDIA

BURMA

THAI.

FRENCH
INDOCHINA

Luzon
PHILIPPINE
ISLANDS
Bataan
Panay
Iloilo
Leyte

BORNEO

NETHERLANDS INDIES

PALAU
ISLANDS
Peleliu

MARIANA
ISLANDS
Tinian
Saipan
Guam

ADMIRALTY ISLANDS
(Bismarck Archipelago)
Manus
Ponam

NEW
GUINEA
Einschhafen
Port Moresby

Bougainville
SOLOMON
ISLANDS

Kwajalein

MARSHALL
ISLANDS

Tarawa Atoll
GILBERT
ISLANDS

FIJI

AUSTRALIA

Remembering

THE GOOD WAR

[1]

War's Beginning

Memories of and Reactions to 7 December 1941

MILITARY CONFLICTS dominated world events in the five years before 1941—a civil war in Spain; the Italian attack on Ethiopia; the Japanese invasion of China; the German conquest of much of Europe. But a strong sense of isolationism contributed to the United States' officially neutral stance, even though relations with Germany and Japan were increasingly strained. Tensions between the United States and Japan, especially, continued to escalate throughout the summer and fall of 1941, but few publicly predicted that war was imminent.

Thus the Japanese attack on the American military installations at Pearl Harbor, Hawaii, on 7 December 1941 came as a surprise. Two waves of carrier-based aircraft, launched from ships steaming approximately 275 miles north of Hawaii, struck the sprawling Pearl Harbor facilities beginning at 7:55 that Sunday morning. Within two hours, six battleships and ten smaller vessels had been sunk, hundreds of aircraft were destroyed or damaged, and more than 2,400 servicemen and civilians were dead. The next day, President Franklin D. Roosevelt addressed the nation and, speaking of the "day which will live in infamy," asked Congress for a declaration of war against Japan. The

American public, shocked by the nature of the attack and the extent of the damage, was galvanized into action.

The first reports on the destruction at Pearl Harbor reached the American Midwest in the early afternoon. Many Minnesotans recalled where they were and what they were doing when they heard the news. But many did not: fully a quarter of those interviewed either could not remember hearing the news or had no specific reaction to the events at Pearl Harbor.

The people whose memories fill the following pages are largely the generation born between 1915 and 1925; thus, with few exceptions they were aged sixteen to twenty-six in the year 1941. While a sense of youth is evident in their responses and concerns, their reactions to the attack—and the declaration of war that followed—differ widely: some remember thinking of family members and loved ones; others, particularly young men of draft age, considered what impact war would have on their lives. Another group viewed the war as far away, as nothing to worry about, as something that would not affect them personally—the geographic location of Minnesota, far from the coasts, is telling in this regard. And among men of military age, there were several who remember rushing out to enlist, or wanting to.

✦ ✦ ✦

Gloria Johnson of Minneapolis was a high school student in December 1941. She remembers the details of that day.

EVERYBODY REMEMBERS that I think, if they lived then. My mother and I were avid movie fans, mostly because my father was a motion picture projectionist. So we would go to the theater, not his theater especially, but to other theaters, neighborhood theaters, two or three times a week. And this was a Sunday, and we had decided to go to a movie. We stopped at my cousin's house so my aunt could go with us. They had the radio on, and that's when we heard it. You know, we didn't have radios on all the time because we didn't have news that often in those days. Obviously we didn't have television.

I think my initial reaction was probably anger, because you didn't want to think of this happening. I was trying to remember if we were aware, or how much we were aware, of the involvement of the United States previous to this, and I don't think most of the people were. It probably didn't penetrate at that point, you know, what was obviously, what was going to be entailed. At least I don't remember; being in high school you've got other things on your mind. [*laughs*]

Lester Marshall (b. 1921) of Cloquet was a skilled machinist, employed at the Navy Yard in Washington, DC. He is animated as he describes the events of 7 December 1941 and the effects at work.

I WAS SITTING with my father in the living room, listening to the Washington Redskins whop the daylights out of the Chicago Bears. The announcer came on and said, "Whoops, folks, we've got to break this up. This is just come through; it's from the White House. The Japanese have bombed Pearl Harbor today." And about twenty minutes later, the telephone rang. A fellow . . . he was a foreman at the Navy Yard, where I worked, he called me up and he said, "You're home. That's good. Is your mother home? That's fine. Have her pack enough lunch to keep you going for at least twenty-four hours. Throw some clean clothes in the sack that you can wear after that, when you get to [work]." Those places are dirty.

I was working at the Washington, DC, Navy Yard at that time. And [the foreman] said, "I'm picking up three other fellows, and I don't know *when* we'll get home. We won't work you more than eighteen hours out of a twenty-four-hour day. But you'll get at least three-hour breaks to sleep and you'll have an hour to eat a couple times during that time. Take what you can to eat, and what you can't, you'll have to buy some."

He picked me up in about fifteen minutes. My mother literally, well, what she did was take a loaf of bread and slice it lengthwise. Then she put butter and ham on one side, and on the other side she put peanut butter, and then she slapped them together. She said, "You can have peanut butter and ham together. Or you can have open-face sandwiches." She threw some pickles in a jar, and some Jell-O. And I had some kind of fruit; it must have been apples, but I don't really remember.

Leon Frankel was a student at the University of Minnesota. Out with friends at a pool hall on that Sunday afternoon, he realized his life would soon change.

A S YOU KNOW it was a Sunday, and the Sunday ritual was that a friend of mine by the name of Sonny Zuckerman, our ritual was to go to a pool hall on Sunday, known as Bilbo's, in St. Paul. It was like a famous hangout for everybody. We were at the pool hall when the news came over the radio that the Japanese had bombed Pearl Harbor.

That's where we were when it happened. It was quite a shocker. Most people had never heard of Pearl Harbor. Didn't know where it was. Slowly but surely we started hearing the news of what took place there, and it sounded pretty devastating.

I think [the other people in the pool hall] all felt about the same way we did. They just didn't know what to make of it. It was such an overwhelming event. We knew that there were all kinds of negotiations going on. Japanese envoys were in Washington and there was all kinds of talk about this, that, and the other. War seemed like so

Enlistment ceremony, 1942. After the Japanese attack on Pearl Harbor, Minnesotans from all walks of life joined the military.

far off. It was going on in Europe, of course, and places in Asia. But we never thought *we'd* ever be affected by it.

I was eighteen at the time. I remember Sonny and I both looking at each other, and of course the draft was on prior to this, and a lot of our friends and people we knew had gone into the army. We both looked at each other and more or less with the same thoughts, that it looks like, being of eligible age, sooner or later we're going to wind up somewhere in the military.

Having finished high school in 1940, Walt Mainerich of Chisholm was working in a Civilian Conservation Corps camp in northern Minnesota. He remembers hearing the news, then wanting to rush out and join the Marine Corps.

I COULDN'T get a job in the mines [after high school], so the best thing was, some of the neighborhood boys were working in CC camps. Civilian Conservation Corps. I was assigned to a camp up there by Big Deer Lake, about maybe forty, fifty miles away from here. I signed up in June of 1941, and I happened to be there in December of 1941 when Pearl Harbor was bombed.

It was on a Sunday. It was a day of rest for us guys. We had a big barracks with maybe thirty guys in it. One guy who was in charge of the barracks was a World War I veteran. He was the only one that had a radio on. . . . This happened to be during the daytime when we got the news about Pearl Harbor. Boy, oh, boy! He made us all stand up, and they played the national anthem on the radio, and we all stood there and anybody looked this way or monkeyed around, boy! He said, "You stand at attention when the national anthem is being played." That's what we did.

Then another friend and I left the camp. We said, "Well, we're going to go back to work in the mine or go in the service." We tried to get into service, him and I and somebody else at that time. We were all hepped about joining the marines. At that time we were going to go to Grand Rapids [Minnesota] and sign up. That day, when we were supposed to go down, there was no truck available so we couldn't go and sign up. I think we were pretty lucky. . . . I almost ended up in the marines. I would have ended up in the Pacific.

For some, thoughts went immediately to the family members, friends, and loved ones who stood to be directly affected by the nation's entry into World War II. One of these was Catherine Lemmer Brueggeman. Born in 1921 in St. Paul and raised in Somerset, Wisconsin, she was in nursing school in December 1941.

I HAD THE FLU and I was in my dorm room listening to the radio, and I heard the call, and pretty soon I had half of my class in there listening to it. They didn't care about whether they were going to catch the flu or not. You just stayed glued to it. It was, we had no television, so it was just the radio, but it was just something that just held you right there, listening to what was going on. It was like watching almost, like the thing in New York [on 11 September 2001], it was just following it, and getting, well, you weren't getting information as fast you get now, but we were hearing about what was happening there. [We were] nervous and scared, I think.

[There was] a lot of emotions, because most of us had brothers or fiancés or cousins, anything, that were all in that age group that were going to end up getting into the war.

In December 1941, Elmer L. Andersen (b. 1909), later governor of Minnesota, was president of H. B. Fuller Company in St. Paul. His first thoughts were of what would happen to his wife and children if he were called upon to serve.

AS TO WHERE we were when the war started, I remember it as clearly as if it happened yesterday. Our first son had been born in '38, and Eleanor was pregnant with our second child, Julian. It was on a Sunday, and we had come home from church. We were having dinner and listening to the radio, and suddenly it was interrupted for the news that there had been an attack at Pearl Harbor. We were just stunned. My first reaction was, what's going to happen to the family if I was called for military service? I certainly thought I might be called. I thought everybody would be called, because there was war declared the next day.

When Elaine Bunde Gerber of St. Paul heard the news on the radio, she, too, thought immediately of family, specifically her four brothers.

I KNOW IT WAS a Sunday morning when it happened. I don't remember if we heard this before we went to church or after. We heard about it, and we couldn't believe it. I think it was President Roosevelt that came over the radio—that's all you had, of course, radio—to tell us that we were being bombed by the Japanese at Pearl Harbor. It was quite a shock when you're thinking you're doing fine. Everything was going well. And then, after a while when you start thinking about it, then you think, "Well, I have four brothers that are all of age to go." They were all older than I was. It was kind of scary when you think about it. We were a close family, and everybody was living at home yet except for my two oldest brothers.

[My parents] were very stable people, and they didn't talk about it to us. I'm sure they didn't like it. My mother, of course, was a little upset with it, having children that would probably be going in the service.

Vivian Linn McMorrow (b. 1920) was a teacher at a country school in Wright County, Minnesota. Unsure of Pearl Harbor's location, she knew for certain that war meant her fiancé, Ralph Gland, then serving a one-year draft enlistment in South Dakota, would be in for the duration.

IT WAS A SUNDAY afternoon. I was sitting at the table. I had my radio on, but I was doing lesson plans for the next week. When they announced it on the radio that they hit Pearl Harbor, I thought, "Now Pearl Harbor, where in the world is that?" I had never even heard of it. It was a possession of the United States, so that meant they had attacked the United States.

[My fiancé, Ralph,] was still in South Dakota. All I could think of was, now Ralph would have to go to war. Now he had to be in active duty. Just being in the service wasn't so bad. I could handle that. [It was only for a year.] You can live with that. There was going to be an end. . . . They gave him a week, and he came home. My school board got together and decided that they would close school for a week so I could have the week off to be with Ralph while he was home.

Clarence Leer (b. 1925) of Abercrombie, North Dakota, a Red River agricultural community, lived and worked on the family farm. Military service loomed, and both Clarence and his parents knew it.

I WAS HUNTING pheasants. We'd always hunt pheasants in the fall. Partly to eat, because it was extra meat. There were a lot of pheasants in North Dakota at that time.

The first thing [my parents] thought about was having somebody who would have to go in the army. Be drafted. I guess that was my worry, too. I thought that I should volunteer, but then my folks didn't want me to do that. They needed me on the farm. Particularly my mother, she didn't want me to go. We talked about it and she said that I should wait to be inducted. Basically [she said] that I was needed on the farm. I don't know if that was the real reason or not. That's the reasoning she used. My dad didn't say much one way or another.

Some stated that the war and the Japanese did not represent anything of serious concern. Bill Amundson (b. 1923) of White Bear Lake, an employee in the actuarial department for Minnesota Mutual Life Insurance Company, admits that he did not take the Japanese threat seriously. He figured his life would essentially remain the same.

OUR FAMILY had stayed in touch with some of our grade-school teachers and, in fact, on that Sunday, we were [in Excelsior, Minnesota,] having dinner with my second-grade schoolteacher. We had spent some time with them, and we happened to turn on the radio and heard that Pearl Harbor had been bombed and that we were probably going to be at war.

My initial reaction was that it shouldn't impact my life at all. The Japanese didn't seem to be a world power to me at that time. In fact, I remember a couple days later, I was at my home in White Bear Lake and walking out to get a ride down to work with my future father-in-law, and I thought to myself, "We'll take care of the Japanese real quickly. There should be no impact on my life from this war, so . . . I'll get on with my life and continue to work."

I didn't consult with anybody, but I think the feeling was fairly mutual that people didn't take the Japanese seriously. I didn't talk with them particularly about this issue, but I suspect that they had the same opinion that I had, that the impact on our lives was going to be minimal. That we would just go on with our lives and start our families and lead a normal life.

Living on the family farm, Waldo (Wally) Meier was in his final year of high school. Initially shocked when he heard the news at a church meeting, he gradually came to believe that the war remained far away and was not something to be concerned about.

I WAS AT A [church youth] rally. We had—I and my brother, and we had a couple of other kids with us; I don't remember now anymore those details—we drove, oh, I imagine it was about a one-hour drive. We didn't have the car radio on for some reason. We got at the rally in the early afternoon, and we had a chapel service. At the end, when the chapel service was over, the minister said, "I suppose you all know we're at war." I could have just about fallen right through the pew at that time. Because this was already about four in the afternoon, and it actually happened somewhere just after noon central time.

Didn't make any mention of it [during the service]; when we came in nobody said anything. So it was kind of a shock. Course at the time, sort of the feeling, "Oh, that's now and it'll be over in a year or two." I really didn't think too much of it at the time. . . . We were hearing radio broadcasts, and they were patching them through so that we could listen to the actual reports. . . . It was getting about midday on Pearl Harbor, and they were still trying to figure out what really had happened. We sat up until after midnight listening to the car radio. We had driven back, and then we just sat in the car and listened, trying to hear something. . . .

[My parents,] I think they took the old German stoic approach. Not a whole lot of discussion or anything about it. It's [*pauses three seconds*] oh, I don't know, it's also sixty years ago. I don't believe there was really any, no panic or that kind of thing. Another thing was, that's practically the other side of the *world*, the way *we* looked at it. You know, you didn't move around a whole lot. I know there was some thinking at the time that the Japanese may try to carry it to our coast, the West Coast and so forth. . . . But it never really got home to us. . . . That middle of the country was as far away from anything as you could get.

Anger at the Japanese was an emotion common to both men and women—and most pronounced among service members. Two interviewees, however, brought unique perspectives to the subject of how to feel toward this enemy. Bill Devitt was a student at the College of St. Thomas in St. Paul. He recalls that some reacted angrily to the news but also that he felt somewhat differently.

WHEN I FIRST heard the news it was on a Sunday. We'd just gotten back from Mass and we were going to have a brunch; it was around noontime. We heard it over the radio . . . at my parents' house.

I don't know if I was up with the current news of the time or not, whether I realized at the time we were negotiating with the Japanese, that sort of thing. It was a surprise. I had never heard of Pearl Harbor. I didn't know where it was, I'm sure. . . .

Maybe [my parents] talked about it, I don't know. . . . My sister's boyfriend was there. He said something about those dirty yellow bastards or something like that, which was uncommon language in our household. He said it quietly, but I remember that. I don't remember that I felt that way.

Some of the people thought the Japanese were sneaky, dirty rotten people. I don't know that I ever thought that way. I thought if you're going to fight a war—I think that now and I think I thought that then—you fight the best way you know how to win, without the niceties of rules and all that sort of thing.

In December 1941 James Griffin (b. 1917) was a part-time officer with the St. Paul Police Department, married, and the father of one. He recalls the racial prejudice of some American whites in the aftermath of Pearl Harbor.

I T WAS kind of a shock. And I do remember, and I got a chuckle out of it, I heard a lot of white fellows say, "Well, we'll straighten that out in about sixty days." And I says, "It ain't going to happen that way, that quick." "What do you mean? Hell, what can they do?" I says, "It's going to be long. This war ain't going to end in no two weeks or three weeks. It's going to be a long haul." But you see, that's the reflection of the people thinking about people with dark skin. "No way for them to be able to beat us." Well, they found out.

Having immigrant parents or strong ethnic ties could play a role in how individuals reacted. Lois Breitbarth (b. 1927), who lived on a farm near Wheaton, in southern Minnesota, remembers her grandmothers, immigrants from Germany, being upset that the United States would now be at war with the country of their birth.

A S FAR AS THE WAR, I remember quite vividly the day Pearl Harbor was bombed. That was December 7, 1941. I was in high school, and it really shook everybody; it was a surprise attack. You know, we had been following what had happened over in Europe, with Hitler taking over the various countries. In high school, in history class, that was a big item, and we talked about that a lot, but everybody was really surprised by the attack on Pearl Harbor, and then that war was declared then right away after that. I remember President Roosevelt on the radio, because there was no TV then [*laughs*], and I remember sitting by the radio and listening to him declare war on Japan. The day after.

My grandmothers, both of them came from Germany, and my paternal grandmother especially, she didn't like the idea that we were going to fight against Germany. She didn't think at that time that Hitler was that bad a person, and she had family and relatives yet in Germany. She didn't really at first like the idea, here the United States was going to fight against her homeland.

Looking back on Pearl Harbor and its aftermath, and considering the experiences excerpted above, it might be tempting to draw the conclusion that, as Gloria Johnson stated, "everybody remembers that I think, if they lived then." But the reality is much more complex: while it is true that many can recall with some precision where they were and how they initially reacted, a sizable minority have only vague memories of that day or of their response to the news that the United States was at war with both Japan and Germany.

The oldest of six children of Mexican immigrant parents, Henry T. Capiz (b. 1926) was a high school student in St. Paul in December 1941. He remembers that the day's news hardly affected him.

I WAS A TEENAGER, and I wasn't doing much of anything. I was hanging around the house, and the news came over the radio. I had grown up with war, so it didn't make too much of an impact on me. During my childhood years and teenage years that's all you heard was war. First it was the Japanese in China, then it was the Spanish Civil War, then the war started in 1939. So it was war, war, war. So it didn't register too much at the time, and I certainly never thought I'd get involved. I didn't give it much thought. I just thought it was another news item. As young as I was, it didn't have a lot of impact on me.

I think [my parents] were a little shocked. As I said, a lot of emotion didn't register at that time. I don't have a lot of memories about that particular day.

Lois Snyder (b. 1922) of Lanesboro, in southeastern Minnesota, had finished high school and was looking for a permanent job. She admits that she did not realize at first how the war would affect her life.

I WAS HOME yet. I had been working up in the Twin Cities for a while, kind of babysitting, maid stuff, not doing much of anything, and I was home for the weekend. That's about it right there. My boyfriend [and future husband, Gerry], he was working and going to school up at Dunwoody [Institute in Minneapolis], and by then I think he was working. [He] had come down to Lanesboro for the weekend . . . and I think we had just been out riding around or something, and we came home and heard it on the radio at my house.

Well, I was just out of high school and . . . I was unbelievably naïve when I think back. I wanted to find a job of some kind, and so far I hadn't done anything very much, nothing special. [*pauses three seconds*] Didn't make that much difference to me. . . . Gerry realized of course that it was war, and my dad had been in World War I, so he knew right away what it meant. Along about then we decided that we would get married. At first we said, no, we will wait till afterwards; then we decided we would get married before he went into service.

Jacob Gondeck of Gilman, in central Minnesota, was working at a CCC camp in the north-central part of the state. He admits that he paid little attention to what might happen next.

WE WERE OUT in the CCC camp [in Outing, Cass County], and all at once, "Hey, jeez, they bombed Pearl Harbor." That went like wildfire through all the barracks and that. Then all these older guys, they couldn't wait to get in. After a week there was hardly anybody in the camp. They all went to sign up. You just went from one desk to another and signed up.

My reaction? You know, at [age] seventeen you don't . . . it doesn't hit you. You don't think. What I was thinking about, well, I was looking forward to having this tryout with the [Minneapolis] Millers [baseball team]. I was a pitcher. But that's what I had in my mind.

Larry Strand (b. 1924) was living with his parents on a farm in then-rural Brooklyn Center. He knows he was working when the attack took place, but his reaction, as he recalls it, was minimal.

I WAS WORKING at a local Standard Oil station. After taking care of a car at the gas pumps, I went into the office and heard on the radio that the Japanese had bombed us. Well, we always had music on. It was always a background. It wasn't so much listening; it was just having a little bit of something in the background. And I was usually working by myself.

I can't describe [my reaction to the news]. At that time I was seventeen. I guess I didn't have much of a reaction, except that I was disgusted with the Japanese. I can say that much. I knew where Hawaii was—Pearl Harbor, probably not. [*laughs*] I don't remember [talking about it with my parents]. I think I kept it to myself.

A junior at Mechanic Arts High School, Bert Sandberg of St. Paul recalls being out with friends when he first got the news, but he acknowledges that he paid little attention—his interest was focused on school and sports.

IT WAS DECEMBER of '41, and it was on a late Sunday night. I'll never forget. We had played basketball, and we were at Bridgeman's, a restaurant, an ice cream store, on the corner of St. Peter and Seventh [in St. Paul]. And we stopped in there—we had an old Model A—and one of the boys came out and says, "They bombed Pearl Harbor!" And nobody knew where Pearl Harbor was. We didn't know what he was talking about. "Where's that?" "Hawaii," [he said]. "But where's Hawaii?" It was very . . . [*pauses three seconds*] kind of a shock.

To be honest with you, I was so wrapped up in sports and that . . . I guess I didn't know much about the outside world, like Germany, Japan. I figured nobody could beat us. I didn't know any better.

And the big shock came as the next day we went to school at Mechanic Arts. It was a Monday, and they had an assembly about the war. I think Roosevelt signed the declaration two days later. And [the principal] says, "And now we're going to sing the 'Star-Spangled Banner.'" And nobody knew it. So he said we all had to go back to our homeroom, study it, and come back in half an hour! We all came back, and then we could sing the "Star-Spangled Banner."

A few others' reactions went beyond the personal and the immediate to a view of the larger impact or the potential longer-term consequences. For Clarke Chambers of Blue Earth, in southern Minnesota, a junior at Carleton College in Northfield, the events of 7 December 1941 were just the beginning of a generation-defining event.

I WAS LISTENING to one of those broadcasts, symphony orchestras, by radio. Was it the Philharmonic probably? And the news broke in. This is my memory. I was active politically in the student body [at Carleton], and we had a little committee about foreign policy and things like that, so we went and got the right professors and put together a symposium that evening in Severance Grand Hall. Right away we were into it.

I think that everybody was just eager to know what on earth this was, and where it was going to turn out. Some of us, obviously, as all student bodies, were better informed than others, but it was information. And also, implicit there with the young men was, "Okay, where do I go to sign up?" At that time nobody knew. But there was a sense of real crisis and emergency that we were going to be the hell out of there.

[As to my emotional response,] I'm sure it was not fear. . . . My closest buddies—and including myself, but they wouldn't have me— within a week they were up at Minneapolis trying to register [for military service]. A lot of the really gung ho guys were going in the marines; okay, if they were physically able and they could see, they went there. But the people were going up fast. I think it was a rush to be part of that generation. I think we knew, my friends—this is not universal—we knew that this was really an important war that had to be won. [We saw this] very quickly.

Twenty-six-year-old Beatrice (Bea) Kellgren was married and living in St. Paul. The Japanese attack represented an opportunity and an adventure for Bea and her husband, John. Within a month they were on their way to Seattle, for John had found a job with the aircraft manufacturer Boeing.

WE WERE living on Grand Avenue in St. Paul. My father-in-law was there for dinner, and we were listening to the radio, and all of sudden this came on. We were all horrified. We sat there looking at each other, thinking, "Now what's this going to mean for us?"

'Cause at that time my husband had just lost his government job . . . with the National Youth Administration. They just closed down, so we knew we were going to have to do something. So we just kind of sat there wondering, because we knew our lives were going to change, but we didn't know quite where to go from there.

I think everybody just about realized the same thing. It was hard for my father-in-law, because he was quite elderly and to think of another world war coming, it was pretty hard on him. But us, we were really young. We knew it was going to be an adventure. I mean, we weren't worried, we knew things were going to open up, because living in Minnesota was sort of, not drab, but we knew this was all happening on the coast. And we were a part of it [in Minnesota], because we were a part of the U.S., but we lived where we weren't that involved in it just yet.

Why did we go [to Seattle]? Because within the next few days, there were ads in the paper for aeronautical engineers for Boeing in Seattle. My husband was not an aeronautical engineer, but he knew he could be one, so first thing he went down, made an appointment, and was interviewed and got the job, and so we left a couple of days after Christmas.

Practically all our friends moved out to California, or of course a lot of the fellows were drafted. We had drafting then, so a lot of the fellows were called up right away. So, within the next few weeks there was a big change. Very scary, especially [for] those that went in the service. Who knew about war?

Earl Nolte was a high school senior living at home in Fairmont, in southern Minnesota. He and his friends immediately saw that their post-graduation plans had likely been made for them that day.

A GROUP OF my friends were out playing football. It was a very nice day on December seventh. We were out playing football and kind of got tired, so we went into the house to get a drink. Then the radio came on saying the Japanese had bombed Pearl Harbor. Most of us there were seniors, and right away it struck you—that takes care of, "What are we going to do after getting out of high school?"

We're going to college, or going to work, or what are we going to do. We *know* where we're going now. It was quite a sobering thought. Again, not knowing what's ahead or anything like that. But as young kids it was still kind of exciting.

As to my folks' reactions, especially with three sons, you know how Mother would take that. She right away was concerned about, "Now what will happen to my three boys?" It ended up that all three were in the service at the same time. This was hard on Mother.

My dad very rarely said anything. He always kept everything to himself. He was just a quiet guy. I'm sure he really was hurt, but he never said much.

Paul Peterson was a high school senior, too, living with his parents in Minneapolis, not far from Powderhorn Park. In his memory, the news was on everyone's mind, and the implications were clear.

THAT'S ONE OF those dates, as President Roosevelt said, "a date to live in infamy." I was at home. It was a Sunday. We had come home from church, and the word came over the radio. We didn't hear it—somebody else did and telephoned our house to let us know. It wasn't long after that—incidentally, it's something that's long since faded into history—that we heard the newsboys on the street hawking the "Extra! Extra! Read all about it!" On Sunday. They published a separate edition. An extra edition of the paper with the news of the attack on Pearl Harbor. It was very interesting because, being a senior in high school, I was pretty self-absorbed and wasn't paying much attention to what was going on in the world, but it certainly was a shock. I think to everyone.

I think we realized—being 1941, I was seventeen years old—what this meant in terms of potential military service. I had a brother who was five years older. My parents were very, very concerned, obviously, that he would be ultimately drafted or that he would wind up in the service somewhere. He did, as I did.

The first thing out of my mother's mouth, I think, was that her sons were going to wind up in service. For them, you have to realize, in 1941, that wasn't that many years after the end of World War I, which they remembered and remembered very well. Although my father never served in World War I.

[In school,] everyone talked about it. I had classmates, high school classmates, who obviously did volunteer. My brother-in-law volunteered as a marine, because his dad was a marine. I talked about it, thought about it, but I decided I was going to wait to be drafted. . . . It was no surprise when [my draft notice] came.

Members of a final group tell still a different story, for in December 1941 they were already in the military. Experiences of that day vary greatly, as do responses. James Beck (b. 1921) of rural Palisade enlisted in the army in 1939. After the assault on Pearl Harbor, he remembers a fear that the continental United States could be attacked by the Japanese.

I WAS STATIONED in Fort Lewis, Washington, and when Pearl Harbor was bombed Fort Lewis was evacuated. Roughly fifteen to twenty thousand troops, I would say, we all went out in the field, you know, away from Fort Lewis, because we expected that to be bombed by the Japanese at any time.

We had, of course, been briefed often about world affairs and what the likelihood was of us getting into the war, so we knew what was going on as well as anybody. So I guess it wasn't too unexpected when it happened. But I was angry.

Dick Mertz was born in 1921 in Saskatchewan, but his family moved to Shakopee, Minnesota, when he was a child. In 1940 he enlisted in the military, spending more than three years in the Canadian service before transferring to the American service. In December 1941 he was in Calgary, Alberta.

I SIGNED UP in St. Paul. They had a recruiting office in the old railroad station in downtown St. Paul. That's where I saw the sign, and that's where I went in to get information. I'm pretty sure the guy that signed me up was a used car salesman. [laughs] I mean he really worked on me to get me in there. I bought a lot of things. I believed him—that was a mistake. He talked about the opportunity of seeing this country and that country. Seeing Canada and seeing England.

Ken Jensvold of Montevideo went to Winnipeg in 1940 and enlisted in the Royal Canadian Air Force. By December 1941 he was a flight instructor, stationed in Lethbridge, Alberta. About Pearl Harbor he noted, "I flew seven training flights on 7 December, from our airfield in High River, Alberta. The local papers covered [the attack], but I didn't take any great note of it one way or another."

That appealed to me. I wasn't anxious to fight; I was anxious to see the world. This was the opportunity.

First of all, the Canadians were very happy about [the United States getting into the war] because so far the battle had been entirely in Europe without any help from the United States. Well, with limited help from the United States, I guess I'd say. So they accepted it rather happily, and so did I. I was in the same position as a lot of Canadians there—anxious to have some help. . . . I guess I considered myself an American in a Canadian uniform, though. I think that [other people] saw me a lot the way I saw myself, as an American boy who was up in Canada training to be in the war.

Walter T. Larson joined the U.S. Navy in 1940, after high school. He experienced 7 December 1941 as an electrician on the battleship USS *Nevada*, which was anchored at Pearl Harbor.

I GOT UP EARLY in the morning and went to breakfast. I was going to wash clothes that day. . . . There were quite a few guys down there and they were talking. . . . Anyway, I was there for a little bit, and this guy come running down the passageway, and he was just *screaming.* "The god-damned Japs are bombing the hell out of us. General Quarters! General Quarters!" And about that time, the General Quarters sounded. . . . We were going to start up to the searchlights [which was my battle station], but this kid, he says, "No, I ain't going up there." I said, "Well, if you don't go to your battle station, it's a general court martial. It's one or the other." He said, "Well, you go first, and I'll follow." So we got up there, and there were two, three other electricians up there and some other guys on the search lights. . . .

There was a guy up there doing special duty, a seaman. He had a machine gun, a .30-caliber machine gun with the old round clip on top. . . . There was quite a bit of fire and stuff. About that time a [Japanese] plane came in and torpedoed *us*. And as it banked away, we all stood there and was watching him. He wasn't very far away from the ship. We hollered at this kid to start to shoot. And we could see the bullet holes go right in the center of the plane, about every six inches down the center. Must have hit the pilot and the guy in the back end right up through the bottom [of the plane]. It crashed right behind the ship shortly, and the back canopy opened up, and this guy started to crawl out, the gunner in the back end. He started to crawl out, but the plane started to go down, and he went with it. So they both must have been wounded. I don't know if there were two or three guys in the plane, but it went down and that was it.

That's when I started to think that a person could get hurt. This is for real! I don't think [that entered my mind before that], because we trained and everything was automatic. You just did it. I had some kids ask me sometime, at one of the schools where we were talking about it, "Did you get scared?" I said, "No, I don't think at the *time* I was scared, but that night when we went to bed, then I got scared." Because there were so many wounded ones and so many dead. You get to thinking that you're lucky that you weren't one of them.

We were up on the searchlights there, and there wasn't much we could do. You don't use the searchlights in the daytime. We were more or less just watching what was going on. Shortly after that the [battleship] *Arizona* got bombed. When that thing went up we were still on the searchlights, and that fire must have gone thousands of feet up in the air. It really was big, and the noise, you can't even *imagine* the noise it was when it went off. And the fire from there hit us like a blast furnace; the heat from the explosion hit us up there.

It was just shortly after that that they ordered us off the search-lights to go below. On the way down we ran into Chief Boatswain's

Mate Hill, and he told us to close a hatch that was on the stern of the ship before we went down below. So there were four of us that went and closed this hatch, and we went down below. We stopped at sickbay; we thought maybe we could help at sickbay. The doctor there, he told us no, we'd be more harmful than we would be good, because we didn't know what was going on anyway.

About that time, there were a couple of black guys that came down. They were burned pretty bad. Their skin was hanging down. And I remember the doctor telling them to go sit in the corner while he took care of some people that were really hurt. So we went down below the armor deck and cleaned some compartments where they'd operated on some of the guys and stuff, and helped wherever we could at that time.

I was more mad than anything. I couldn't believe that they would do something like that without notice or something. But actually, I don't think we really thought too much about anger or anything else. The thing was to help who we could and get things going as much as we could after the bombing was stopped. After the bombing, the electrical gang, we tried to get as much electricity going throughout the ship, because most of it was out already. And I was picked to go up to this number five casement and pick up some of the bodies and bring them down so they could be identified. I helped carry two of them. That was all I could carry. They figured I'd be a casualty, too, so they told me to leave [before I got sick]. . . . Some of the guys I picked up I went through boot camp with. I lost two electricians that were very close. And I don't know how many were wounded. But there were quite a few. [*emotionally*] I lost quite a few friends.

Toshio Abe was born in 1919, the son of Japanese immigrant parents. In April 1941, while a college student, he was drafted into the U.S. Army. He was stationed at Fort Ord, California, in December 1941. He initially took offense when asked how he felt about the Pearl Harbor attack.

YOU MEAN [how I felt] as a Japanese American? I didn't even think about it. The enemy attacked Pearl Harbor. People like you ask that question because we are Japanese Americans, and, consequently, we may have had some negative thoughts about patriotism. [*somewhat irritated*] "How do you feel? What's your attitude toward the Japanese and being an American?" I think 99 percent of us didn't even give that a thought. It was the enemy versus us, as Americans. [*pauses five seconds*]

After Pearl Harbor social attitudes might have changed. I think a lot of people were confused as to how they should regard us, Japanese Americans in uniform, in the U.S. Army uniform. In answer to your question, my reaction is somewhat neutral. I never even thought about that other than possibly there might be some few people that would really let you know how they felt positively or negatively about it. Probably I think in the minds of many of the majority of people, being Caucasians, they might have had negative reaction, yet I don't recall any unpleasant incidents.

Herman Hinrichs of St. Paul (left) was a machinist on the USS *Oklahoma,* stationed at Pearl Harbor on 7 December 1941. He vividly remembers escaping the torpedoed ship with a crewmate: "The starboard portholes were still open because the ship was on its side, so . . . we got a hold of the upward bunks, pulled ourselves up, and got out through a porthole, and dropped into the water. Of course by the time we got out, the water was all burning—it was all on fire— and [Japanese aircraft] were *strafing* us. So, all you could do was dive down, swim under water, come up and get a breath of air, and *swim.*" Herman spent 1942–45 in the Pacific on the battleship *Massachusetts.*

Alois (Al) Kopp (b. 1918) grew up on a 640-acre farm near Raleigh, North Dakota. He enlisted in the U.S. Navy in 1937, and in December 1941 was a pharmacist's mate on the cruiser USS *Houston,* then in the Philippines. Al remembers a false sense of security after the first Japanese attack and a sense of arrogance toward the enemy.

YOU ALWAYS think it's in the future, so when it suddenly happened, then you get a shock. A surprise. . . . You had thought about it in the past. We just knew that it would happen sometime.

We were in Iloilo on the island of Panay, an island just south of Luzon. We were in their capital port taking on fuel. I was sleeping. Still in bed. It was about like four o'clock in the morning of the eighth. The ship's General Quarters alarm went off. We heard the general alarm go off, and everybody was blasting over the loudspeaker that the war was on. "They're bombing Pearl Harbor." We took off. We got out of there, and we hadn't gotten out of the harbor and they were bombing us.

[The Japanese] knew exactly where we were. They were bombing us, and it didn't do much good. The bombs didn't even get really close to us, which, we thought, "Well, this is great." We found out differently afterwards.

We had this feeling. It's crazy how kids think, but we were real proud of the navy, and our gunnery was the best. . . . We'll take this war and we'll take these Japs on. They all have big Coke-bottle lenses and buckteeth, and they can't read, and they can't shoot. We were looking at three months, and then we go back to school.

[2]

War's Broadening Horizons

New Experiences, New Locations

THE UNITED STATES simultaneously fought in Europe, Asia, and the Pacific during World War II; to meet these extensive commitments, the military expanded tremendously. From a December 1941 force of approximately 2.1 million (in the Army, Navy, Marine Corps, and Coast Guard), the military grew to more than 12 million by mid-1945. In all, a total of 16 million men and more than 300,000 women served in the armed forces during the war years—far more than in any of the nation's wars before or since. The Selective Service Act of 1940, which ultimately made all able-bodied men between the ages of eighteen and forty-five subject to military service, alone was responsible for the induction of 10 million men into service.

Basic training and daily existence in the military transformed lives through regimentation and numerous restrictions; duty stations far from home, in many cases in foreign lands and among different people, broadened horizons and exposed service personnel to new ways and cultures. Even those who served within the United States but in a new region of the country—and men and women from the Upper Midwest are prime examples—could be confronted with ways of thinking unlike those they had previously known. Once in uniform, some men and women found doors opened to new opportunities; others were forced to face existing stereotypes or even open discrimination. Few returned home unchanged.

Different groups felt the impact of the stereotypes and discrimination of 1940s American society. People of color, specifically African Americans, Japanese Americans, and Mexican Americans, often endured some form of discrimination. Their individual reactions differed depending on circumstances, but many recall some level of prejudice and intolerance. Women, too, faced discrimination. Although they enlisted in record numbers during World War II, surmounting obstacles including sexism and routine assignment to low-skill jobs was difficult, as the military resisted equal opportunity and treatment throughout the war years.

Leaving Home, Staying Home, and Basic Training

WHETHER AS CONSCRIPTS or volunteers, millions of men and women served in the armed forces during 1941–45. Some men of draft age remember being anxious to volunteer, and some actually did, but the vast majority entered the military through the system of conscription.

Numbers tell only part of the story; complex situations and emotions determined how and when a particular man or woman joined the service or if he or she joined at all. The majority of men recall some form of pressure to serve, whether real or perceived. Some have memories of acting on this pressure, of wanting to enlist or be drafted; others remember not being able to serve, for various reasons. There was also parental pressure, on one hand to join the military and on the other hand to stay out—in both cases young men struggled with decisions that may have displeased their parents. And as the war dragged on and selective service regulations were changed to make it easier to draft married men, some men with families admit to being less than enthusiastic about leaving their loved ones behind for the uncertainties of war.

Once inducted, all shared the experience of basic training. For some it was primarily a psychological or physical experience; others recalled the controlled and disciplined surroundings; still others focused on one aspect of the training, from weapons and constant movement to the weather or the food. One overriding point connects them: enlistment meant personal transformation.

✦　✦　✦

Fritjof "Fritz" Lokensgard, the son of a Norwegian Lutheran pastor, was raised in rural western Minnesota. Ordained a minister in 1937, he was with his wife and three small children serving a small parish in North Dakota when the United States entered the war in 1941. He admits to feeling pressure about military service, even though as a minister he was automatically deferred.

[I]N EARLY JUNE 1942] my wife and family were visiting her parents in Chatfield, Minnesota, and she had our car down there. There was no bus or anything, so I hitchhiked. You could do that in those days. A young fellow picked me up, and we were driving down on the way to Rochester. We talked about the war. He said, "I'll be going in next week. I've been drafted. I'm 1-A." He said, "What are you?" And I had to think for a minute. I hesitated. Then he said, "Are you a 4-F?" I said, "No, I'm not a 4-F." A 4-F—that's not physically able. "What are you then?" So I stuttered and stammered. Finally I said, "I'm 4-D." He said, "4-D? What's that?" [*pauses briefly*] I said, "Deferred." As a minister I'd be deferred unless they absolutely needed me. I felt about as high as an ant at that time.

That same month, Fritz heard a sermon that convinced him he was needed in the chaplain service.

I went to a church convention in June [1942], in Minneapolis. One of the speakers was a chaplain from Great Lakes [Naval Training Center]. . . . He gave a sermon that really made up my mind for me. His approach was this: he said, "I joined the navy in order to preach to the sailors, but things have happened differently. They preach to me." And he told about the influence those young men had on him. And on his life, his spiritual life, his whole being. . . . The next day I went down to the recruiting office in Minneapolis.

Elmer L. Andersen, later governor of Minnesota, was president of H. B. Fuller Company of St. Paul, a manufacturer of industrial adhesive products. Though he was in his early thirties, a family man, and head of a firm that had government contracts, he still felt compelled to inquire about how he might serve.

I T WAS STILL in my mind, wondering what my personal responsibility was, so I thought I at least had to go down to the recruiting station and talk it over with them. So I went down and met with an officer and said that I wanted to do my share, and I had a family and had a business and it would be quite a wrench, but I wanted to know what I should do. He said, "Where do you work?" I said, "H. B. Fuller." "What do you do?" "I'm president of the company." "What do you make?" "Adhesives." "Anything for the war effort?" "Yes. We've succeeded in producing a water-resistant adhesive, and we're selling quantities of it to many packers of war materiel so that it can be dumped in the water and safely floated to land." He said, "Well, my gosh, you can do more good staying at home running that company than going into the army, so just go home and turn out a lot of good glue." That was an enormous relief.

It kind of took a burden off my mind. I didn't want to be a slacker, and I didn't want to duck away from it, but I certainly didn't relish the idea of leaving my family and business and dislocating my life if there was any suitable alternative. So his words of encouragement kind of eased my mind. There was no question about it. I never got drafted or bothered about it.

Clarence Leer lived with his parents on a Red River Valley farm in Abercrombie, North Dakota; as the only son, he received a farm deferment. He remembers, however, a form of pressure to be part of the military.

I KIND OF wanted to enlist [in 1944], but then because my folks needed me at home I didn't think I should. My folks had to apply for the deferment with the Selective Service Board. Of course they knew everybody on the service board. There were several automatic deferments, if you needed it, if somebody needed it to work on the farm. . . . I guess I felt that [I was contributing by working on the farm]. Yes, I was helping the war effort working on the farm.

In early 1945 the deferment was allowed to expire, and Clarence was soon drafted into the army. Emotions were mixed.

I think the deferment . . . probably could have been extended for another year, if [my parents] had insisted. . . . They left it up to me if I wanted to go, and I said I would just as soon wait and see if I can't get drafted.

My mother was pretty upset. I don't know how my dad felt. He didn't say much. When I got on the bus to go to . . . be inducted at Fort Snelling . . . that was pretty sad. [It was] tough on my folks. I guess it was kind of tough on me, too. First time I'd ever really been off the farm.

Alice Pieper (b. 1925) tells the farm deferment story from a different perspective. Although her family lived in St. Paul, immediately prior to U.S. entrance into the war her father moved them to a small farm in rural Sunfish Lake, hoping to obtain a farm deferment for her brother. For reasons of his own, her brother rejected the deferment and ultimately joined the Marine Corps. Her parents' worst fears were almost realized when he was badly wounded in 1945 at the invasion of Okinawa.

I WAS MOSTLY raised in St. Paul. Then just before the war my father bought a piece of land out there in Sunfish Lake, but he kept driving back and forth to work in St. Paul. They figured that my brother would probably have to go into the service. [He was] thinking that it would save my brother from going to the war [by getting him a farm deferment]. . . .

Farmer boys were deferred. Not if there were three or four boys, but if just one, he would work the farm. My father, he thought that my brother could stay on the land. My father had been in World War I and been through that, and he had been overseas, and he just felt that it wasn't a very pleasant thing to go through, and if he could save his son from doing so, he would do it.

But my brother was not interested in that; that wasn't his idea. He said that he owed it to his country. He signed up and went into the marines. He didn't right away, but he did later on. He was in the invasion of Okinawa [in April 1945], and he drove one of these [landing craft] that went up on the shore. Anyway, he was bringing a load of men to the shore, and they were bombed. Then when he came to, he was onboard a hospital ship.

They notified us that he was onboard a hospital ship, but they gave us no clue as how bad he was injured up until he got to the States, and then they notified us.

Maurice Raether of Duluth witnessed abuse of the farm deferment system firsthand.

D URING THE WAR there was a worker shortage. Farming was rated high; it was "essential." My wife's father had this dairy farm. He had his son in the navy, and they had this other young man, he died up in the fighting in the Aleutian Islands. He was married to the boss's niece. Well, a couple of fellows came there to work. We called them draft dodgers, boys from Chicago. They had never milked a cow in their life. They were working our farm just to stay out of the service.

They knew the right people. My wife's father must have signed for them to be on the farm. I knew he had a couple of young men there. I didn't have anything against them, but they didn't belong on a farm by any means.

Other young men of draft age also had experiences with deferments of one kind or another. Some were held out of service because of work they did or a skill they had; others were classed 4-F, or medically deferred, because they had failed an induction physical.

Lawrence Myking (b. 1916) was married and working for a wood products company in Cloquet when the United States entered the war. Like many men in town, he reported for an induction physical soon after the attack on Pearl Harbor. For Lawrence, that induction physical was the end of the road—in 1942 his employer acquired a deferment for him as a skilled machinist. Lawrence recalls being puzzled as to why he received a deferment when some other men had not, and he remembers wanting to serve with them.

I DON'T REMEMBER how long after it was, but . . . some other guys at work told me before noon that they had called their wives and that the mail had come in, and in the mail was their letter to report for induction. I just went home. I looked in the mailbox, and I had the same letter to report for induction. I said, "I'm not going to work this afternoon." Then I waited. They worked until three-thirty. I waited until about four-thirty. I knew nobody would be there by then. I was a machinist, and I had a hand box. My special tools were in that hand box.

I was in getting some other stuff for my other toolbox that wouldn't fit in the hand box, and the personnel manager happened to come by the door, and he came in and asked me what I was doing. I said, "I got one of those letters to report for induction." He said, "It's a mistake." I said, "I'm all set to go, and all the rest of the guys are going." He said, "You'll have to go to the draft board and see." That was just across the street, across the tracks, so I went over there. I showed them the letter. They said, "Yes, that's a mistake. You shouldn't have gotten that letter." I said, "I'd just as soon go." They said, "It's hard to get out of it. You've got a deferment." They said it's hard to get out of a deferment.

I was working in the machine shop. That was essential work. I don't know exactly why, but I was needed. . . . One of the guys in the shop had been to Dunwoody [Institute in Minneapolis, a technical school], and he had taken a trade, and *he* got orders to go. And another one of my friends from church, he had to go.

After graduating from high school in 1943, Don Marinkovich of Chisholm received notice to report for his induction physical at Fort Snelling, near Minneapolis. Mentally prepared to enter the military, he instead was classified 4-F, medically deferred. Guilt plagued him as the town's other young men continued to leave for the service.

ALMOST WENT into shock. The guy put that big red "X" on my card. I said, "Is that 4-F?" He said, "Yes." It was a punctured eardrum. I had ear problems when I was ten years old. Swelling inside the ear. A horrible thing. Once the eardrum bursts the pressure is gone and the pain is over, but that infection stayed. . . . I never considered it a big deal.

This was bad. I felt embarrassed. Terribly embarrassed. I talked to other 4-F guys, too, that felt the same. . . . Every place you went, "How come you're so young and you're not in uniform? My kid's in the army. Look at you." If they didn't say it, you felt they were *thinking* it.

Augustine Martinez was a twenty-five-year-old father of two working at American Hoist in St. Paul when in 1944 his deferment expired and he was drafted into the army.

[O NE DAY] they came around, they called me in the office. "Hey, Martinez, you've got to go. We can't do anything. You have to go." Oh, no! There I went. I had to report to Fort Snelling, for examination, physical. They examine you and all that stuff. Everything went all right. Number one [1-A draft classification]. I said, "No, no, no. I'm old. I can't go. I have a wife." They said, "Sorry, Martinez. There's nothing wrong with your hands. You can hold a rifle, can't you?" Oh, boy! That was it.

I didn't like it, because I had children already, and a wife. They're left behind, you know. Work and food and things like that. I didn't feel good. Hey, what's going to happen here? You go away for months and months, and during a war you never know if you will come back or not. Everything was on my mind there. You cry. You just don't feel good.

It was terrible. We cried. The kids cried. We went to the train depot here in St. Paul. That's where I left from. Yes, that was hard. Oh, my, it was hard. I'm not kidding you. Oh, I remember, I cry all the way. It was terrible! It's worse than war, leaving your family like that.

Once a part of the military, young men and women were confronted with intense and new experiences, often in far-distant places. Many recalled how difficult it was to leave home for the unknown. Manuel Aguirre, for example, grew up in a close-knit Mexican immigrant family that in the 1930s settled on St. Paul's West Side. After being drafted into the U.S. Navy in September 1943, he experienced his first extended period away from his family.

I WAS NEVER out of the state of Minnesota, other than Iowa. I was never any other place. . . . It was kind of lonesome [at basic training]. We got our thirty-day leave after basic training was over. We were glad to get back [home], and then we had to go back again. I went to California. Mother and Father and the family there, they kind of hated to see us go. I know when I went back after that leave from

Manuel Aguirre (back row, left) served in the Pacific during 1944–45 on the USS *Ozark*. The pilot of a small landing craft that transported both men and supplies, he participated in a number of invasions. He recalls the one at Iwo Jima in February 1945: "You could hear the bullets whizzing by and splashes all around. I didn't think about it. I knew what I had to do, and that's what I was doing. . . . I had to get the boat in there and get the guys off. . . . If we had some wounded to take back to our ship, I had to do that, because we were a hospital ship."

boot camp, they went to the train depot [in Minneapolis]. I told them not to go up there, because they would all start crying. "No," they said, "we won't cry." So we went to Minneapolis depot. Then they all started crying. My mother, she was crying. That was hard. That was hard.

I didn't see [my mother] any more after that. She passed away [in December 1944,] when we were gone. That's the last time I saw my mother. That's what hurt me more, for a long time. It still hurts me, because that's like somebody losing a boy in the service. He gets killed. Only it happened the other way to me. I went through . . . all the invasions—Luzon, Iwo Jima, Okinawa—over a year before I came home.

She died on December ninth, and I made the first invasion at Luzon January ninth, exactly a month later. I found out on the way to Luzon for the invasion. That must have been about the middle of the month, the middle of December or later, because I got a letter from home before they gave me the notice. An officer just came and told me that my mother passed away.

In December 1942, Larry Strand volunteered for the U.S. Marine Corps. He remembers the start of basic training and the loneliness that eventually caught up with him.

WE WERE technically sworn in, put on a troop train, and went down to San Diego, where I was put into the recruit depot there. I remember this was in December, and it was cold. I used to wear long underwear when I was working as a carpenter, and I still had that on when I got to San Diego, and they told us to take our clothes off. I'm the only guy standing there with long underwear on, and I really felt like a farmer, I tell you. . . . [*laughs*] In that bunch I was the only one with long underwear on. I didn't need them any more down in San Diego.

I hadn't been out of Minnesota hardly. This was a big experience. Really a big experience for me. . . . I wasn't lonesome because, I think, we were so busy. The only time I got lonesome was . . . after two years being in the Marine Corps, I got liberty from the hospital, and I went by myself to a movie. It was the first time I was out. It was *Holiday Inn* [with the song "White Christmas"]. I sat down in the movie, and I watched for about twenty minutes, and I got so lonesome I couldn't stay any more. I had to get out because it brought back all my family memories. I couldn't stand it. I don't know if I ever have seen that show. I know I couldn't watch it because I got so lonesome.

For others, basic training represented something new, something positive. Osmund "Ossie" Olson (b. 1923) of Warroad, in far northern Minnesota, had polio as a child, yet he was classified 1-A and drafted into the army in 1943. Passing through basic training helped boost his self-confidence.

MY FEET are crippled. I wear a seven triple-E shoe. The muscle in my left leg is about three-quarters of an inch shorter than the right one. Then when that second time I had polio [as a teenager,] I lost the sense completely in my right thumb. But they drafted me anyway. I was warm.

Anytime you're learning something, I think it's an experience that's good for you. You're seeing the country and they're teaching you things that can help you. I kind of think I enjoyed the basic training, because I was able to do things with the rest of them that I didn't think I would be able to handle. . . . I thought a lot of times I wasn't going to be able to keep up. But I managed, and I got through it all right.

At the time the United States entered the war in 1941, Tom Takeshi Oye (b. 1918) lived in Oregon with his Japanese parents. His being drafted soon thereafter meant a duty to fulfill.

THE DRAFT STATION for our area [was] about six or seven miles away. A friend of mine came to pick me up, because my folks didn't drive. As I got ready to leave, my dad came down the pathway from the house, and he said to me in Japanese, "You're an American citizen. You owe your life to your country." He said, "I'm not a citizen, but you are. Be sure you do your job." He took the time to tell me that. He came out of the house when we were about ready to leave for [the draft station].

[My parents] were carry-overs from the feudal system of Japan, and under the feudal system what the lord or master said was the law. They translated that to the U.S. citizenship, that whatever the country says, it's your duty to respond to that. That was the attitude of my dad in particular. My mother was not quite as articulate as he was, but she felt the same way.

Walt Radosevich (b. 1921) enlisted in the Marine Corps in 1942. He remembers basic training at Parris Island, South Carolina, as an intense experience, physically as well as psychologically.

BASIC TRAINING, that was hell, really. Hotter than Hades. It was nothing but sand fleas and fiddler crabs. Those darn little crabs. And sand. Sand, sand, more sand.

Four o'clock in the morning our drill sergeant would holler, and we'd have to get out, run, get into formation right away, count off, line up. And then we'd start our routine, and this was before breakfast. . . . And everything was move together; your whole squad, or your whole platoon, would move together. We'd do all our exercises, our drills and everything, before breakfast. Then run to the chow hall, have breakfast. You all stood up in front of the table, sat down, got your food, back up again, same routine. Then out to drill again, they just kept drilling, drilling, drilling, until, well, from four in the morning till dark.

But they kept pounding in through our heads, "Nothing like a marine; you're a marine; there's no one in the world is going to beat you. You can't be beaten by *anybody*." Actually, I'd say they brainwashed us.

Walt admits that homesickness was part of life for new recruits. Not everyone made it through.

My first time away from home, I was lonely as hell, really. I know there was one young marine from Cleveland, a young Jewish boy,

Besser, his folks had a big shindig before we left for basic training. And he cried all the time he was there in the boot camp. . . . Besser was practically [*pauses three seconds*] going insane because he didn't want to have anything to do with it. He was so homesick that they finally had to let him go. . . . They discharged him because they couldn't do a thing with him. . . . I'd say 90 percent of us were homesick. We were all eighteen to twenty years old. I was homesick too, but I figured, "Well, damn it, you're a marine. You don't cry, you don't do this. . . . You asked for it, so take it."

Frank Soboleski (b. 1925) grew up on a farm near International Falls. For him, basic training at Fort McClellan, Alabama, in the heat of summer was a real adjustment.

Frank Soboleski in International Falls with his mother, 1943, before shipping to Europe

WELL, THE FOOD was terrible, the housing was terrible, it was hot, they had chiggers, they had mud, and colored people all over. They had funny food, like hominy. . . . After what you eat up here [in Minnesota], good nourishing food, they had just enough to get by and survive on. All the people down there were skinny and unhealthy, and too many of them in one room. It was just a mess.

We always went swimming; we had our own swimming pool up here [in International Falls]. The first thing, there was a creek going behind the barracks, and this person that was in charge says, "Whatever you do, don't go in that water." Well, it looked pretty nice; there were little riplets on it. Water was running down you, and everybody had sweat under their sleeves, just hot. I turned around and went back, took my clothes off, and dove in. I come up and shook my head, and I looked, and there was two snakes there wiggling at me. And they were coming right at me. Well, Jesus Christ walked on top of the water, but I bet I'd have beat him! I got to shore and then found out later they were water moccasins. Now I know why they didn't want us to jump in that creek. That was my first experience in Alabama. I figured I had better listen to the bird with the stripes on his sleeve.

Frank remembers feeling contempt for those in his unit who did not take the training seriously.

I didn't like the South, but I wanted what [the army] had to offer in Fort Benning, Georgia. I wouldn't miss that for the world, because I had read about it all through basic training in Alabama—and I wanted to be a paratrooper. They were a special outfit. They weren't just . . . [*trails off*]. What did it was in basic training, when they had ammunition. Some guys would be back there lighting a cigarette, and you are supposed to be in combat. [*disgusted tone*] That's the enemy out there—either they get you, or you get them. These birds weren't taking it serious. This is my neck, and I want to save it. I want to train with people that have the same ideas on surviving as I have. But they weren't that way in basic training.

We're crawling under barbed wire, on a firing line, with live ammunition over your head. They'd just lay down there, and when it's over with, then they'd come out. Well that's a hell of an attitude. That's not the guy I'd want next to me; I didn't want any of these. . . . They had families and children at home, and they didn't want any part of that. They were going to drag their feet as much as they can, maybe get a discharge one way or another. And that's the type of people that were in there. A lot of them *did* get discharged. They'd be there, and the following week they weren't there. They must have pulled enough strings with someone they knew. I was thoroughly disgusted with basic training. I went in, and I *wanted* to go. [*pauses three seconds*] I couldn't wait to get out of there.

James G. Kirk, Jr. (b. 1920) worked in war-related industries and was deferred for several years. In 1944 his deferment was not renewed and he was drafted into the army. Basic training at Fort Bragg, North Carolina, was a disciplined and controlled existence.

IT WAS THE regimentation. Knowing that you had to get up at a certain time, you had certain duties to do, you make your bed in a certain way. Doing everything on time. Everything had to be just according to army rules. Marching. Everything was *so* regimented at that time. It was strange for me, but as you continue you get used to it. . . . I just sort of knew that I had to, that it had to be done. No sense in me trying to avoid it. So I just got on the bandwagon.

The segregated military meant all recruits in his training unit were black, but James, educated in Minnesota, noticed an important difference.

Strangely enough, most of the blacks that I met, the majority of the blacks that I met, were not so well educated. In fact, I used to have to write letters to their families for some of them. They couldn't read or write. My education was superior . . . to what they had been used to.

Augustine Martinez was sent to Camp Robinson, Arkansas, for basic training. He remembers the hot weather and the constant rush from one thing to the next. Although he missed his family, he learned to adjust.

BASIC TRAINING was hard. And hot. Every morning twenty miles with full field pack and your rifle and whatever, shovel, bayonet, whatever it was. There we go. Sometimes, once in a while, "Okay, run now!" Running. Stop. Then we walked. Stop. Then we walked. No rest. All the way down about five miles, then, "Okay, take a five-minute break." [*panting sounds*] "Okay, let's go again!" Here we go again. Full field pack. Hot.

I remember they used to take us in that truck. Full field pack. Everybody together like sardines in there. Hot! "Okay, hurry up, hurry up, hurry up, hurry up, hurry up! Okay." We sat in the truck for a half-hour to forty-five minutes or an hour. And the truck was hot! "I thought you said we were going here." "Never mind, you stay there." I think they wanted to teach us [to] hurry up and wait. There you go—hurry up and wait. It was hot, though. Hot!

I didn't like [being so far away from my wife and kids], but as we looked at each other, it's just like brothers. We're all brothers. Same uniform and all that. Same necktie and everything. Same thing. Basic training. . . . Going to eat, training. You kind of forget a little bit about home. You forget about your house, your wife and kids. Just keep on with this. They got your mind on doing something else here. They kept you busy so you can't keep track of your wife and so on. But any time when you're alone, you sit up. Oh, I wonder how they're doing, and things like that.

Frederick Branham of Scanlon, near Cloquet, was also sent south to Arkansas for army basic training. His most prominent memories are of the weather—and of learning how to use the bayonet.

C AMP JOSEPH T. ROBINSON, Arkansas. It was terribly hot when I got down there in September. Didn't like their food, to start with. [*laughs*] Of course, infantry training is an awful lot of physical work. That's a positive way to put it. In the morning your fatigues would be fairly dry and clean. You had probably washed them the night before. And when you came in you looked like you'd lived in a hole for a week. Your feet ached and your back ached.

I think during my training down there I had enough training in bayonet to be an instructor. You had to be like a ballet dancer with that stupid thing. That seemed to be my free periods. I felt picked upon, but that didn't change anything at all. And you can't guess what happened when I got over in France—I threw the bayonet away. Along with many other infantrymen. Figured if we got close enough we're going to shoot them. If we're out of ammunition we'll surrender. . . . You can kill quite easily with a bullet, but to stab somebody and feel the flesh and everything else that you're destroying, I don't think you can do that.

Don Stephenson (b. 1925) of Spring Valley received his draft notice in 1943 and decided which service branch he preferred. At his induction at Fort Snelling, however, things did not work out quite the way he envisioned.

LIKE A LOT of kids my age, flying was the real thing, and that was in my mind. When they said my eyes weren't good [when I tried to volunteer], why then I knew that was out, so I just let the draft catch me. So when I got to Fort Snelling here in September '43, I thought, "Well, I'll try the navy." I was standing in line. I was one in the first of this group going through. There were about fifty or seventy-five of us from [Fillmore] county. I was one of the first ones to get through and make my choice, and I was standing in line to sign with the navy.

This buck sergeant came walking by, and why he picked me out, I don't know, but he says, "I want you in the Marine Corps." I said, "I thought we had a choice." He said, "I have a quota to fill." As soon as he said quota, why I knew what that meant. So I knew I was stuck for the Marine Corps.

In October 1943 I headed to San Diego and went to Marine Corps boot camp. . . . [Being far away from home was] scary. I had no idea how to deal with people or strangers or what have you. . . . Of course the first thing they did was take *everything* away from you. All your civilian clothes. They more or less stripped you down to nothing. Then they gave you a box to ship it home.

Not all recruits headed to points south: Toshio Abe, for example, came north—to Minnesota. Soon after the war's onset, the U.S. government recognized a need for trained Japanese linguists, and a military intelligence school program was established at Camp Savage, south of the Twin Cities. In June 1942 Toshio arrived with the first group of trainees, all Japanese American; he remained in the state until late 1943, and during this time moved his mother and brother to Minnesota from an internment camp in Arizona.

IN JUNE OF 1942 they started recruiting the linguists. . . . They started recruiting from various camps. . . . Out of the hundred and seventy-five guys at Camp Wolters [Texas], they called out twenty names. I was one of them. They sent us up here to Savage, Minnesota, in June of 1942.

We were in class eight hours a day, five days a week. On top of that we had two and a half hours of studying at night. We knew that we were going to be involved in the translation of documents and interrogation of prisoners of war. We knew that was why we were going through all of this.

It wasn't easy [adjusting to] Minnesota winters, because most of us were from Hawaii and California. In fact, the first winter here, I looked at an outside thermometer. It said thirty-six degrees below. I told myself, "I swear to god this will be my last winter here!" We didn't even know how to dress. The idea in cold climates that you put on layers of clothing, loose clothing in order to keep warm. Not knowing how to dress, many of us suffered frostbite on our feet and hands and ears.

As a Japanese American, Toshio immediately noticed a difference between Minnesota and his home state of California.

[T]he difference [is like] between night and day from the West Coast. Because here, we'd go into town and the civilians didn't look at you like you're some kind of subhuman animal walking down the street, like they did on the West Coast. People were pleasant, friendly.

[We were in uniform when we went to town,] because this was wartime. You had to be in uniform. Prior to Pearl Harbor you could wear civilian clothes when you were off base. But anyway, we were in uniform. Which reminds me—when we first came to Savage there was no transportation, no bus service or anything to town. We used to hitchhike. There was another guy and I, I remember one Saturday we were hitchhiking and a guy picked us up. We were in uniform, and this guy asked us if we were prisoners of war. I thought, "Why would a guy ask us that question and still pick us up?" [*laughs*] He was friendly. We told him that we weren't prisoners of war. . . . There were a lot of civilians that saw us around there, but they really didn't know why we were there.

Walt Radosevich of the Marine Corps, 1942, prior to shipping out to the Pacific

Most young men eventually adjusted to the rigors of basic training and life in the service, but not all did. Some tried to escape the military or stayed away past the end of their approved leave; others were convicted of criminal activity. Marine Walt Radosevich spent part of 1942–43 assigned to duty as a guard in the naval prison in Philadelphia. It was an eye-opening experience.

WHEN WE GOT to clerical school it was filled again, so that's when they put me in the naval prison as a guard. Between there and Portsmouth, Virginia, they had two big prisons, and they were big and rough, I mean, really. Standing in these towers, like you see in these prisons here, the same thing. They were all navy deserters, marine deserters, army deserters. Criminal activity also. It was really a prison for all enlisted men, or drafted men, that had gone over the hill or done things they shouldn't have. There were a lot of them in for theft, and there were special groups and that.

Well, there was probably twenty-five hundred prisoners in there, deserters, AWOL boys—boys that come in late, they're called AWOLs. We didn't have any major dishonorable discharges in there. . . . Most of them were guys that just wanted to go home. They took off without leave, and when they came back they had to go into prison. They'd be there for two, three, four months at a time, I guess, and then they'd try them again or discharge them. If they were discharged, then they got a bad conduct discharge or a dishonorable discharge, whatever they came up with on their verdict.

I hated that job. Because I felt sorry for a lot of them, you know, because they didn't want to be in. They were like I was, first time away from home, and they were lonely and everything else. Ninety percent of them that we had, that I got to know in the time I was there, were homesick kids. I mean, they were young, eighteen-, nineteen-year-old kids that had never been away from home. None of us had.

U.S. Army statistics count more than forty thousand deserters during World War II.

Perceptions of Race and Racism

WHEN THE UNITED STATES entered World War II, America was already a multiracial society. Even so, racism existed at many levels and in many forms, and the military was no exception. African Americans, for example, had long been relegated to a second-class status within the armed forces. Even as the size of the American military increased under the Selective Service Act of 1940, there were still fewer than 100,000 blacks serving in the army in November 1941 and a smaller number in the navy; the Marines Corps and Army Air Corps were closed to blacks entirely until 1942. Although Mexican Americans and Japanese Americans did not face these same legal obstructions, they often endured discriminatory treatment. Manpower demands whittled away at certain barriers, however, and the number of people of color in the armed forces grew. By war's end, 1945, hundreds of thousands of Mexican Americans, Japanese Americans, and African Americans served throughout the military. While numbers increased, discrimination and segregation remained in place, taking on quite different forms.

Throughout the war, blacks remained largely limited to support functions, in units performing manual labor, handling munitions, or providing transportation. In the navy, the vast majority of blacks served as stewards. Only a small number of black servicemen were placed in combat units, and relatively few of them ever saw action. A notable exception was the Air Corps' segregated 332nd Fighter Group, which served in North Africa and Italy in 1943–45.

Japanese Americans were suspect, partly due to existing racism in American society but especially because of the attack on Pearl Harbor. The U.S. government interned thousands in camps, but young *Nisei* (second-generation American) men were still inducted into service. There were segregated units, but some did see combat: of these, the highly decorated 442nd Regimental Combat Team stood out.

A total of 350,000 Mexican Americans (and Mexicans residing in the United States) were eventually drafted into the military. But while discrimination can be documented, for example, in lower rates of promotion and assignment to less-skilled jobs, no separate Mexican American units were formed and no official policy of segregation existed.

Men and women from Minnesota were part of this social fabric, witnesses to and participants in social change. Their experiences, and how they remember them now, years later, offer a fascinating window onto a changing world.

✦   ✦   ✦

The reactions of service personnel to segregation and institutionalized racism differed greatly, as did their willingness to speak openly about it. A number of white servicemen interviewed for this book observed and condemned racism. Carl Johnson (b. 1915) of McGregor, an Air Corps mechanic stationed at the 8th Air Force Replacement Center near the town of Stafford, England, distinctly remembers the bigotry as well as being ashamed of how some others acted.

WE HAD very few blacks. I think we had two. They worked just like we did. One of them did some mechanical work; the other guy cleaned up the trucks. I myself never had any gripes, but we had some southern boys. I know the one was from Oklahoma. He and I were walking down the sidewalk one day, off base. We were both staff sergeants. We were talking, and he looked up, and here was a black master sergeant[, who outranked us]. And he looked up, and he says, "Get off the sidewalk you black son of a b." And I felt so bad. The black master sergeant probably thought the same thing about me as he did [about this other fellow]. He couldn't stand to meet him on the sidewalk. The black sergeant just politely stepped to the side, and when we got by he stepped back on the sidewalk. . . . I felt ashamed, because they were there for the same purpose as we were. But there was a problem.

Delbert Kuehl was born and raised on a farm outside Alexandria. Ordained a minister in March 1942, in July he enlisted in the army as a chaplain, and after basic training he volunteered for service with the paratroopers. He served in Europe with the 82nd Airborne.

YES, WE HAD some men in our unit who made racist comments. Quite a few of our troopers were from the South, and there was still a lot of antagonism and prejudice against blacks by some of the southern troops. Not all of them, but quite a few of them. I would hear them talk, and that bothered me. "They aren't as talented as we are. They are trying to undercut the whites in any way they can. They are lazy." These kind of things. I told them I didn't think it was true. Now I couldn't talk from experience, and that was too bad. I could not talk from any experience of close relationships with blacks—we didn't even have *one* in Alexandria, where I grew up.

For the years 1943–46, Walt Radosevich was assigned to the marine contingent aboard the battleship USS *Iowa*, which was in the Pacific. Confronted with racism onboard ship, he empathized with the black sailors.

THOSE POOR GUYS. I got to know five or six of them, from the Carolinas. They were down on the third deck. They were just cooks, mess boys; they worked in the galley all the time. Stewards they were, really, for the ship. They were always in the officer's quarters. That was their special job.

They were good sailors. They were real nice. See, I was born and raised there in Ohio, five miles from [the town of] Oberlin, and that was underground railroad for the blacks. So I grew up with blacks, and I still have very, very good black friends back there in Ohio that I grew up with, went to school with, danced with the girls and that.

Some of the fellows didn't like it, especially the southern boys. . . . We had a lot of southerners, and they just *hated* them. . . . "You don't talk to a nigger." That was what they said. The blacks would come through our apartments to go to their jobs and to go to the mess hall—they had to come through ours—and these southern boys would just be on them all the time. I often said, "What are you guys hollering at them for? They're here like we are. They're the same as we are." . . . They were there, they had a job to do, and they did it. . . . Why there was, why there *is* so much hatred for them, even today, I don't understand it.

Aileen Duffeny Krusell (b. 1922) of St. Paul was a Navy WAVE (Women Accepted for Volunteer Emergency Service); she worked in Washington, DC, for the Office of Naval Intelligence.

THERE WERE no blacks at Hunter College [in the Bronx], where I had basic training. When I got in Washington, DC, there were a few blacks, but they were in custodial work and in the kitchens. Their jobs were maintenance or cooking. They didn't mingle with any of us at work. We didn't bother *them* and they didn't bother *us,* but there was a friendly atmosphere between all of us, believe it or not. But there weren't a lot of them there.

Aileen Duffeny Krusell,
Navy WAVE, 1943–46

Some Caucasian service personnel admitted to racist attitudes or an insensitivity toward people of color. Some were changed by their experiences—and some were not. In the following section, several names have been omitted: speaking about attitudes and actions in the 1940s, many were ashamed of themselves but still willing to talk. The first excerpt is from an enlisted man who served the entire war in the navy, including three years of front-line duty in the Pacific.

ON THE [battleship I was on], there were more colored than there were Filipino. But they were all mess stewards. That was the only thing they were. They served the officers, cooking and serving their tables. They were not with the whites at all. They were entirely, 100 percent segregated.

If we had liberty for an evening, blacks and whites did not mix, not at all. It was so segregated that there wasn't any attempt to do it. No one even thought of mixing.

The first time I ever saw a colored guy who was a machinist's mate [like me] was when I was down at the repair base in San Diego. That was in 1945, right after the war. I had a horizontal boring mill down there, and I got a second-class colored machinist's mate. . . . He wanted to be friendly. I ignored him; I'll be honest with you. Just like he ain't there.

Born and raised in rural northern Minnesota, this serviceman had no contact with people of color. The situation changed when he joined the army and was shipped south for training.

WE ENCOUNTERED blacks, but just on the street. You know, you'd have an evening pass, or a weekend pass, or something. The colored people didn't really impress me. Like, two of us were on a pass [when I was stationed in Alabama for basic training]. We walked down the street. We were going to get a cup of coffee, or whatever. And seven colored guys are walking abreast. Well, the two white guys have to go around them, off the road. [*pauses three seconds*] And little things like that kind of just put a taint on.

[The blacks were] in service units. They were truck drivers and maintenance people, where there were vehicles. When we were getting ready to jump, they were out there pulling the blocks out from under the wheels [of the airplanes]. None of them were paratroopers.

We ignored them. Because most of the guys [in my unit] had had little encounters like I'd had in basic training. You know, they were 4-Fs, they were draft dodgers, and whatever they were. And seven or eight of them would pick on two guys. Well, you can't lick seven of them, because we tried that. So we had a dim view of those people.

One Pacific theater Air Corps veteran is bitter about the attention given to some black veterans. From his perspective, discrimination did not exist.

THIS GREAT emphasis on that famous squadron of black pilots in Europe, the Red Tails [the Tuskegee Airmen, the 332nd Fighter Group]. . . . These guys, every one of them, is a god-hero. Well, just because they were black and they were just doing their job, like we were? I went through much more hell than any one of them did. I'm just a guy nobody knows, one of the thousands and thousands of pilots and air crews that were over there. [*pauses three seconds*] *Everybody* contributed during World War II. After the fact to blow it into something beyond what it really was is a little bit unfair.

By the way, over on Tinian and Saipan, of all the thousands of crewmen, I didn't see one black. I don't think they were discriminated [against]. I think they just didn't try out for that. The people that tried out for it got to be pilots. I don't know what the demographics was of getting into training and various, I don't know what that was. . . . Why there weren't any blacks? There just weren't.

In a naval hospital for skin problems, marine Larry Strand of Minneapolis had an encounter that taught him a life lesson.

I HAD A personal experience with a black in the hospital, and we became very good friends. I didn't know a whole lot about blacks, but I thought they could take a joke like anybody else. At that time we didn't have a lot of blacks [in Minnesota]. We had quite a few in south Minneapolis, but I hadn't been associated with very many of them. I went in and washed my face. This was in the hospital, and this guy was going to go in to wash his face. I said, "Why bother? You won't know the difference." God, he went and got his knife! A six-inch knife! And he came after me! I said, "I'm sorry! I'm sorry! I didn't mean to offend you. I was just making a joke." That was the best thing that happened to me. I've never forgotten that one. That was a good experience for me as a young man. . . . I learned my lesson there for the rest of my life.

Four African American servicemen speak about discrimination and the segregated military; their experiences yielded very different perspectives. The first, James Griffin of St. Paul, was a twenty-eight-year-old father of two when he entered the navy in May 1945. He began basic training at Great Lakes Naval Training Center just as the navy started to desegregate its facilities. Jim remembers tension when his group of African American trainees was ordered to move from all-black Camp Smalls to formerly all-white Camp Downs.

S O WE GOT together and marched off. And like I said, they called a couple of drummer boys down [*laughs*], so there were two drummers in between sixty-four guys. And we marched on off to Camp Downs.

So we marched out of there. The guy who was pushing us through boots, name was Blount, he was tough, and he knew how to handle men. . . . They called him Pops; he was about my age. Most of these guys were kids . . . youngsters.

Got around the bend from Camp Downs, not quite in sight of the gate there, and this guy called halt. He says, "Now, fellas, I don't know what's going to happen when we hit this camp, but if there's any problems don't settle it yourself. You tell me about it, and I'll handle it. And another thing, when we march into camp, I want those guys to see the best marching camp outfit they've ever seen." That's one thing about black soldiers and sailors: they were always good marchers. He called us to attention, and we shoved off and marched in there.

He took us down there and got us our barracks and so on and so forth. We started putting our gear away, and [we were told] what time we were supposed to be there to eat. We said okay. This one fellow said, "Wait a minute, better look around." This guy that was pushing us through boots, he said, "You see that up there?" They had a noose hanging up there!

Hell, them guys in the camp put it there! So [Blount] says, "Don't do nothing. Take it easy. We're going down to chow now, and I'll go down and talk to the officer of the day." Of course, I wasn't there, but everybody found out what he said. He went down and told the officer of the day, he says, "We came in here peacefully. You go hanging nooses around here, we might have a riot here." The officer of the day, the guy that had the hat on that day, had good sense. He says, "That won't happen again." And we never had a bit of trouble.

Joe Gomer of Duluth, born in 1920 and raised in Iowa Falls, Iowa, enlisted in the U.S. Army in 1942 after graduating from college. He was accepted into Aviation Cadet Training at Tuskegee Army Air Field, Alabama. Tuskegee was home to the all-black 99th Pursuit Squadron, later the 332nd Fighter Group, formed in 1942. For Joe, arriving in the South was a journey into another world.

I *knew* [segregation] existed. For example, [as a boy] I went with a group. They were all white, except my brother and me. There were two of us. We were flying our model planes in Waterloo, Iowa, and we went into this lunch place. As they got my order, they put it in a bag and told me I would just have to take it outside and eat it.

I'd never been south before as an adult. . . . We were the first group out of the Midwest [heading to Tuskegee]. Two other individuals went with me and went across the Mason-Dixon Line. That's when I realized we hit the South, because when we went to the diner [car], they escorted us to the table at the back and then pulled the curtain on us. Of course I got up and pulled the curtain back a couple times and then finally walked out. We were going to take our meal back to the Pullman, but the trainman came by and said, "We'd be pleased. We'd like to have you come out." So we did eat the rest of our meals, but behind the curtain.

From Joe's perspective, wearing a uniform did not seem to make a difference in how blacks were treated off base in the South.

Well, it depended on where you were. They didn't have much use for us in Tuskegee, Alabama. And there was a white sheriff there that made life pretty miserable for the military. Just for blacks. The uniform didn't really help you. And there were places where, even as officers, white airmen or soldiers would refuse to salute me. That didn't happen too often. . . . If you could get their attention, [you could] arrest them or something like that, but usually it was too much trouble. They'd just keep on going, and there wasn't much you could do.

I felt mostly powerlessness. Because there was nothing you could do. But there were others who were just the opposite so . . . you can't lump them all together. There were good and bad. Whites going south also had their first introduction to segregation, and it bothered them. They would be in with the blacks, and they would be ordered to get up and go to their section.

Following fighter pilot training, in May 1943 Joe was commissioned a second lieutenant and then shipped overseas to a duty station in Italy. He flew sixty-eight
combat missions before rotating out of the 332nd Fighter Group and back to the
United States in December 1944. Returning home meant re-entering a segregated society.

I should also tell you about my reality check after coming home [from Italy]. There are combat troops, combat veterans, and there are black combat veterans. When they turned me loose, they took me over to Naples, and I had to wait for transportation. [It was] December '44. I think I was the only person of color in all the thousands of people. We came back on the SS *America*. We had to wait for a troop ship. It came time to board ship, and I was with a group of officers. I was a first lieutenant. There weren't a lot of officers there, but . . . the officers went aboard first, naturally.

There was a short, fat, redneck captain standing up on this little box. When he got to me, he just looked and ordered me to the end of the line. Now I was a combat veteran. I'm on my way home, a war hero. And that guy probably had not seen a day of combat in his life. Well, the second time he ordered me to the end of the line . . . [*trails off*]. I wanted to come home—I picked up my duffel bag and bell pack and went to the end of the line, behind everybody. Everybody. I was the last person to board ship. But I knew I was coming home. I tell you what, if I had felt toward the Germans the way I felt toward that honky captain, I would have been an ace many times over. [*laughs*] That's the only time I ever had a real killer instinct. . . . But what could I do? . . . I don't know what he would have done if I had outranked him, but it'd be kind of an embarrassing situation for him if he had to order a higher-ranking person out of the line.

The first place I went was home. We got leave. [I was] reunited with my wife, all that sort of thing. . . . For a few days I was a war hero, and not a black combat veteran. I was just a combat veteran.

Wilbert Bartlett (b. 1921) of St. Paul was in the U.S. Army and stationed during 1944–45 in Greensboro, North Carolina, at an overseas replacement depot. His primary responsibility was basic training for new recruits of color. He learned that, in the eyes of the military, race was a fluid concept.

I DON'T KNOW for some of them [in our training area] if you would call them African Americans. They had this African American group. Some Mexicans, some Indians, some of the darker races. If he was dark, if he was a Mexican—they have many black-skinned Mexicans—if they were dark, they ended up in that group. And they didn't hesitate to put them there, either. That caused some friction sometimes, too, because a lot of times these people knew what they were. Sometimes they wondered why they had to be in a so-called— it was Negro then—why they had to be in a Negro outfit, when they were Mexican. It was because they didn't have an all-Mexican outfit. They didn't feel that they were any kind of color at all. They thought they should be in a white outfit. The discrimination was from color and race.

Wilbert attended college in Jefferson City, Missouri, and while in the army was stationed at Jefferson Barracks, near St. Louis, before being posted to Greensboro. He remembers clear differences between these locations.

You noticed a difference. When I went to Jefferson City, in Missouri, I knew what things were going to be like, but when I went to North Carolina, then you saw just a little bit more of the Jim Crow [system]. It was really—There was no doubt in your mind what things were. When you got into town, into Greensboro, in the town itself, you knew right away that you were going to the black restaurants, you're going to the black entrance to the theaters, and things like that.

It started getting better at the end of our time in Greensboro[, in 1945]. Things were breaking down a little bit. You noticed a little change. It wasn't something that you could get up and holler about, but you noticed a little change. We had MPs that were black in Greensboro, black MPs, and they drove their own cars. The MPs drove their cars around, military cars. They went into places where sometimes they had to go for a mix-up of whites and blacks. They didn't just have the car, they had the .25[-caliber] pistols and hats and everything. Regular outfit just like the white MPs.

They worked together sometimes, the MPs, because sometimes it wouldn't be prudent for the black MP to go into a white area by himself to try to break up something, so they had the radios in the cars. Especially when there were blacks and whites involved. Blacks wouldn't go into a place probably anyway, if there were just whites involved. It just wouldn't be done like that. But if there were both races involved in something, they would even call on each other. They seemed to work pretty good like that. It was more prevalent in Greensboro than in St. Louis.

For a black man in uniform in North Carolina in 1944–45, there was a period of adjustment to the South and its entrenched racism. But fighting the system at that time, Wilbert concluded, simply was not worth it.

A lot of these drugstores still had the old counters where you sit down and eat. Now that wasn't—You couldn't do that. But some of them tried to do it. We got politely asked to leave. It wasn't done, to sit down at lunch counters and eat at that time. [In uniform or not in uniform, it] didn't make a difference. It was terrible, too. Being in the service and you'd get the same old answer: Go to the black drugstores.

It wasn't that you didn't have places to go to; it was just the idea that you should be able to go anywhere you wanted to go to. That was the drawback. You either make up your mind if you want to try—you make up your mind that you're maybe going to run into trouble—or you just kind of say what the heck and forget about it. Those from Minnesota that would go over there and find out they can't go to a drugstore and sit down and get sandwich or something, they got to rebel. First thing you know, somebody's going to get loud, start talking, cursing. It's going to bring problems. And that's when they call in the police.

Lawrence Brown was born and raised in Minneapolis. In June 1942, at age twenty-two, he was drafted into the army and assigned to the segregated 604th Ordinance Ammunition Company. Commanded by white officers, the unit received, stored, and distributed a broad range of ammunition for assorted small and large caliber weapons. A noncommissioned officer, Lawrence served with this unit in North Africa (November 1942–August 1943) and in Sicily and Italy (August 1943–February 1945).

IT WAS SO foreign to me, the concept of segregation. The way I was raised, I never thought that way. Being born and raised in Minneapolis it was a little bit different. I never had to think about people as being in boxes: blacks here, whites there. That's how silly I was probably. I never saw things in a color deal. . . . A lot of guys said, "I'm not going because of segregation," and all that crap. That didn't enter my mind. I'm not stupid. There was a little thing in the back of my mind, but it never was a big thing. . . . So coming from the background that I did, the military was horrible. It was just demeaning. I was like a farm animal or something. Back of the bus. Upstairs in the theater.

I was the most angry guy in the world in the service. I was angry about what I was forced to do. Others were, too, but most of them resort to, to physical violence, and that's where I'm not stupid. I feel that I want to win. In a battle I want to win. And if you get killed, you don't win. And if you go in with a plan being very hopeful that you'll win, if you don't win you can go back and fight again the next day. And given the circumstances that I was in [trying to fight the U.S. military,] I knew that the chances of winning were almost nil; the odds were too great.

Basic training was a hurry-up, get us ready to be stevedores. You don't have to train stevedores to be expert riflemen. We were on the rifle range probably two days, three days maybe. But we had no rifles. You know when we got rifles? On the boat when we were on the sea [heading to North Africa]. We finally got rifles, and this one little guy says, "Now we're all equal." But nobody had any ammo. Later we finally got ammunition for our guns.

Although Lawrence wanted to fight a system he perceived to be unfair, to do so openly would have been impossible. He remembers taking some action, within the system's limits.

You fight a system like that, but you fight it with the best weapon you have available—your head. And you're fighting a lot of battles. You're fighting a battle with yourself. How do I keep my sanity in this situation? How do I keep from punching this idiot, this asshole [white officer] over here who is trying to make me a little guy because he's so small himself? Can't do anything. How do you deal with this? You pinch yourself. You think about running away. I thought about going away, but, hell, stationed in North Africa, there was a thousand miles of land and ten thousand miles of water.

We had all these minority papers: Chicago *Defender,* Pittsburgh *Courier,* and whatnot. . . . My buddy and I, we got the papers [through the mail]. And the papers were writing about, they're not using our guys [blacks] to the best advantage and all this stuff. So when I get that stuff and cut out the things that I thought were of interest to the people, I put it on the bulletin board. This was not what the segregated army wanted.

I got called in. "Sergeant Brown, are you the one who put this on the board?" "Yes." "You put any more on the bulletin board, court-martial." I said, "When I send letters home or when I get letters from home they're usually censored. If you don't want the things that are in the papers to be put on that board, then you censor the *papers* when they come in. The papers come in here through the mail. Until you do that I am going to put this stuff on the bulletin board." Now that took a lot of courage. But I knew I was right. I thought I was right, I should say. So that was the way I fought this thing.

With strong anti-Japanese feelings evident after the attack on Pearl Harbor, Japanese American servicemen faced an especially difficult situation. Although citizens and in uniform, they still felt the effect of U.S. government policies that discriminated against Japanese Americans and led to the internment in relocation camps of more than 110,000, 64 percent of whom were American citizens.

Tom Takeshi Oye, a second-generation American, was drafted into the army in 1941 and served during 1944–45 in France and Italy in the Nisei 442nd Regimental Combat Team. He points out the irony of the separate facilities he encountered at a base in Arkansas.

A S A JAPANESE AMERICAN, I didn't feel singled out at all. Just part of the army. We were under orders to go to Camp Robinson in Arkansas, and that was it. That would have been the latter part of February [1942 that we arrived there].

The only thing that I remember about Arkansas is that Arkansas had separate facilities for the blacks and the whites. One time, going into Little Rock on a weekend, I used the black facilities because I didn't know the difference. And when I came out, a white person approached me and said, "You know, you're not supposed to use the black facilities. That's for black folks. You use the white." So this was interesting, because the army had transferred us off of the West Coast because we weren't fit to be there [after Pearl Harbor], and here we are in Arkansas and they're telling me that blacks are black and you are not a black, so you have to use the white.

Toshio Abe, the son of Japanese immigrants, grew up in California. A college student when he was drafted into the U.S. Army in April 1941, he too was moved from a California duty station after Pearl Harbor. At the time Toshio was sent to Camp Wolters in Texas, his family was interned in a relocation camp in the Arizona desert. He recalls feeling powerless about the situation.

W E WEREN'T HAPPY about it. Here again, we felt that there was nothing we could do about it. There's an old Japanese phrase, they say *shikataganai,* which means "there's nothing that we can do about it." I mean, it's happening and that's it. We learned that from our parents. You see something happening that you don't quite agree with, and yet if you don't have the power to change it you have to more or less "accept" it. I think most of us [Japanese Americans] in the service saw our friends and parents being sent to these camps. It was something that we weren't all that happy about, and yet there was nothing we could do about it. Our attitude was that we all accepted it. . . . We in the service, I would say that we were insulated from all these unpleasant details of evacuating the civilians, our friends, our relatives. We didn't really realize what they were going through. Our friends and our relatives didn't have time to be writing to us and telling us what they were going through.

Mexican American veterans recall a different reality from that described by either African Americans or Japanese Americans. These recruits had to leave Minnesota for military service, and all of those interviewed remember being anxious about what they might encounter—some had heard from parents or friends about negative experiences in Texas or elsewhere in the South. Yet none claim to have personally experienced overt discrimination or racism while in the service, even though they witnessed it.

Augustine Martinez of St. Paul, 1943

Augustine Martinez was born in 1919 in Mexico; his family, migrant workers, moved to St. Paul when he was seven. Drafted into the army in 1944, and at that time still a Mexican citizen, Augustine identified racism in the military. But, he says, it was not directed at him.

THE PEOPLE in Arkansas, [where I had basic training,] they were all right. I mentioned the colored people. They still didn't like too much about those people, the colored people. I noticed that. Because we used to go in the park, the guys, and bum around. You have to go to the white toilet and the black toilet. They were separate in those days. And buses downtown—the blacks were in the back and the whites in the front. I noticed that. I don't dare say anything. . . . It isn't right to be like that. I said, "We're all equal. We're all together here. What the hell—we're all human anyway." I sat right next to a colored guy, just to make it. There's no big deal in that. . . . Now today, everything is changed.

They treated me like a white person. I'm white [referring to his light-colored skin]. They treated me as white. No big deal there. They can see the color black, but they got me as a white. I used to go to churches just to eat, me and my partners. Go around singing. Just to get a sandwich, because we were hungry. We sang, hallelujah and things like that, just to go eat. They treated us good, though. . . . And there were places we would go for a beer or something. They would treat us good.

Henry T. Capiz was born and raised in St. Paul, the oldest of six children of Mexican immigrant parents. Sent to Camp Hood, Texas, for basic training, Henry identified differences between recruits of Mexican heritage.

As MEXICAN AMERICANS, we weren't segregated at all. We were integrated into the military population. . . . [During basic training in Texas,] I don't recall anybody segregating themselves into groups. But I think the Mexican Americans, they had a little more grouping among themselves. Those from the South or Southwest, they always got together and spoke Spanish in little groups. . . . I kind of found it foreign to be with those [Mexican American] guys from Texas. They had their own language and their own customs. It was a little foreign to me, which they picked up on right away. I was from Minnesota.

I did speak a lot of Spanish with them. I also spoke English with them, because at home we spoke both languages. Even my mother— my mother went to school in Texas, so she spoke English, too. We spoke both languages. I was fortunate that my grandmother taught me Spanish. I was able to speak both languages. . . . I tended to socialize mostly with the European Americans . . . sort of back and forth. [The Mexican American guys] wouldn't have any of that. They thought I was trying to be better than they were, but that was not the case.

Henry's father, who was from Texas, warned him to expect discrimination when he arrived there, but he says he did not find it.

I knew that there was discrimination in Texas; that was always in the back of my mind. I was aware that from the stories my dad used to tell me of how he'd go to work for a farmer, and the farmer would chase him off with a shotgun and not pay him. That was in the back of my mind. I was somewhat concerned about what might happen.

One of the first things I noticed was the discrimination against the blacks. They had to sit in the back of the bus. When we would catch a bus into town, they had to sit in the back of the bus. But I found no discrimination at all, because I would wander around the towns—Killeen, Delton, Temple—and I found no discrimination at all in those areas. . . . I was a little leery about it, but I never found any problem. I went in all the shops and all the restaurants. I said, "Where's the discrimination?"

Women in Uniform

WOMEN HAD SERVED officially in the U.S. military since the first decade of the twentieth century, in both the Army and Navy Nurse Corps. But nursing was a traditional female role, and numbers remained small. World War II changed the situation. Although many U.S. military leaders initially resisted establishing separate organizations for women, as manpower requirements increased they saw that creating auxiliaries, or female units, could release more men for front-line duty. By 1945, all the service branches had launched auxiliaries.

Women in uniform initially performed traditional female tasks: they were secretaries and file clerks, postal workers and storekeepers. While the majority of women continued to be assigned such jobs throughout the war, as the fighting wore on auxiliaries received newer duties. Navy WAVES (Women Accepted for Volunteer Emergency

Service), for example, worked in communications; others were trained in meteorology. The pilots of the Air Corps' WASP (Women Airforce Service Pilots) program worked as instructors, trained male flight crews and pilots, and ferried all types of aircraft—including heavy bombers—across the country.

Women entering an auxiliary force faced numerous challenges: they were assigned to low-skill positions; they encountered sexism on the job; their training was minimal, less than a male soldier would receive to perform similar work; and black women remained in segregated units. Women in uniform endured public misunderstanding and were in some cases labeled as promiscuous or as lesbians. And always there was hostility from the service establishments, which saw in the auxiliaries a threat to the traditional, male-dominated order.

But there were also advantages, the most obvious among them that military service—outside of nurse corps units—became a real option for women. In the service, some women acquired new jobs, mastering tasks denied them in the civilian world. Joining the military represented for some a way of moving forward, away from home or family or small-town life. Minnesota women in uniform had duty stations in many corners of the country—and even the globe: from Washington, DC, to San Diego, from the Philippines and New Guinea to France and Germany. Many recall the sense of accomplishment they gained from managing new responsibilities, and several described a self-awareness and a self-confidence that remained even after the uniform was exchanged for civilian clothing.

✦ ✦ ✦

Elizabeth (Betty) Wall Strohfus was born in 1919 and raised in Faribault. She was working in town when, in 1942, she had her first airplane ride. She immediately decided to pursue flying.

THIS PERSON hadn't had a license too long, and he loved to give people thrills. We got in his little Piper Cub, sixty-five horsepower, and went up about thirty-five hundred feet and into a stall and a spin. He turned around and looked at me, and I said, "One more time!" After six more times he didn't look around any more. He landed that airplane, and he was a little green. He excused himself and came back and said, "You know, whatever you do in this life, you've got to learn how to fly. I've made everyone else sick. You are the only one that has made *me* sick!" [*laughs*] I knew at that time that I *had* to learn how to fly, because for me, it was an experience. I had to learn.

In 1943, Betty volunteered for the newly formed WASP program, which was to perform a variety of duties stateside, relieving male pilots for overseas combat assignments.

WASP pilot Betty Wall Strohfus of Faribault, 1944

In '43 I started flying more [with the local Civil Air Patrol]. Then we got a notice from the government that they needed women to take over men's jobs in flying, because they needed the men to go to war. They needed women that knew how to fly, to do the ferrying and the training done during those years. We needed either thirty-five hours of flying time or a private license. I never got around to getting a private license; I just got my thirty-five hours of flying time. By this time, I had also talked to my sister, Mary, who liked to fly, and my friend, Kay Murphy. The three of us headed down to Avenger Field in Sweetwater, Texas, for training.

Training was a six-month period. You see, we had a more rapid training than men, because we had to have that little bit of flying before we were accepted. They knew that we could handle an aircraft by that time. . . . Now the ground school, for me it was very difficult, because I never got a pilot license. When I got into engines and meteorology and physics, I felt such a bad stomachache. It was really difficult. But I knew if I wanted to fly airplanes, I had to do it. I cried a lot of nights, but I passed the ground school.

Of the 1,800 women accepted for the new WASP program, just 1,074 finished the rigorous training at Avenger Field and graduated in early 1944; Betty was one of them. She was stationed at Las Vegas Army Airfield, Nevada, where she flew a variety of aircraft, did gunnery training, and provided in-flight instrument training for male pilots.

[The male officers] were very cautious when we first came to Las Vegas. We were checked out in everything we were to fly, because they did not *believe* that we could fly the airplanes. But they checked us out and saw that, yes, we could handle these aircraft just as well as, if not better than, them. You see, if we weren't better than the men, we couldn't fly the airplanes—we *had* to be better, and we knew that. We did do a really good job. If they didn't like us there, they could send us home. At that time we were not [officially] a part of the military, so if they had told us we had to go home, we'd have had to go, because we were not going to be taken into another service like the WAC [Women's Army Corps] or the WAVES. So we knew that if we didn't do a good job, we'd get sent home.

After some time they needed instructor pilots, so I went back to Sweetwater, Texas, for a very intensive instruction course. Then I went back to Las Vegas Army Airfield and taught instrument flying to the fellows. To begin with I had a little trouble. There was this big tall guy, about six foot two. I'm going down [to the plane] with my two cushions and my parachute on my back, and he's really dragging with his parachute. I said, "You don't want to fly with me, Jimmy?" He said, "No." I said, "You're afraid of flying with me?" He said, "Yes."

We were flying an AT-6 trainer at that time. But it was equipped with the hood to go over the cockpit, to teach instrument flying. We got in; I didn't put the hood on. I said, "We'll take it up to thirty-five hundred feet, and when I wiggle the stick, I want control." So I did a lot of maneuvers and scared the hell out of him. I wanted him to know that regardless of the position he put our plane in, I could pull it out. That was his worry. When he's under the hood, he can't see outside—you could be going straight down and think you're flying straight and level. So you have to trust your pilot, your instructor. Once he found out I had the skill, I had no problem. I did that a few times, and then I never had any more problems with the fellows.

Betty's military flying career ended in December 1944 with the government's decision to deactivate the WASP program. The women pilots were simply sent home.

When I heard the WASPs were being deactivated, it was really hard. I really wasn't expecting the deactivation. You see, we were so busy doing what we were doing. We thought, "How could they get along *without* us?" We were doing all this training and all this ferrying. It was a shock, but, also, we knew that we went in to relieve the men for combat duty. [By late 1944] they had enough men pilots. . . . They had enough men coming home from overseas. They needed the men to do the flying now, to get their flight time.

Betty Myers Sarner (b. 1923) had spent part of 1943 working in a shipyard in Richmond, California, before returning home to St. Paul. Restless, she talked to her mother about joining the Navy WAVES.

M Y GIRLFRIEND Margaret had already joined. I said, "Gee, Mom, that sounds like a good idea." "Well," she says, "you think it over." At the time my mom needed a little help along the way. Financially. But then I found out that I could use her—she would be my dependent, and I would get money in the service for her. So consequently that made me feel a little bit better that, if I did leave her, I didn't leave her in the lurch financially. She did get something every month; it came out of my check. I don't have any idea what it was; it was probably a pittance, but it was worth something. . . . Needless to say, I wasn't too wealthy in the service. I never went to any fancy nightclubs; I went to the USOs [United Services Organizations]. They were a good place to meet people and have fun.

Betty joined the WAVES and spent 1944–46 in service. She recalls that once she became part of the navy, men and especially women her age treated her differently.

I felt that I was a part of the war effort. But we girls in uniform, you know, were not looked on as very—Well, a lot of guys and other girls didn't look on us as very good citizens. They just thought we were in the service for one thing—to get a man, and things like that.

I tell you, when I came home on leave to St. Paul the one time, the part that I recall more than anything is when we were in a nightclub. You know, when you're in the service you've got your uniform on, and all the guys have got their uniform on. You have something in common, and it's much easier for a guy to come over and talk to you, because you have that uniform on. That's the way it happened. Well, naturally, the civilian girls didn't like that one bit, because it was just like they were being shunned. So they just made little snide remarks like, "What *we* really need is a uniform." Stuff like that. I could brush it off. It didn't bother me any, because the guys were coming over and talking to me. So I could care less. [*laughs*] It worked real good.

Another Navy WAVE, Pat Cavanagh Ethier (b. 1923) of St. Paul, recalls that in 1943 her fiancé, Orville Ethier (b. 1921), tried to convince her to stay out of the service. She also describes certain perceptions that existed about women in uniform.

ORV AND I were engaged then, and he was very opposed to my going in the navy, *very* opposed. I think he felt that, you know, that I'd have the opportunity to meet other men and, sailors being what they are, I think that he was concerned about me being away. He tried to talk me out of it, but of course [he was onboard a ship in the Pacific], so it was long distance. He said that he wished I wouldn't do that, but of course I was determined that I was going to, so I did.

As far as relationships with other servicemen, the ones that I encountered always were fairly respectful. I think that maybe part of it was the fact that we [women] had this feeling of needing to keep our behavior at a level even above what the ordinary person was, because of this stigma sometimes attached to women in the service. [*pauses five seconds*] I don't necessarily mean stigma. . . . I think that there may have been the perception that, there could have been a little bit of—Oh, you were in the navy because you were looking for men. [*laughs*] And that maybe your behavior would be a little suspect because of that. I don't know; maybe this was just a perception. But

I think we had the feeling, the girls that I was with, we had the feeling that we needed to be a little above and beyond the average person, because we needed to bring that respect to ourselves.

In January 1945, Pat was stationed in San Diego. Orville was on stateside leave after his ship, the *Ward*, was sunk during action in the Philippines. At home in St. Paul that month, they made a spur-of-the-moment decision—to get married. Pat's description of these events is filled with a sense of urgency, in some respects a real-life version of the wartime film *The Clock*, in which Judy Garland and Robert Walker race against time to marry before Walker ships out with his unit.

Orv and I both had leave at the same time. I had gotten home to St. Paul before he did because I got a flight, so I was home to greet him in Union Depot when he came in. We were home—I'm trying to think how long we were home—and we decided that we might as well get married. It was a Saturday, and we decided that we would get married. This was Saturday; we were married on the following Wednesday. We're both Catholic, so we had to go out and talk to the priest about this. We had to get a dispensation from the church to get married without the customary three Sundays of banns. And we had to get a waiver of the waiting period at the county office. Somehow we got all that done, so we got married!

The honeymoon, Pat recalls with a smile, consisted of several days at her sister-in-law's house in St. Paul and a train ride back to San Diego. Then separation.

I don't even recall how many days we had at home. We had a reception, but we just had family, of course, that's all that was there at my sister-in-law's place [on Goodrich Avenue in St. Paul]. My brother Jim was in the service, but my sister-in-law Marie had the house and we had a reception there with family. Orv and I went to the Saint Paul Hotel that night after the wedding, and we figured we could stay there until we were going to go back to San Diego. But my sister-in-law said, "Well, why do that? You take the house here, and I'll move down with your mom and dad." [*laughs*] So we stayed in her house until we went back.

We went back to San Diego on the train then. . . . Orv went back to San Francisco and then was transferred to Mayport Naval Air Station [in Florida]. . . . We were a whole continent apart.

Veda Ponikvar was born and raised in Chisholm, on the Iron Range. The oldest child of Slovenian immigrant parents, she graduated from Drake University in 1942 with a degree in journalism, then enlisted in the Navy WAVES. She received an officer's commission and training as a linguist.

I WAS ALWAYS fascinated by the navy. As a person with a college degree, I knew that I would have some interesting assignment. I didn't know what it was going to be, but I didn't think that with my degree and my background that they would put me in some room pushing a pencil.

I was sent to the military language school in Frederick, Maryland, which was a terrific experience. I spent thirteen weeks there. . . . I concentrated on the Slavic languages. It was rough, especially because I had to learn at least the key words and sentences for both Czech and Polish.

We were in class at six o'clock in the morning, five days a week. And many, many times we would have our dinner at six o'clock and be back at our desks at seven. It was very intensive, but nobody ever protested or ever asked why, because I think we were all aware that this was very crucial and very important. . . . We all felt that we had to do very well. It was strange—there was an urgency to everything. Somehow we had to get the war over with, and we couldn't prolong this.

There were more men than women in my class, but a fair number of women. . . . [Fair treatment by men in uniform] never seemed to be a problem as far as I was concerned. . . . There was a job to do, and we had to get it done. There wasn't any time for any foolishness.

From 1943 to 1946, Veda served in the Office of Naval Intelligence in Washington, DC, interpreting information on Eastern Europe and Yugoslavia, briefing both government and military policymakers.

My job was to decode, for one thing. But the other was to work with the other branches of the military. We would gather all of the information of where the armies were, where the navy was, where the marines were, the number of casualties, the number of reinforcements, all that sort of thing.

Early in the morning, and we'd start at seven o'clock, your lower-grade officers would come. Like ensigns from the navy and lieutenants and captains [from other branches]. We had great big maps all over the place, and then we had these pins with colored heads. Each one meant something. We would fill that whole area with those pins, and then we would give them an overview of what was happening throughout the world. Then the next level of officers would come in, and from an intelligence standpoint they would get a little higher briefing, and so on up the ladder until we came to the admirals and the generals. Then they were the ones that went and informed President Roosevelt.

I never found any delineation [between men and women in uniform]. There were some difficulties in some offices, but not in the intelligence sector. We knew we had to work together. . . . I don't know if it was so much my rank that was respected as the fact that they were pretty much aware of the material that I put together was very accurate. And also respected and appreciated by those higher up.

Ardice Brower was born in 1921 on a farm near the small town of Kennedy, in far northwestern Minnesota. She was working for a radio station in Omaha, Nebraska, when in 1943 she made the decision to join the Marine Corps, becoming one of the early women enlistees in this branch of the military. She recalls that a woman in uniform was sometimes viewed critically.

I HADN'T EVEN especially thought about joining a women's group, and I just thought those marines were terrific. We heard all the stories about the fighting in the South Pacific, getting teletypes [at the radio station] about the fighting and the losses. I don't know if I thought I was safe when I said, "I'll join when the [women] marines are formed," but that's what I said. And that's what I did when the women marines were formed.

My family, they just accepted it. My family was not a controlling family, so they didn't say, "You're going to do this or that or something else." I don't think I exactly had a pat on the back [*laughs*], or anything *negative* either—just more acceptance is probably the word.

I joined because I wanted to help end the war and was responding to "Free a Man to Fight." But it definitely wasn't because I thought I would be happier, or because I thought I would have a lot more dates—because there were no men around—or because I was a "loose woman," as many people thought *happened* when you joined the service. In fact, I talked to a woman here in town who joined, and she didn't even like to tell people she'd been in the service because people would think that she was not a very moral person if she did that. [*laughs*]

You have to remember the times. . . . Women didn't *do* things that men did. Women started working in war plants, and that was totally new. Joining the service? That's about as bad as you could do. [*laughs*]

Following basic training, Ardice was stationed in 1944-45 at Cherry Point Marine Corps Air Station, North Carolina, where she worked as secretary to the station legal officer. Living in quarters on base, she explains, produced a sense of community, of women sharing a new experience.

Ardice Brower (left) and sister Bea, shown here in 1945 at Cherry Point Marine Corps Air Station, North Carolina

We had a big barracks, several stories maybe. . . . There were just bunk beds—one big open room. You know, you have these four bunks that are facing each other, the top bunks and the lower bunks, and those make for a *real* close community. And a tiny little locker and locker box to keep things in. . . .

In the barracks, we had the same group of women all the time. So it was a pretty stable feeling. There was a lack of privacy; that part was different. But you do, you just become good friends, you just become close. I became friends with people from all over, learned some of their stories and where they were from.

Living and working in North Carolina brought Ardice face-to-face with very different attitudes about race, in situations that were not always comfortable.

Occasionally we would go off the base to Newburn, North Carolina, the closest place. And there was Fort Bragg, and then sometimes, too, there was a place just for recreation, a beach area in Morehead City. But I don't think that the civilians appreciated having men and women in uniform around all that much. They were never rude or anything like that, but I just never felt particularly accepted.

For me, this was not only my first experience out of the [Upper Midwest] but certainly the first experience in the South, where there was a difference as far as blacks and whites. I had one experience when I got on a bus, and there was one other person on that bus, who was a black man in uniform—we were both in uniform—and I sat down not with him, but close to where he was sitting, and the bus driver said, "I will not start this bus until you move up closer to me," because he was black. We were both in uniform. I just did what he told me, but I don't know today if I would've been so . . . [*trails off*]. The way I'd been brought up, it was not the thing to do. I can even remember a conversation in our office [on base] with one of the other lawyers, who was from North Carolina. We were talking about racial matters some way, and he said, "You take care of *yourselves,* we'll take care of *ourselves* here in the South, and you just leave us alone!"

[3]

War Experienced

Minnesotans on the Home Front

GOVERNMENT and business cooperated to mobilize American industry for the war effort. Almost overnight, companies large and small retooled their production lines to manufacture everything required to fight a modern war. The big automobile firms, for example, produced tanks and other military vehicles; smaller companies made everything from prepackaged foods to replacement parts. Aircraft manufacturing and shipbuilding firms had thousands of orders for all service branches. To meet demand, factories added shifts and workers put in longer hours—by 1943, the average manufacturing workweek had jumped to forty-seven hours, up eight hours over 1939.

The production boom stretched the existing labor pool and created an enormous need for workers, skilled and unskilled. For men not in the service—and of men aged eighteen to thirty-five, only one in three performed military service—jobs were available and wages were good. Many others also benefited from this dearth of workers: millions of women, youths, elders, and people of color who had previously been unemployed or in low-paying jobs found new and better opportunities. In the West and Midwest, cities boomed due to wartime production: St. Paul and Minneapolis resembled urban areas like Los Angeles, Detroit, or Akron. Beyond the Twin Cities, ship-building rejuvenated Duluth-Superior and Iron Range mines operated around the clock.

Women Working

WOMEN PLAYED A vital role in America's wartime economic expansion, working in factories large and small. Perhaps the Rockwellian image of Rosie the Riveter comes to mind. If so, with good reason: nationwide, hundreds of thousands of women took industrial jobs that had been considered "men's work," in construction, manufacturing, and mining. Many moved to new locations to take these jobs, some of them leaving home for the first time. Outside of industry, many of the opportunities were in offices, and although countless women performed traditional clerical or secretarial jobs, others gained positions of some responsibility as men were called to service.

Still, working women faced real challenges, and Minnesota proved to be no exception in this regard. There was sexism on the shop floor, and African American women clearly recalled racism at their jobs in the Twin Cities. And while one woman riveted together bombers and another assumed what had been a man's position in an Iron Range mine, many were still employed in "traditional women's jobs," specifically assembly-line and clerical work. Women's pay lagged far behind that of male coworkers, even when performing similar work. Finally, working mothers raising children on their own tackled the issues of making ends meet and finding housing and childcare.

The Minnesota women speaking here illustrate several national trends, above all mobility. They found work in places like California, Georgia, and Washington, DC, at a variety of jobs, some in war-related industries like aircraft factories and shipyards. Pay, they recalled, was often more than they could have earned in Minnesota. But these women left home for more than just money: there was a chance to get away, or the search for adventure, or the desire to join a military husband. Other women moved to the Twin Cities from small towns and rural areas, lured by the opportunity for a better-paying job.

✦ ✦ ✦

Frances Olson Arcement (b. 1926) grew up in Northeast Minneapolis in a working-class family. Not long after completing vocational high school, she was attracted to the opportunities available in war production, specifically on the West Coast. In early 1944, she and a friend answered a newspaper ad and soon found themselves on a train, headed for the Boeing aircraft factory in Renton, Washington.

WE WENT TO work for Boeing in Renton, Washington, right out of Seattle. We went to work on B-29s [Superfortress heavy bombers]. My one girlfriend Chaddy and I went. We were both in the same position: we were both kind of tired of everything. . . . I think I was glad to get away for a while. They had a deal in the newspaper where they would pay your fare and find you a place to live, and I think we got a bonus if we went. So, we both decided to go, and off we went!

We'd come from all kinds of places. When we got to Renton they had places for you to live. It was like patio homes, but they were all hooked together. My girlfriend and I had a living room, and one bedroom, and a small kitchenette. . . . There was a bus, but we walked most of the time, because everything was kind of more or less close, you know. So a half an hour's walk was nothing.

Now at the main entrance [of the factory] we had to show our badge. Had your name and number on it. You had to have a badge to get in, that's a fact, or you wouldn't have made it in. I mean, it was war times.

Everybody worked a different shift. When we started, we had to go in for training, we had to learn how to rivet, and, oh, they had to show you everything. . . . On a B-29 I worked right where the nose—where the cockpit is—joins to the body of the plane, the fuselage. What I did [motions with hands, fitting together two parts], I had to put all these rivets in with a rivet gun. . . . I had to learn how to rivet on the side of a plane.

There was other people, but when I was finished with my job, then you went to another plane. But the planes were loaded with

Frances Olson at home in Northeast Minneapolis, 1943, with her boyfriend and later husband Bud Arcement of the U.S. Navy. During 1944–45, Bud served in the Pacific onboard the submarine *Pampanito*.

people working; everybody had their job, and that was my job. . . . *We* would move [to the next plane] when we were done, because a lot of the other stuff took longer to do. It seemed like nothing was in a hurry, and yet we produced planes like crazy. . . . We were putting those planes together for the war, that's why we were there. I think we all thought about it, we knew they needed them, and we got them out.

When we first started we were "C"—we had ratings—and then if you got better, you had a "B," which I had a "B" rating. And then when my girlfriend and I decided well, it was time to go home, it was getting towards Christmas [1944], then they offered us a pay raise to keep us. More money involved. Financially I was doing fine, better than when I was home. We were working forty-eight, probably fifty-four hours, six days a week. Sunday, that we had off. . . . It was a good place to work. I sometimes wish I'd stayed. . . . But we decided no, we were going to go home. I liked being away from home for a while; then I got lonesome, and it was time to go home.

After returning from Washington at the end of 1944, Frances found employment in war production locally, at the Twin Cities Ordnance Plant in New Brighton, Minnesota.

Yeah, that's right, I worked there, and I worked on the assembly line, as an inspector of .30-caliber bullets. The job was advertised in the paper. They were looking for help. I figured if I could do it. . . . I was more than glad to get the job, go in and help. The pay was good there, too. I can't tell you how much, but it was good for the time, you know. . . . We were working sixty hours [a week].

There were a *lot* of people there. That one, there again I worked shifts.

I had a machine that just sent bullets through, and I had to check them. I was an inspector. I had to check them, to see that there was nothing wrong with them. You had a light and a mirror, and it rolled by and you had to be fast enough to pick them out. You had to look for nicks or whatever. Just like on a belt, they came right by you like that.

We had more, more women than men there because most of the guys were in the service, so you figured the guys that *were* working there didn't qualify to go in the service.

[Financially I was doing okay,] because I used to give my mother some money. In fact, I remember my first paycheck from there. . . . I bought my mother a new coat, a new hat, a new dress, new shoes out of that first paycheck. And my second paycheck, I bought her a new kitchen set.

Betty Myers Sarner was living with her mother and sister in St. Paul when, in early 1943, the opportunity arose to move to California and work in a shipyard. Never having lived away from home, she saw a chance for adventure.

MY GIRLFRIEND saw this in the papers and thought it would be a real good idea. Shipyard jobs. She said, "Wouldn't that be fun?" And, of course, I had never given it a second thought. . . . I said, "No way. I'm not leaving St. Paul." Within two weeks I was out in Richmond, California.

We got our bags packed. I had a suitcase that we had to have a rope around it just to hold it together on the train. Nowadays you would be embarrassed to tears to even walk down the street with that kind of a suitcase. [*laughs*] I mean it was terrible, when I stop to think of it now. But you know, when you're nineteen years old not too much fazes you. [*laughs*]

My mom was quite shook. But she said, "You'll be back shortly." I think I lasted longer than she thought I would. . . . Being far away from home was hard; it was quite hard. But luckily I was with two girls that I was close to. . . . Even so, I wrote home quite a bit.

We thought there was a job waiting, but when we got there, no. But when we did go down and apply we didn't have any trouble at all getting the job. I was doing office work, forty hours a week. You had kind of like blueprints of different ships and stuff, and I had to file all those things. It was anything to do with the ships. That was about it; it was strictly office work.

At the time I thought the pay was okay. It was okay for what we were doing. But I never knew what it was to save money. [*laughs*] I mean, let's face it . . . we lived from payday to payday. Like most kids at that time. Enjoyed life. At that time that was all you lived for, was to have fun.

In late 1943, tired of living far from home, Betty returned to St. Paul. She worked there for several months; then, in May 1944, she joined the Navy WAVES.

✦   ✦   ✦

Florence Andersen Glasner was born in 1922 and raised on Minnesota's Iron Range, in the small mining community of Pool Location, near Hibbing. In 1942, with the departure of large numbers of local men for military service, Florence found work at the nearby Oliver Mine. Her position was in a central tool room, where other workers came to pick up and drop off various electric tools; a male worker had previously held the position.

IT WAS CALLED Oliver Shops. It was a warehouse and electric shop, a mechanic shop, and welding shop. . . . Because of the shortage of men, U.S. Steel was now hiring women to do certain things. . . . There were women in the welding shop and the warehouse. Then there were women working down in the mine, driving trucks. I don't think there were any in the mechanic shop that I remember. We wore overalls. And we had steel-toed shoes.

[At first we] fixed electric cords if they were frayed. We learned how to do that. And at one time we were wrapping coils. . . . Then I ended up in the tool room. . . . I was the only one in the tool room.

[I worked] with men. All electricians. Most of them were married with children. There were a few younger ones. . . . They would come in the morning and get their tools that they had to take out, and then we'd be on our own during the day. There were a few men that worked in the shop repairing stuff.

Most of them were very protective of me. Didn't want me lifting the heavy stuff, which a lot of it was. They would come and get it themselves. There was a gate there, and I could unlock it.

Some of them thought they could come into the tool room and maybe pinch you. I wasn't used to that, and I didn't like it one little bit. [Often] it would be the same fellow that would think he could come up and nudge against you.

If I was harassed by anybody, all I'd have to do is mention it to anybody around and they'd say, "Well, if he comes around, we'll be up here too." Which made me very happy. . . .

When we would go for lunch there were about ten or twelve of us women, from other divisions. There were five of us that were about the same age, that went to school together. The others were a little bit older. . . . [At lunch we talked about] what we were doing at home and what our husbands were doing, and what we'd heard from them. I didn't have children then, but most of them had children.

With fewer men in town, weekend entertainment meant certain changes.

A bunch of us girls would go out on a Saturday night. Many times my dad would drive us and let us off, and then somebody else would come and pick us up. We all liked to dance, so we all went out on Saturday night. Sometimes you danced with women, and sometimes with the other men that weren't gone to war.

I think it would have been tough if all my friends didn't have their husbands gone, too. We got together, and we played cards. We went to shows. Once in a while we would go out and dance. I think because we had such a good friendship with other women that it helped us. We looked out for each other and were worried about where their husbands were, too. One of the girls, her husband was in the navy, and he died before the war ended.

Florence's husband, Tony, served with the army in Europe and saw front-line duty in a tank destroyer unit. She had anxious moments when she learned he had been wounded in action.

His tank destroyer was hit. Four of the fellows were killed. Two of them got out. He was one of them. He was sent to the hospital because he had hurt his eye. . . . He got a Purple Heart.

I got a telegram. I was working, and my sister called me. I got hysterical. My boss brought me to my sister's. I thought he was hurt, and he was not going to come back.

Later I would get cards saying that he was convalescing. Then when he got out of the hospital, he wrote. He was back with his unit. Didn't want to go back on the front line, but as long as he was okay, they sent him.

Florence felt that the war inspired a stronger sense of community in her town.

I guess we were pretty patriotic then. I know when boys were drafted and they were all going out, there would be a big group of people down at the train station. If they had someone going or not, they'd be there to say good-bye.

I know the war brought our little town, Pool, closer together. You met somebody on the street, and you'd say, "How's he doing? Where's he at now?" Because everybody had somebody in the war.

Velda Beck (b. 1925) grew up on farms in South Dakota and Minnesota. In early 1944 she moved to Macon, Georgia, where she married her fiancé, James Beck, then serving with the army at nearby Camp Wheeler. Velda and Jim remained

in Macon for the next year; during this time Velda worked for a local manufacturer—and had her first exposure to life in the South.

I FOUND EMPLOYMENT working in a pecan factory. Sorting all kinds of stuff out of pecans. . . . I first started out on a belt where you'd have to sort out the brokens and the shells and so forth. These are all women on the belts. Many of them were servicemen's wives. There was no blacks working there on the belts, just whites. I was in charge of the belt.

My employer was from New Jersey, and he saw that all of us northern women worked really fast and hard, so he gave us all a raise of five cents, so we got fifty cents an hour. Some of these people would complain when I'd see that they could step up their operation just a little more and get a little more out of them. I'd open up this little knob you'd turn and a lot more pecans would come out. I had them really working hard, and they didn't care for that. I don't think they liked me as a boss very much.

Only men that were there were black people that they would use. They were the maintenance and also supplied us with the pecans that we would work on. They were all black.

It was the first time I had encountered black people really. In Duluth there might have been an elevator operator that was black, but course in Duluth you didn't have very many blacks. . . . [In Macon] I would be friendly, talk to them. These southern ladies, they were upset to think I would want to talk to them. The blacks were human beings, after all.

Velda Beck of Palisade with husband Jim, 1945

I guess slavery hadn't really left them yet. They felt that they could make them do degrading work, and they didn't care how inconvenient it might be. [In Macon] we moved to another place, next door, it was a little nicer, and this landlady had this black woman come in and wash clothes. She didn't have a washing machine, so she had to bend over the bathtub to scrub them with a board. And I know there were washing machines available, but, you see, that was it—they could get them to do it. And then they had a black man that, instead of mowing their lawn he had to use a little hand scythe, and scythe and scythe the whole lawn with a little hand scythe. It was just like as if, well, you're going to get paid but we don't care how hard you work for it.

Lavinia Stone Murray (b. 1917) grew up in rural Shelby County, Kentucky. In 1940, searching for better opportunities, she moved to St. Paul to join family. In 1941 Lavinia married James Murray, who the following year was drafted into the U.S. Army, where he spent the next three years.

WHEN THEY announced about Pearl Harbor, that's the first thing I began thinking about—my baby that I was expecting, and about James leaving.

For Lavinia, the period 1942–45 required some adjustments. She did not have enough money to live on her own, so she shared a home with her in-laws. In 1944 Lavinia found a job at a St. Paul department store. Her position brought her face to face with a certain amount of workplace racism.

My aunt was working there; she had been there for years. And they needed help. So she told me about it, and I went down there and applied, and they hired me. Merchandise. I did all the stamping. Put a marking on, like on markdowns. Cutting off the old price tag, putting on new price tags, keeping the clothes in order. That type of thing. At that time they didn't have any black salespeople. I could assist with the sales, but for me to have my own [sales]book and go around, you know, as a salesperson . . . I didn't. There were no black salespeople in any of the stores.

There were a couple of prejudiced people, but one lady, an elderly lady there, she would always speak up for me. I know I got disgusted with one of the women, and I said I was going to quit, and she said,

"Don't you let anybody ever run you off a job!" She said, "You're as entitled to a job as much as anybody. You're an American citizen." She was Catholic, an elderly white lady, but she was really a good person. She was always in my corner. She was the one that encouraged me to stay on there.

I banked my whole check, my allotment check [from my husband], after about the second month [on the job]. I started working, and the first month I had to buy some things for my baby. After the first three or four months I just would save my whole [allotment] check. I wouldn't cash it. I would put it in the bank, and I lived on what I made from my job.

Lois Snyder grew up in the small town of Lanesboro. After high school she moved to Minneapolis and, in 1942, got married. The next year her Army Air Corps husband Gerry was shipped to England, and Lois was alone and pregnant in the Twin Cities. Following the birth of her child, she got a factory job and struggled with issues of work, childcare, and affordable housing in an era when working mothers living alone were not the norm.

S OMEHOW THE IDEA of looking around and being responsible for work didn't, didn't really sink in until after I had the baby. . . . A girlfriend of mine that I had known, she had a girl staying with her that was working at Northwest Plastics, and that's how I got in. With somebody taking me by the hand, literally.

I was working eight-hour shifts. Actually, I worked second shift, so it was eight hours, and then a half-hour of that was lunch break. I worked at Northwest Plastics for about two and a half years. Part of the time of it second shift, part of the time graveyard [midnight shift]. We made fairly good money. . . . I think it started out at a dollar an hour. . . . There wasn't—The fellows weren't paid any more than we were; we got the same pay. The scale rates were the same, at least where I worked.

There was a few young fellows working there that were either too young to go into service or in some way had been classified differently. . . . Then some of them came back [from the military], and

Margaret Amundson (pictured in 1945 with fiancé Bill, a navy pilot) worked in a St. Paul dentist's office during the war. The office's location garnered certain advantages: "I would hear about a store in downtown St. Paul, a grocery store, that had, say, pork or chicken or something that day, so I would spend my lunch hour standing in line, hoping that by the time I got to the counter they would still have something left. And you bought whatever it was; it wasn't deciding, 'Oh, I'm going to have leg of lamb this week' or something. Some of that stuff was just nonexistent, and you just took what you could get and made do."

then there were some older fellows. I remember one, an old school-teacher, and there was a lot of girls, ones my age and several of them considerably older. See, back then I was like twenty-one or twenty-two years old, and there were girls that were ten to fifteen years older than me. Some of them had raised their families, even, and some that were able to get away had help [around the house]; they could come to work.

There were different jobs in the place. There were certain molds that the fellows used, because [the molds] were heavier. They put stuff in the mold, and they would have to pry it open. The girls didn't do that kind of stuff, because the hydraulic presses opened automatically. We'd put what we called preforms—the premeasured blocks of plastic powder—we'd put them in the machine, and then there would be this thousand pounds of pressure and heat that would squish them into whatever they were supposed to be.

We were making cases for periscopes, cases that they put a glass prism in. They used them in tanks, because there were no windows to see out in tanks. They would look in the mirror and they could see out. So that was one thing that we made. Another thing that we made were the little tiny throat microphones that the fliers wore, the aviators.

Lois lived in several different Twin Cities apartments during 1943–45 as she struggled to find affordable housing in a difficult market. Childcare was another worry.

As far as the one neighborhood was concerned, I had my landlady
downstairs, and the only thing in the neighborhood was like a grocery store and a Bridgeman's [ice cream parlor] down the next block.
It wasn't as though I knew people in the neighborhood; I only knew
the people next door who had a tailor shop, and their daughter
would baby-sit while I worked nights. She would come over after
supper, and I would get [my son] Dickey to bed. Then I would take
a nap and try to remember to wake up before it was time to go to
work. [*laughs*] One time I went to sleep waiting for the streetcar.

We had ration books for meat, but with just me and my kid sister and the baby, it wasn't as if I had to do a lot of cooking. So, it isn't
like when you cook for your husband or boyfriend, where you had
to have hamburger, pork chops, and roast beef and stuff like that. We
lived a lot easier than that, and [*laughs*] we ate a lot cheaper than that.
We had a lot of Spam; that was a mainstay. It was to make sandwiches
for work, and it went a long way. When you haven't got much money
to spend, you don't eat big. I remember when a neighbor kid was
taking care of Dickey one time, she ate up all that was left of the open
Spam that was going to be my sandwiches for all week. [*laughs*] She
lost her job in a hurry.

Doris Shea Strand was born and raised in Minneapolis. After graduating from
Central High School in 1940, she worked until 1944 in the main offices of Minneapolis Moline, in Hopkins. Normally a manufacturer of farm equipment, the
company retooled its production line for the war effort. Doris clearly remembers changes around the office.

W E WERE A farm implement manufacturing company, but we
immediately changed over to wartime production. It's always
amazed me to think that they could make that change so quickly.
Change the dies and the whole production effort.

The company policy changed, whereas prior to the war a married
lady could not work. If you got married you were dismissed, because

they wanted to give the gentlemen the job, because they were supposedly supporting families. But immediately, the war changed
everything. It didn't make any difference if you had a family or
whatever. The men were off to war and the gals just filled in the
blanks. There were no restrictions at all.

I remember the first fellow from the office got his draft notice. It
was just as if the energies were sapped. We just couldn't believe that
Irving Watts was going to have to go to this army camp. That was the
first one, and from then on it just really . . . I would say from 50 [per-
cent women] to 50 [percent men], it probably went to about 85 [per-
cent women] to 15 [percent men].

It was mostly women in 1944 when I left there. The gentlemen
that were left were more the older men, department heads and that
sort of thing. All the young men had either been drafted or volunteered for service. Most of the women were about my age group,
maybe a very few were older. What we used to call spinsters. . . . It
was mainly younger gals.

We did work quite a bit of overtime. Maybe it was the company
not employing enough people, but we did work quite a bit of overtime. I think it was because we were understaffed. We had to absorb
the extra work for that. . . . You were maybe doing a job and a quarter instead of your regular hundred percent job. You were putting out
a little extra effort because they didn't have staff enough.

I started at sixty-five dollars a month. Of course we got paid for
overtime and that sort of thing. I think after having been there for
four years I got seventy-eight dollars a month when I left there in 1944.

**In December 1944 Doris married Errol Fox, then serving with the Marine Corps,
and went to San Diego to be with her husband. From January to June 1945 she
worked in the inventory audit department for a company manufacturing planes
for the U.S. military.**

I found a job. Jobs were plentiful; it seemed like I could just apply
and was taken in. I worked at Consolidated Vultee Aircraft Company,
called Convair. They manufactured airplanes. Big planes, military aircraft. They had government contracts. I was a part of the inventory
audit department there.

They had a government contract, and there was something like "cost plus ten percent." But I'm sure it was just padded even more than that. It was to their advantage to have a huge payroll. It was almost a shame to be a part of it, but I needed the money too! [*laughs*] I don't remember exactly what the pay was, but it was much better than I had ever had back [in Minneapolis].

While jobs were easy to find in San Diego, locating an affordable apartment was almost impossible. Conditions could be cramped.

Housing was at a premium, no matter where you were. We had a friend in San Diego who all of a sudden found one room with kitchen privileges for five dollars a week, and we were glad to get it. It wasn't cheap, but it was average. . . . [The room was] probably ten [feet] by twelve [feet]. It had just a double bed and a dresser, a couple chairs, and a card table we had in there, too.

Anyway, I went down to San Diego, and we moved into this one room with kitchen privileges. Errol was still in the Marine Corps, stationed at Camp Pendleton, so he was in a carpool. It was fifty-five miles from San Diego to Camp Pendleton. [They drove that] every day.

This was an old house, an old structure, and there was a wall down the center with a stairway on either side. As I'd come home from work about four or four thirty, there would probably be two or three gals on either side of this wall with a can of something in their hand. And the minute you'd hear the hook go up on the kitchen door, whoever could run the fastest got to use the kitchen. Hopefully it was to just heat up a can of soup or something, and they wouldn't be in there long, and then the next person could run in there and do a little bit. It was just very meager. We got in there once in a while, but not too often. Agility was the secret there! [*laughs*] But you just lived with it. It was just a part of life. Nobody was mean about it. If you had longer legs and could run a little faster, you ate earlier that day. [*laughs*] [The bathroom] was shared with, I suppose, seven or eight other rooms. You had to take your chances on the kitchen and the biffy! [*laughs*]

Men Working

MEN RECALLING their civilian work experiences during 1941–45 mentioned many positives. The surge in employment opportunities brought tangible benefits: more hours per week and plenty of overtime meant improved pay packets, whether one was a plumber, an Iron Range mineworker, a skilled machinist, a munitions worker, or a bus driver. While some left Minnesota for employment, most found ample opportunities within the state—in the Twin Cities or in places like Cloquet, South St. Paul, Duluth, or Chisholm—and had no desire to relocate.

For some men, the increasing numbers of women on the job—sometimes in new or different positions—represented a challenge. Adjustments needed to be made, and, some admitted, the transition was not always smooth.

Wartime opportunity brought new job possibilities for Minnesota's Mexican American and African American populations as well. Those who remember the war years tell how they moved from underemployment or even unemployment to regular positions in metal foundries, slaughterhouses, or ordnance factories. While whites may have avoided this work or left such positions during this time, for many people of color these jobs represented a step up the social ladder. Racism was still evident, but economic times were improving.

✦ ✦ ✦

Martin O. Weddington (b. 1917) grew up in St. Paul. In 1941, as the United States geared up for possible war, Martin found employment at the expanding Twin Cities Arsenal complex in suburban New Brighton. He worked primarily in a plant that manufactured, inspected, and tested .30-caliber machine gun shells.

IT JUST HAPPENED that I heard from somebody that they were hiring out there at Federal Cartridge, is what it was known as. I just decided I might as well try and see if I can get a job out there. . . . I only worked for Federal Cartridge for a short time, from fall '41 until spring '42, I think it was. . . . I started as a janitor.

Then I finally decided that, hey, I'd better get with the government. And sure enough, I was able to get hired by the War Ordnance Department, because I'd already passed several Civil Service exams. I assume they took individuals from these exams that they'd already passed rather than go through having more exams to hire for that particular thing. So I was hired.

When I went into the War Ordnance Department I was an inspector . . . for finished cartridges. Thirty-caliber shells. Later I was in the actual testing, firing of bullets and tracers. . . . It was pretty good pay.

Transportation was being made available for people in the metropolitan areas to get [to New Brighton]. Bus service to get you out to the arsenal and back to the neighborhood.

Employed in a key war industry, Martin received deferments from military service. He spent the period until early 1945 at the arsenal and lived in St. Paul with his wife, Sallie, and son Martin, Jr. (born 1941).

I got my greetings from Uncle Sam. But because of my employment and the position that I had, the ones that were running the plant would tell them I was needed. I'd say, "Hey, I been drafted for such and such a date," and they would say, "Well, we'll see about that." And so . . . they'd tell the draft board to defer, and I'd wind up not going. But, oh yes, my name came up.

Martin's deferment eventually expired, however, and in April 1945 he was ordered to report for military service.

I guess I was ready for it, more or less. I knew it was coming. . . . I had almost been told before that they just can't keep getting the deferments. You were mentally prepared for when the next one comes.

James G. Kirk, Jr., graduated from St. Paul's Central High School and attended college for two years. When the United States entered the war in December 1941, he was working as a railway car waiter.

OR AFRICAN AMERICANS here in St. Paul, post office, packing-house, or the railroad were the main jobs. So that's what you took. My father had been on the railroad for so many years. I just felt that I would feel more comfortable doing the same thing that he had been doing all his life, or most of his life.

I started out as a waiter. . . . All the waiters were black. The cooks in practically all instances were white. And the dining car stewards were white. I had probably been working there about a year when they promoted me to waiter in charge. I did that until I left the railroad in 1942.

James found work as a laborer in local war-related industries, first for International Harvester (1942–43), then at the Twin Cities Arsenal (1943–44).

I knew that I would be drafted [once the war started]. . . . The main reason I left the railroad was to avoid the draft. At International Harvester I was a janitor [but was] included in the work force of something that was war production. . . . As I did, people were changing jobs in order to stay out of service. There were friends of mine who were doing the same thing, trying to stay one step ahead of the draft.

At the arsenal I was a laborer. And not a good laborer at that. [*laughs*] Not having been a physical man at any time in my life it was kind of hard for me to do the laboring work. I dropped a bucket of hot tar one cold winter night, and it bounced up in my face and closed my eyes with the hot tar. I had to have the nurse put cocoa butter on it to open my eyes.

Married since 1941 and the father of two children, James was nevertheless drafted into the U.S. Army in April 1944.

✦   ✦   ✦

Thousands of wartime workers were drawn to the Twin Cities Ordnance Plant in suburban New Brighton, which manufactured .30-, .45-, and .50-caliber ammunition

Maurice Raether (b. 1910) worked for the Duluth Transit Authority. A bus driver since 1937, he lived in Duluth with his wife and three children during the war years.

ONCE THE WAR started I worked longer hours. [*emphatically*] A *lot* of hours. . . . The runs, they had up to ten hours in a run most days. And then they had these extras during mornings and evenings, during rush hour. They tacked those on to that run, you know. . . . And the foremen, they were bothering *everybody, every day,* to do more work. . . . So I think I worked sixteen hours a day there for a few years. [The bus company] had trouble finding drivers, [because] there were more people working, you know, working in defense.

On the buses, we were just overloaded *all* the time during the war. Yes, right to the door. They used to shove one another in the door and they'd say, "Shut the door," and they'd shut the door and somebody would let out a little yelp because they pinched their butt in the door!

Pay was 53 or 54 cents an hour when I started [in 1937], and . . . we were froze at 75 cents per hour during the war. During the war years the company gave us a six-dollar-a-month bonus, or seventy-two-dollar-a-year bonus. Men could go to work in the steel plants for $1.24 an hour, you know, so they didn't hang around the bus company very long.

I suppose I did [think about getting another job]. I could have if I ever did want to. One thing that kept you on the bus run, at the bus company, wages were low—we knew truck drivers were getting more than we were—but there was always overtime. [And] I kind of liked driving the bus, I guess. After all, it wasn't hard manual labor. You were halfway dressed up in a uniform all the time. I wasn't all greasy and sweaty, you know.

Mel Boggs (b. 1918) finished a plumber's apprenticeship in 1941 and spent two years working in the trade before volunteering for the Air Corps. Married in 1939, Mel became a father in 1942.

A T FIRST I didn't think about going [in the service], because we didn't have any idea how long the war was going to last or what it was going to amount to. There were a lot of arms plants being built, and factories. They started working overtime in the construction business because they tried to build ammunition factories and things like that.

I stayed in the plumbing business. I had enough of my apprenticeship in that I could pass the test and get my license, so I was working as a journeyman. . . . Everybody was making a lot of money because we were working so many hours. . . . You could work seven days a week if you wanted to. And that's what I did. And got paid overtime for it. Time and a half. . . . That was all figured into the cost of the job when the contractor bid it. He knew that he couldn't get enough help to do it on a five-day week. They'd have to work overtime.

The place I worked at was just an average-size place. They just took as much work as they could do. If a job came along and they had the manpower and the time to do it they'd take it, and if they didn't they just wouldn't. . . . To get additional help wasn't all that easy. There weren't that many people available. . . . There was a man-power shortage. There was a lot of construction work going on but not enough mechanics to do it. And because there was a shortage they worked longer hours.

Henry T. Capiz was raised in St. Paul, the oldest of six children of Mexican immi-grant parents who before the war had labored as migrant workers. During 1943–44, as a high school student, Henry also held down a job at Swift and Co. packinghouse in neighboring South St. Paul.

I WAS A contributor to the household, because there were ten of us. There were six of us kids, my mother and father, my grandmother, and my cousin Rita that lived with us. That was a bunch of people to support. My dad needed help.

I started [at Swift] September of '43. I tried to get out of it, because it made for a long day. Going to school and then going to work, until ten thirty at night usually.

I was in a clean-up gang. I was assigned a certain part of the build-ing where all the processing machinery was. So in the clean-up gang I used to use a big steam hose, a pressure hose. We had to clean all the machinery with the steam pressure. And after it was all clean, then you followed up with a spray of mineral oil, to keep it from rust-ing overnight. Just like that it would rust. . . . You had to clean the walls and the machinery and the floors. And the chutes where all the meat went down through.

Normally it would be [unusual to have a seventeen-year-old in a job like that], but at that time, 1943 and 1944, there was a manpower shortage. They were taking everybody. Women. My mother started to work, too. She actually went to work. . . . She worked in process-ing meat, like baby food. Not real heavy labor. She eventually retired from Swift. It was not uncommon. They had a lot of kids working and a lot of women working.

These jobs had positive impacts on Henry's family and the household.

There were some changes [around the house], yes, but my grandmother lived with us so she sort of stepped into the void. She took care of a lot of things. I know she pretty much raised me, and she also raised my younger brother, Stevie. She took care of a lot of the details.

It was pretty good money for someone my age, and then I turned that over to my dad. I'd get an allowance for expenses. For the streetcar, which wasn't much, ten cents for a streetcar ride, and for incidentals. I was a contributor to the family. . . . It made quite a bit of difference.

My father said, and I don't think he was being inappropriate, he said that World War II was the best thing that happened to the Mexican American people. They were brought into the mainstream. Brought them out of the *barrio* and into the mainstream, and that was true.

Before entering the army in 1943, Harry Gurrola of St. Paul found that the war brought new opportunities far from home—in Sausalito, California, in the shipbuilding industry: "It was going day and night. I wasn't a welder then, but I got there and they sent me to school. The ship builder there, he sent about twenty of us. We got full welder's wages while we were going to school. It was a real good deal. Then we could work all the hours we wanted."

Angelo Legueri (b. 1916) grew up in a mining family in the Iron Range town of Nashwauk. He worked eight years in the iron ore mines before being drafted into the army in 1943. U.S. entry into the war, he recalls, meant a boom period on the Iron Range.

I WORKED AS a common laborer to start off with. Then they promoted me to a brakeman on one of the electric locomotives. Then they made another change: they got rid of all the locomotives, and they got diesel trucks to do their work. I got to be a truck driver until I was drafted in the army.

They needed a lot of ore because they needed to make tanks and things. I'm not exactly sure about how many million tons of ore were mined at that time, but, boy, it was terrific. So we worked seven days a week, twenty-four hours a day, even after it got cold and the ore would freeze in the chutes. They had to put heaters on there. . . . We had to work overtime hours. They had a certain quota to make, and we had to be there until it was done.

When I was working, we made more money. I got better income, because I remember we had to borrow money to build our house and we had payments, small payments each month. Well, when we started to work more and make more money, we increased that payment. The bankers told us we didn't have to hurry up and pay it off, but we wanted to pay it off. We put the money into the house. And whatever we needed, we could pay cash for it.

As the war continued and many men left for military service, replacement labor was needed. Some jobs were filled by men from outside the area, Angelo recalls, others by women, who began to work on the Iron Range in larger numbers and in different jobs.

As men were being drafted, they were replaced by people from other parts of the country. They came and took our place. . . . . . They were probably about ten years older, but they had all come from the farming communities. They came here and took our jobs.

In some cases women became samplers. When they loaded the ore they had to take samples from each car and then check the samples so they could determine the ore content, the iron content in each one. So they took those jobs. And other jobs, too. I don't remember jobs in the pit. Driving truck; they were truck drivers. Some of them were really good at it, too. Those women I worked close to I thought were really good. They did a real good job, but not all of them.

More women working at the mines required universal adjustments and at times generated conflict.

Definitely there were some adjustment problems to having women on the job. We had to have private dry house for them. Private lavatories. They couldn't be the same place as the men had them. They had to have their own.

Of course there were problems, because you get a bunch of men and women together, there's going to be male and female problems. That eventually happened. Some of the guys would come along and they would pester the women. Maybe even worse than that, if they could. And the women, the only way they could defend themselves was to turn them in. Some of the men lost their jobs because of that. Because they were pestering the women.

Don Marinkovich (b. 1924) grew up in the Iron Range town of Chisholm, one of eight children of Croatian immigrant parents. After being classified 4-F, or medically deferred, in 1943, Don spent the remainder of the war years working in the iron ore mines.

I GOT ON AT the Oliver Mining Company, the Morris Mine. . . . I had to be a hundred forty-five pounds to go in an underground mine. I really weighed a hundred thirty-five. But that would show up in their physical. The personnel man . . . said, "You weigh a hundred forty-five pounds?" "Oh, yeah," I said. So I went in at a hundred and thirty-five. . . . That was physical work.

I was a motorman. . . . I was hauling the ore out. Electric locomotive, a small thing. I hauled three five-ton cars per trip. I was hourly, but the miners got paid by the cars that I hauled. So this, to me, was a big deal.

Going in the mine was like going onto another planet. . . . We grew up in the area and would hear the old timers talking about the mine. We heard a *lot* of talk about what went on in the mine. . . . I didn't know anything about it until I stepped in there. "Oh, *this* is what they were talking about!" It was a different world. When I found out that the miners were satisfied with my work, that I was giving them good motor service, this was a thrill.

Everybody was working every hour they could. We worked six days every week. We'd get an extra shift in the mine when we worked day shift. They called it cleaning track. Every man shoveled three five-ton cars. At a hundred thirty-five pounds, I'd ache till the next week. Never dreamed to refuse that extra shift, though—that was time and a half.

No women in the mine. Never underground. . . . There *were* women working, and they were doing jobs that a man used to do. Some were lining switches at the [Oliver] Hull-Rust mine [in Hibbing]. Locomotives come up out of the pit, and you switch them onto the tracks. And some were in the sample crews . . . in the crusher house. Samples [from each load of ore] are ground and separated.

Once I got out on the pit, working on the tie tamper; it's like a jackhammer. Son of a gun, I worked opposite a woman. I was embarrassed—I had a tough time keeping up with her. When it was over I had to lift the jackhammers up. I lifted mine up; then I took hers. My arms were sore! But I couldn't show it.

Don recalls certain shortages in the local stores, specifically of the food he took to work.

I remember I used to like sardines in the dinner pail at work. I used to like King Oscar sardines, and I couldn't find them. Once I got a hold of a can of anchovies. Didn't know what anchovies were. Took it in the pail. Opened it up, and that stuff was so salty every tooth in my mouth hurt. This was a problem—what do you put in the pail? Meat was always in short supply. We had chickens at home. Sometimes I had that in the pail. You heard about black market, but I never saw anything. You had to have connections, I guess.

Lester Marshall of Cloquet was a machinist and later a tool and die maker. He spent the war years working at the Washington, DC, Navy Yard, a sprawling defense facility. As a skilled worker in a key location, Lester received a deferment from military service. He clearly remembers the nonstop pace of work at the Navy Yard.

BEFORE THE WAR, they worked an eight-hour day. But when it looked like we might be getting into the war, they doubled it to two shifts. And as soon as Pearl Harbor banged up, then they went to seven days a week, twenty-four hours a day. . . . I worked seven days a week.

I came home from work on the [*pauses three seconds*], it would have been the fourteenth of November of 1942. I was working midnight.

I said to my mother, "I'm going to take a bath and change my clothes, and I'm going to go downtown." She said, "You've got to sleep." I said, "I'm not working tonight; I'm taking Saturday and Sunday off. I'm going to go downtown, and I'm going to see so-and-so and some other people I want to see. I haven't had a day off since Pearl Harbor. I've been working seventy-four hours a week. It's time for me to take a day off."

They wouldn't *make* us work Saturdays and Sundays. . . . We were *encouraged* to work Saturday and Sunday, and sometimes we had a job that had to go. They'd come around and say, "Marshall, we have to have this job tonight" or "we have to have this machine manned tomorrow night." And that's the way it would go.

[By October 1943] I hadn't been allowed to take *any* vacation time at all. We earned twenty-six days a year annual leave, as they called it, and fifteen days a year sick leave, and then we were supposed to have so many holidays. I know we *didn't* get them. [*laughs*] They weren't letting us take days off. I got paid for my holidays that I didn't get, time and a half. But the vacation time. . . . When the war was over in '45, I had ninety days of sick leave, and I think I had a hundred twenty days of annual leave earned. Prior to the war, you couldn't let it accumulate more than forty-five days.

Outside of work, Lester volunteered as an air raid warden in his neighborhood.

They had neighborhood defense units, they called them. I think they sent a card or something to every household asking for a volunteer. My dad said to me, "You just volunteered" or something to that effect. Men and women that weren't going to war, we went around and got everybody to black out their windows, or help them put up blackout curtains that one of the government agencies came out with. We didn't want any light showing outside after it got dark. And there weren't any streetlights; they were dark except for maybe [one] or two per street or so. We had blackouts, too.

Then they brought hard helmets around for us. They were nice, like those jungle helmets. They were metal, and they had a headband in there, and then it had the red, white, and blue badge on the front. Behind that it said "National Defense." Well, I was *important!* [*laughs*]

Housing was in short supply in the nation's capital. Lester and his wife, Jo Ann, whom he married in October 1943 in Cloquet, lived in a small rented room and spent months searching for a decent, affordable apartment. Lester recalls he acted fast when he found something in the evening paper.

I happened to be reading the paper one night, the evening paper, and it said, "For Rent—furnished apartment. 109 Maple Avenue, Takoma Park, Maryland." I said to Jo Ann, "Grab your hat, we're going someplace." She said, "Where we going? I got something on the stove." "Well, take it off. We're going over here." I didn't know if [the apartment] had been in the earlier editions or not, but it was only about a fifteen-minute walk from where we were. Jo Ann said, "If you're going to run, I'm going back." I wasn't running; I was just walking fast. I didn't know what the house was like, but I knew where it was, and I just wasn't going to take any chances.

There were so many people looking for apartments to rent, particularly furnished, because so many people came to Washington from all over the country. I know fellows that I worked with that had wives and children back in Frederick, Maryland, or over in Roanoke, Virginia, and they couldn't bring them in [to Washington] because they couldn't find a place to live. They were mechanics, they did different work, but they worked the same place [that I did].

Lester and Jo Ann got the apartment; Lester traded labor on some repairs for a slight reduction in the rent.

Homemakers and Mothers

HOMEMAKERS and mothers faced numerous challenges during the war. There were shortages of almost everything, it seemed: with industry focused on the war effort, numerous products were either unavailable or limited in supply and rationed. Whether food items like sugar, fats, or meat or consumer goods like fuel oil, shoes, clothing, auto tires, or building supplies, scarce provisions forced people to adjust to the ration system—and to keeping track of booklets filled with ration stamps of myriad colors. Women described the various effects of shortages and rationing, from facing empty shops to standing hours in line to just doing without. Many revealed strategies they devised for making do, whether it was trading foodstuffs or ration stamps or holding a little back for special occasions. For one Minnesotan who spent the war years living in Japan, however, the shortages were more severe, and by 1945 constant aerial bombardment added a new dimension—terror.

Other challenges were of a more personal nature. There was loneliness when husbands and loved ones were drafted into the service, anxiety about safety when they were sent to a combat zone, uncertainty when a telegram announced that a brother had been reported missing, and the sorrow of loss when information arrived that someone had been killed in action. Some handled adversity well; others had difficulty adjusting.

But in these situations opportunities emerged. For some women, having a husband in the service meant the chance to experience someplace new, someplace far from Minnesota. For others who stayed in the state, there was the prospect of getting involved in the war effort. And from virtually every woman came a sense of pulling together, of depending on family—and on each other.

✦   ✦   ✦

Beatrice (Bea) Kellgren was born and raised in St. Paul, but immediately after the United States entered the war her husband, John, found employment as an aeronautical engineer with the aircraft manufacturer Boeing, in Renton, Washington. They spent the entire war in the Seattle area, where, as a homemaker, Bea came into direct contact with rationing and shortages and found various ways to provide for her family.

WE GOT SO MANY stamps for coffee, for sugar, for shoes, for meat, for butter. . . . But people got so that what they did was, things that meant more to them than it did to us, we changed stamps. Because we'd get a book every, I don't know, every month or something. My neighbors next door, meat meant a lot to them. Well, coffee meant more to me than meat did, so we'd exchange. Her husband was in the Coast Guard. She was alone a lot, so we got to change stamps with her. Shoes didn't mean that much—Well, you couldn't get shoes anyway. The shoe stores were all closed. Once in a while you'd see a sign saying, "This store will be open. We just got a new bunch of shoes in; you'll be able to buy from two o'clock to five o'clock on a certain day." Then everybody would converge on the store.

Meat markets were a disaster. I can't even remember what kind of meat we used to get, but, of course, the ration stamps didn't allow you to have very much. The chickens weren't any stamps at all, if you could find them. And we used to go and stand in line. There would be a sign; all these things were advertised. They would say, well, there's going to be chickens available at a certain time at a certain place. Then we'd go and stand in line. I remember standing in line for two hours to get *one* chicken. We wanted some meat. . . . Sometimes you'd think it would be fun to have some more sugar or something, or some meat that looked like meat. But you just did without it; it was okay. . . . It was what you had to do.

Eager customers wait in line at People's Meats in St. Paul, 1945

My brother worked on the railroad at that time, and sometimes he would get butter. I don't know how he got it; I never asked him. He brought me two pounds one time, and that butter lasted an awfully long time. Sometimes he would bring some lunchmeat off the train. I think he was a cook; that's why he got some of that stuff. I don't think it was completely legal, but that was not the question. He knew we didn't have it. And he would never eat when he came to our house. He would always wait until they got back on the train, because the train had food. He wouldn't eat at my house, which bothered me. And sometimes he'd be there for a whole day. . . . He wouldn't eat. He might drink some coffee, but otherwise he wouldn't eat, because he felt as though he was robbing us.

Bea recalls how something as simple as a pair of stockings could become the focus of attention.

There were a couple of department stores. We could go in and buy, like underwear, lingerie. No stockings. No nylons, same pair of nylons for five years. They were darned up, I'll tell you that. The pair I had were good, the legs were fine, but the heels and toes were pretty awful. I remember once, our organist at church was going to get married and she didn't have a pair of stockings. She didn't quite know what she was going to do, but somebody got her a pair of nylon stockings, and I think that we sat and looked at her legs more than we looked at the wedding! We were all just wishing somebody could give *us* a pair. . . . The little luxuries were very special.

Doris Shea Strand, who lived and worked in Minneapolis during the war, describes how life at home and in the community underwent a transformation. She shares memories of rationing as well as strategies for making do.

OF COURSE we had the bond drives, to help support the war effort. "Buy savings bonds." There was generally a feeling of, what can we do now? Or, are you involved in this? Participation in little extra things.

Rationing. Oh, it was just something to get used to. We had meat coupons, I know, and sugar coupons, and butter. Butter was rationed, or maybe that was a part of the meat thing; I don't know. Anyhow, we got along fine. But then there was some bartering. If some family did not eat meat, maybe they would trade for some sugar coupons or whatever. . . . On the sugar bit, my two sisters were both married in 1946, in February and in May. Even then my mother had to take the sugar coupons to the Hasty Tasty Bakery to let them bake a wedding cake for the girls.

You had to settle for something less. But even shoes, you had to have coupons for shoes. I remember I had a very favorite pair of shoes and I didn't have coupons to get any. It wasn't uncommon to buy half-soles at the dime store and glue them on the bottom of your shoes to make them last longer. Many times we just cut out cardboard shapes to put inside your shoe. Of course, you changed those quite often because the cardboard didn't last very long. You just roll with the punches.

Doris remembers that her mother joined the work force for the first time.

My mom did so many things, especially during the war. She was a cook, and she helped build gliders. She spent the real war years building gliders up north of the city. Part of the war effort.

That was when ladies, we didn't wear pantsuits as much as we do now. They would just wear men's pants and taper the legs or put something down around the bottom so they wouldn't be catching on machinery and stuff. They wore nets and bandanas around their heads. She was a worker.

[Before the war] she did some what they called "day work," you know, like house cleaning. She made pies at a restaurant for quite a while. But no real "job" job. [My parents] maybe were doing better financially because my mother prior to that hadn't worked a full-time job. She got this job making gliders, for the military. So looking at it that way, they probably had twice the income that they had when it was just my dad. Not twice, because she didn't make as much as dad, but it embellished their finances a bit.

For Doris, contributing also meant helping in the neighborhood and lending a hand to servicemen stationed in the area.

One thing I remember is that communities were divided into sections for an air raid warden type of thing. Mr. Miller had a hard hat and a big long flashlight. A girlfriend and I went around with him if they had publicized a brownout, to lessen our use of electricity. If we'd see somebody with all the lights going we'd tap on the door and ask if they'd cooperate. "We're having a brownout tonight." Just to make people aware, although in the Midwest it wasn't nearly what it was on the East or West Coast. It was just to make people aware of what was going on.

On Sunday afternoons I joined a group down at the YMCA in Minneapolis. They called it the GSO, the Girls Service Organization. A lot of the servicemen would come down to the Y. They had buses come from Fort Snelling and the navy base. So we'd just talk or help write letters or play pool or dance or eat. I'm sure there were a few romances involved in that, too, but overall it was just to give a level of comfort and know that somebody cared when they were away from home. We'd arrange picnics for maybe a half a dozen service people. Whatever we could get in a couple cars, or on a bus if we didn't have gas coupons to take them that far. We'd go out to Minnehaha Falls or just try to arrange a few recreational things. A lot of times organizations would give a bunch of tickets to a concert or to the circus or to some special event.

I think letter writing was a big thing, too, because I know there were a couple of fellows from the Dakotas and they were not used to the big city and knowing how to handle life outside of their small rural communities. So we'd help them write letters and try to make them feel comfortable. I think we really needed to help these fellows that were just new on the planet, so to speak, in this new experience. I think it eased the pain or the anxiety for them.

Looking back and looking at some of the old pictures, you think we were all just little kids. How could we handle that? It worked out fine.

Aileen Frazier Boggs (b. 1918) was married and a mother of one when her husband, Mel, entered the U.S. Army Air Corps in 1943. He remained in the service until late 1945 and spent more than a year overseas. Aileen adjusted to being a single mother managing a household; she felt no desire to join the work force. From her perspective, rationing and shortages were not a problem.

W E HAD quite a bit of rationing. You got little slips, or little coupons. Sugar was rationed. Shoes were rationed. And gasoline. Everybody got these coupons. But my parents lived in town, and they were a big help to me. I would give my gasoline coupons to my parents, and then my parents, they would give me their shoe coupons. After [our son] Steve got to walking he'd need new shoes more often, so they would give me their shoe coupons. Then I would give them my sugar coupons, because we didn't eat that much sugar. We'd trade back and forth that way.

I believe we had ration coupons for meat. Of course, our little guy—he was eleven months old—and I didn't eat a lot of meat. If it was meat, I gave [the coupons] to my parents. Nothing that I wanted wasn't there. . . . Rationing affected me none.

However, Aileen remembers something intangible that did affect her—loneliness. She eventually invited a friend to move into her house and provide company. Sharing the experience of having husbands in combat, the women provided moral support for each other.

Ginger was my friend, and I was getting pretty lonesome there staying by myself. Evenings were really hard.

[The decision to ask her to move in] was personal, [not financial,] because she paid such a little amount. She wanted to do this. Then she would pay so much if she'd eat with me. Like if she'd eat supper she would pay, I forget what the amount was. It was a meager amount.

It was really great to have Ginger there because we had so much in common. Just being in the house. . . . Every night we would write our husbands. She'd write her husband, and I'd write Mel. It was just nice to have her coming home bringing office talk and things that happened at work and everything, and have somebody to eat with. It was just great. We just got to be such good friends. . . .

She liked [our son] Steve so much, and she'd wrestle with him and have a good time playing with him.

Anna Tanaka Murakami was born in 1929 in Minneapolis, one of two daughters of an immigrant Japanese father and a German mother. By 1932 her father was struggling to make a living in the depression economy, so he sent three-year-old Anna and her sister, age five, to Japan to live with their aunt and uncle. The girls would spend the next nineteen years of their lives, including the entire period of World War II, in Kure, a coastal city on the island of Honshu, ten miles east of Hiroshima. Anna remembers being ostracized as half-American and enduring severe shortages of food, but her strongest memories are of the American bombing attacks of 1945, which leveled parts of the city and killed many civilians.

O F COURSE, you know, we were having bomb attacks, so we constantly had sirens. The minute you hear the siren, you were supposed to run to the shelter. These were American B-29s [Superfortress four-engine heavy bombers]. . . . You are scared. Scared stiff, really. When the siren goes off the planes are coming; then you know you are going to get bombed. You could hear the planes coming.

We always run to the shelter, either a public shelter or you have your own shelter in your house. You dig a six [foot]-by-six [foot], probably about five feet deep, and then you put a lot of stuff on top, and then you go in there. . . . Many times we went to those shelters.

On one side of Kure is the ocean, and on one side is the mountains. The B-29s came and dropped bombs all by the ocean and by the mountain. They dropped a big one in the center, so that no one could escape. But we were lucky; our house was safe. My school was in the center of the city, and it was destroyed completely.

When Kure was bombed, because there was so much on fire, the sky was just lit up like day. That time we went to public shelter because it was a big thing. So much fire, we thought our house was going to burn, too. Public shelters, they made a big shelter that you can go in. That's why we went there that time. But that was really scary. Then you just wait until it's over. Then you can come out; they tell you, "you can come out."

You know, it happened so many times. . . . It's too bad, but you get used to it. [*pauses three seconds*] You get used to it.

To this day, when I hear the siren on the first Wednesday [of the month, around the Twin Cities], just give me shelter. I just couldn't stand this sound; it was really scary. And of course at night, you weren't supposed to show any lights, so we had to block all the windows. We had fabric to cover the window and all that. People would go around, and if they see the light on, they would say, "The light is showing! You're not supposed to show anything." They didn't want [the American bombers] to know where the houses are. It was *pitch black* at night.

Kure was bombed maybe five or six times, but the last one was the big one. I think they just came to show us what they can do. We were wondering why Hiroshima didn't get bombed, because it had an army base and everything. Then they dropped the big one [the atomic bomb]. They were waiting for that, the Americans.

On 6 August 1945 an American B-29 Superfortress bomber dropped the first atomic bomb, on the Japanese city of Hiroshima. Anna recalls the time of the attack and its aftermath.

Well, the day before the bomb was dropped I was at the Kure train station buying tickets to go back to the country [where my relatives lived], and just before me they put up the "Sold Out" sign. So the next day I was walking to the station again, at about eight o'clock in the morning, then I saw the big sun, and then I saw the big cloud, like a mushroom. . . . It's just a few miles away; you can see it.

Then everyone said that Hiroshima was attacked by a poison bomb, because we didn't know what kind of bomb it was. Then my cousin, who had a restaurant business, he was going to buy things in the country, so he give us a ride to Hiroshima. He dropped us off there.

At this time my sister was in Hiroshima, at the hospital, as a student nurse. And she was there, so that's why we went to see her; we didn't know if she was safe or not. My aunt's cousin was going to buy stuff for the restaurant, so he gave us a ride in the truck. So we went there, and he dropped us off there, and we walked to the hospital, and we asked for my sister. Somebody said, "Yes, she's here." We saw her, but we could just say hello, that's all, because she was so busy taking care of people.

We went to the other rooms, and people, they were packed in like a can of sardines. Dead. And it was summertime. We went the next day, but already they were burning the things. And the wind was blowing, and the *smell*. It was awful. [*pauses three seconds*] But after we saw my sister we started walking toward the station to go back to the country, and that time a B-29 came. Way up there. My aunt said, "Take cover," because the siren had gone off. But of course I was a cocky teenager, and I said to her, "They're not going to do anything, because they just came to see what they did." But she took cover in the ditch—she was that kind of person—but I just looked up in the sky.

The plane was just a little starlight. But we could hear the noise, and that's how we knew it was a plane. Then we left Hiroshima and went back to the country. . . . [M]y aunt got sick the next day. She lost all her hair, and her temperature was way up high. We put an ice pack to her head to keep the temperature down. It was radiation sickness. But I was lucky, being a cocky teenager. [*laughs*] Nothing happened to me. . . . [Years later] my aunt died of cancer.

Vivian Linn McMorrow was born and raised in the small town of Howard Lake. She taught at country schools during 1939–43 and then moved to Minneapolis to be near her family. In 1942 Vivian married Ralph Gland, then serving with the army. In late 1943 Ralph was at an army post in Texas, set to join the thousands of young men shipping out to Europe.

H E WAS MY childhood sweetheart. We were king and queen of hearts on Valentine's Day in sixth grade.

I remember the last day at Paris, Texas, when we went, another army wife and I went down, to say good-bye to [Ralph and her husband]. I know Ralph expected me to say good-bye and just turn around and walk away and don't look back. So that's what I had to do. It was hard. [*pauses three seconds*] It was terribly hard.

Vivian Linn McMorrow with
her country school students,
1941 or 1942

Ralph participated in the Allied D-Day invasion of France on 6 June 1944; he was wounded during the landing and died eleven days later.

I just don't remember D-Day. It just meant to me . . . now he's in the fighting. . . . I got the first telegram on a Friday after work, about the first of July, that he had been "slightly wounded in action," and my thought was, oh good, now he'll be coming home. . . . Then on the Fourth of July I was visiting a girlfriend who I had gone to high school with, and Mother called me up and said another telegram had come and they would bring it over to me and come and get me. I said, "What does it say? What does it say?" That he had died of his wounds. He had lived eleven days, but he had never regained consciousness. So now I knew. On the seventeenth of June he had died, and I got the notice on the Fourth of July. . . . And so all this time I had lived the whole month of June, and here he was already dead, and I had no idea.

I was devastated. I cried and I cried and I cried. And I told my mother, "Are you sure that this isn't hell that we're living in right now?" That's how devastated I was. It can't be part of the good earth. It's got to be hell. What did I ever do to deserve living in this hell?

I stayed to myself the first week. Then I went back to work. I had to go back to work. . . . I taught night school. Worked in the office daytime and taught night school. So I kept busy. . . . I had to keep my mind on something else.

Vivian remarried in December 1944 and relocated to San Diego with her navy husband, Tom McMorrow, but she did not adjust well. Unhappy and pregnant, she returned alone to Minneapolis and lived with her parents.

I shouldn't have gotten married. I was in no condition to get married. . . . Well, it had been over a year since I had seen Ralph, and we really hadn't been together. It was always—All my life, I was waiting and waiting and waiting. We were together twelve weeks, and that was at five different times. The longest we were ever together was five weeks, and we were married nearly two years. So when Tom came along and he wanted to marry me so badly, I knew that I liked being married and wanted to be married, and I knew, thinking about it, I'm not going to be able to have Ralph, so what difference does it make?

Things got worse when we went to California. In the first place, I got pregnant right away. I was sick, and Tom was so immature. He couldn't take care of me or put up with me, and we couldn't find any place to live. There was just nothing.

I was very unhappy, and we didn't have enough money. I got a job, and I was sick every morning. But I got a job working in the office of the department store, and I could see that these other sailors were working part-time in the store, so then I thought Tom should have gotten a part-time job, too, and take the pressure off of me. Why should I be working? I was sick and I was miserable. I was crabby and the living conditions—Everything was awful. So he sent me home. He was going to be shipped out anyway. And after I got on that train and after I got home, I was never sick another day.

Vivian and Tom divorced in January 1946, four months after their daughter was born.

On the Farm During Wartime

MINNESOTA FARMERS made one point consistently: the war years were good years. In stark contrast to the depression 1930s and a federal policy of crop restriction, farmers now found themselves encouraged to produce—and abundantly. Congress offered an incentive by setting farm price ceilings at high levels. As a result, during the war crop production increased by 15 percent, beef production by 37 percent, and pork production by 63 percent nationwide. Higher prices and increased production meant bigger profits: net farm income increased from $5.3 billion in 1939 to $13.6 billion in 1944.

Since farmers grew their own vegetables and raised their own livestock, few of those interviewed complained about food shortages or the ration system. As one farm wife put it, there simply was very little that she needed to purchase to sustain the household—a self-reliance echoed by others. One farmer met the challenge of obtaining spare machine parts by welding or fixing the old or by improvising—there was always some way to keep things going. But others recalled a darker side, too: scarcity brought black markets and influence peddling.

A downside to farm life during the war was the shortage of labor, which at times bordered on the critical. Millions of Americans left the countryside: some joined or were drafted into the military; others were attracted by higher-paying opportunities in cities. The federal government sought to support farms with deferments for agricultural workers and by encouraging people to work on farms, but such efforts were only partially effective. Across the state, farmers were forced to work harder; to rely on younger family members, including daughters; or to scrounge for any available temporary labor. When these measures proved inadequate, as sometimes was the case, other solutions had to be found. On numerous Minnesota farms, German POWs supplied the extra hands.

✦   ✦   ✦

Married and the mother of three, Lucinda Holst (b. 1912) lived on a farm near Austin. During the war years, the farm supplied most of what her family needed, just as it had before 1941.

WELL, I CAN'T SAY life changed; we just went on living. We were living on the farm; we just had to go on. I can't remember that there was anything different. . . . We lost many soldiers from this community, you know, [we had] a lot of young widows. I always felt sorry for them. A dear friend of mine lost her husband; she had two little children. They lost their daddy. So it was hard.

We were exempt. There wasn't any of us [in the service]. See, our children were too little, and my husband was a farmer, so he had to stay home. There wasn't anyone in our relations that was involved, that I can recall. . . . My husband was the youngest in his family . . . and there just wasn't any of his relatives either that got in the service.

We were farmers and were not affected. My brother was a pastor in Washington, and they could not make their ration stamps . . . reach for their family. They had to struggle, where we could make our own butter. We were so diversified with farming. We had cows, and chickens, and everything, so we had our meat. I churned butter. You know, the only thing that affected us was sugar and flour. That was a struggle, and shoes for the children. We had to have stamps [for shoes], but our kids went barefoot in the summertime, which stretched it out.

My garden was about the same size it was before, and I did lots and lots of canning. . . . I came out of the garden with pails of green beans. And cucumbers. Carrots by the bushels. We weren't suffering that way. For food we weren't suffering. Well, I suffered because I couldn't bake as much as I'd like to, because of the lack of flour and lack of sugar. We used syrup a lot, for sugar. A good substitute.

While it was not difficult to keep the family fed, Lucinda remembers that shortages of certain manufactured items, like machinery parts and tires, affected rural households just as much as urban families, if not more.

One spring day in 1944, my husband was working the fields for planting when the clutch broke on the tractor. So he went to all the nearby implement dealers to try and find a clutch for the tractor, but there wasn't one to be found. One dealer phoned another implement dealer in the town of Red Wing, Minnesota, to see if he had one. Sure enough, he did.

Well, Red Wing was eighty miles from our farm. . . . We left shortly before noon. We didn't get very far from home when a tire on our car went flat. The men patched it up and off we went again, but before we arrived in Red Wing we had a total of two more flats. Our tires were old, but we couldn't buy any new or used tires during the war, and you had to have a permit if you could even find one.

A Red River Valley farm in Abercrombie, North Dakota, was home for Clarence Leer. His memories of the war years are of self-sufficiency, of good times for his family, not of rationing and shortages.

ACTUALLY, WHEN I THINK BACK, I didn't really notice it too much. . . . We always had enough to eat. I don't think it impacted us that much. My mom and dad always did some [canning], but I think they did more of it during the war. . . . All you had to buy was sugar. You didn't need to buy meat; we had that on the farm. Churned our own butter; didn't have to buy that. Didn't have to buy milk. That takes care of most of it.

Grain was usually hauled in. We raised a lot of grain for feed. Used on the farm. Stored on the farm. Then we had wheat and flax and things like that that we hauled in to the elevator right away when we harvested. It was sold right then. [Prices during the war years] were better. . . . [Prices for beef and pork] were pretty good during the war, too. Better than before the war.

I think [my folks] were better off than during the thirties. Prices were a little better. Of course it cost more to live, but they pretty much evened out. Took a five-gallon can of cream and sell it to the creamery right there. Then the eggs, too, sold to the creamery. Usually take in twelve dozen eggs in a crate, and a five-gallon can of cream, that would buy enough groceries to last for a week.

Things like tires and parts for the equipment, for the machinery[, were hard to get]. Parts were hard to get. [When we needed a part and couldn't get it, we] mostly improvised. My dad was a very good welder and blacksmith. He could make a lot of the things that he needed and get some part and figure out how to make it fit. . . . People relied on each other a little more, yes. You know, if you're missing a part and you can't get it, maybe you can borrow your neighbor's truck and do whatever you had to do.

During harvest season . . . in September, we needed extra help. Most of the time we got help from the neighbors. They all got together, most of them. You could usually find somebody in town that was willing to come out and work for a few days.

The youngest of six children, Priscilla Starn (b. 1929) grew up on a 160-acre farm near Sleepy Eye. When two brothers went into the service during the war, she was the last child remaining at home. Much of the farm's work fell on her shoulders: the teenaged Priscilla helped care for livestock, worked in the field, and also assisted with cooking, canning, and other housework.

I WAS THE hired man. I did everything. *Everything.* I was a strong girl. I would work out in the fields, shock grain. I rode a tractor in front of the hay wagons when we had them, before we had the combine. Other than that . . . I did everything. Milked cows. Shoveled manure. I remember that! [*laughs*]

At that time we had a cream separator that you had to turn a handle. You put the milk into the thing, and it separated the cream. It had to be turned by hand at that time. The cream was separated from the skim milk. Then we sold the cream and the milk actually to the dairy, and they'd come out in a big truck and pick up the cans. I did a lot of lifting.

Mom had a lot of chickens, and we used to help feed those. Pick eggs. She used to do a lot of canning, and I helped with that a lot. I did a lot of baking. Then we had the corn pickers, the pea viners—we raised corn and peas for Del Monte, too. I was out helping pitch peas onto the truck, too. . . . Did most everything.

I remember one time I was raking hay out in the further forty, had a team of horses with one of those dump rakes. . . . It's a rake that you—The horses pull this thing and it has tines back there. Then you pull up your leg and it dumps the pile of hay. And a bunch of hornets or wasps or bees came along and were stinging the horses, and they went home as fast as they could. I just barely hung on to this dump rake. They turned up in the farmyard and stopped. [*laughs*]

We used to go to [high] school . . . from about nine to four. Chores were after school, too, anything that needed to be done. Dad would bring the cows in, and we would shovel silage or whatever to feed them. Give them oats and whatever they had. Corn. Just a variety of things.

During harvest time I can remember we had this little elevator going up into the granary. Someone had to be up in the granary to shovel the grain apart so it wouldn't just land in one big pile. I was scared stiff one time. It's high up. Like the surf coming in, it sort of drags you. I thought I was going to get sucked in.

Life on the farm continued largely as it had before the war. Self-sufficiency—and a simpler lifestyle—were key.

We weren't hurting for gas, because we could get gas for the tractor, for the machinery. At that time we got all our own meat. We butchered our own pork, pigs, and we butchered our steers or cows or whatever. And chickens. We had everything we needed on our own except for sugar; we had to get that. Actually we grew sugar beets, so we could make our own sorghum.

**Work on a farm...
this Summer**

JOIN THE U.S. CROP CORPS

SEE YOUR U.S. EMPLOYMENT SERVICE OR YOUR LOCAL COUNTY AGENT

The farm labor shortage led to government calls for extra workers

Mom was a good German cook. She grew her own cabbage and made her own sauerkraut. She made a lot of that. We had apples. She made applesauce, and made lots of apple pies. We rendered our own lard from the hogs, so we had that. She made her own soap.

[Life was in many ways the same] as far as our family was concerned. Our living was the same. We didn't really suffer anything on the farm, I don't think. We never had an abundant life. We didn't do much socially except get together with the neighbors for cards and go to church. We really didn't spend anything. . . . But there wasn't anything to spend money *on*.

Before the war, farmers had commonly hired extra help when it was needed. Now, with many young men serving in the military and others working more lucrative jobs in the cities, there was a serious labor shortage in the rural sector. At certain times on the Starn farm, prisoners of war were used for labor.

[We had] German soldiers that helped out during World War II. Because of no help available, German POWs came from [the town of] New Ulm. They came with their uniforms, their black boots. They were brought there in the morning. There was a guard that brought these two or three gentlemen to the farm. Then he had more in the truck, and he was dropping them off at different farms. They would come—In particular this one time they were shocking grain because we just needed help doing it. They worked for a couple days doing it. They just shocked the grain, and that was it.

Of course, being German, my parents could talk to them. I think they felt so much at home. Mom fed them like she would feed anybody else. She treated them just like she'd treat anybody, like her own sons.

Then the next time we saw them we were taking a load of sweet corn into the factory, and they were working there with the big forks pulling sweet corn off the trucks. I don't know what else they did at the factory, but I just happened to see them there. I was driving the truck at that time, too. [*laughs*] I can recall standing back there while they took the sweet corn off, and they would smile at you.

During the war, Eldor Breitbarth worked on his parents' farm in Truman. He also remembers German POWs supplying labor at harvest time. Of German ancestry, his parents were comfortable with the prisoners helping out.

I CAN REMEMBER during the war that during harvest—in those days they shocked oats and threshed it—we had some German prisoners of war. German prisoners helped us thresh the fields. Of course some of them, you had to tell them just what to do. Some of them we felt sorry for.

It was [provided by] the state; they were German Army. They could only work for you one day, just one day, and the next day they were someplace else. I can remember we had one guy, he was really nice, and, in fact, we wanted him to come back the next day. By golly, he did come back, and they were good. You know, I'm German, and I could talk a little German. . . . My folks could talk German [to the prisoners], and that's what they enjoyed.

Albert H. Quie, later governor of Minnesota, grew up on a 240-acre farm in Rice County. After graduating from high school in 1942, he had a farm deferment until October 1943, when he entered the U.S. Navy. The Quie farm was located between the towns of Dennison and Nerstrand, and Al recalls conversations focused on the war and how local men were contributing.

THERE WAS a great deal of talk [in town] about the war, between people, about their sons who were in the service. Big talk. And so those who did not have sons in the service were keenly interested in learning what other people's kids were doing that were in the service. And when somebody was killed there was a grief that came upon the whole town.

Our minister's son was killed in France, and that was really a shock when that came through. Another one of his sons was flying a fighter plane and crashed, but he lived. He was in the hospital for a long time, and that was a matter of conversation. A great deal.

There was deep patriotism. Nobody would have thought of going to Canada to get away from it. . . . That was totally unacceptable for that to happen. People were watched pretty carefully on whether their sons would go or not. It would have to be a pretty significant reason why they wouldn't. It's interesting, staying on the farm was a significant enough reason because of the sense of patriotism of providing food for the people. . . .

I don't know if I would use the word "guilt," but [working on the farm] surely was not as important as being in uniform. Being in uniform was the way to serve your country at that age. So I had a strong desire to do it, and I did not want us to come out of the war without me being in the service, because that would hang with me the rest of the time.

Waldo Meier spent his childhood on the family farm and remained there until he entered the navy in 1943. While farm life meant daily necessities were not an issue, he recalls certain shortages that affected his teenaged years.

FARMING, OF COURSE, was sort of a protected thing. The smaller farms provided more of your food individually, so we were in kind of a good situation. We didn't have to worry about meat rationing, because we had our own meat. Some of the other groceries, sugar, was one of the things that would affect us most. . . . As you went into a store, there were coupon values on products there, and you had your coupon book, and you tore out the coupons that matched whatever you purchased.

Gasoline was one of the things that affected us most, as a teenager, naturally. There was no such thing hardly for any of us to have our own cars; that wasn't the normal sort of thing. Usually we got to use the folks' car or something like that and drive around. . . . On the farm we did have ration stamps for [gas for] agricultural use, and those were somewhat unlimited. I don't recall specifically how many stamps we got; those were "T" stamps as I recall.

The other things, as far as rationing was concerned, it was simply a matter of things weren't there. Shoes were something you couldn't get, so that was one item. I remember that you weren't supposed to have cuffs on your trousers, and also the patterns got comparatively narrow on the pant legs and things like that, to conserve fabric and so forth.

Also, the speed limit was moved way down. Then everybody was asked to turn in tires: you could keep one spare tire for your car; you shouldn't keep any additional tires. When I got to Fort Snelling [to be inducted], here was a pile of tires that was about a hundred feet high and about a block long. I think they were here at the end of the war yet. So all these tires we turned in stayed here and collected water and mosquitoes all during the war.

It was kind of disheartening. You always had a few spare tires around, it seemed like, and we turned in everything. Boy, later on we sort of paid for it with the problems we had. Tires were not available, and they sold tire liners, as they called them. What they amounted to was an old tire that had been stripped of the sidewalls, and you put that inside of the other tire just like an inner tube. Of course, everything was out of balance, but we were only supposed to drive at about forty miles per hour, so you weren't going to get fast enough to have a problem.

Born in 1915, John Behlen farmed 400 acres in western Swift County, Minnesota. When the United States entered the war, his first concern was for the future of his farm. He soon realized that prices for farm produce were much improved over the prewar years.

IN THE FALL, I kind of liked to raise fall pigs. I had time in the winter to kind of look after them. . . . One day [in 1942] we penned up the biggest ones, and we backed up that old truck and loaded it. They were heavy. I was going to take them to Dawson because there was a buying plant there. I went down to Dawson and unloaded the pigs. They gave me five hundred dollars—it was five hundred dollars, and I think I had either four or five more truckloads at home. And it affected me so that I got engaged. [*laughs*] I was really flying high.

We must have been making some money, because it came to be that [in 1945] the war ended. . . . Then I ordered a new tractor. That came, and I

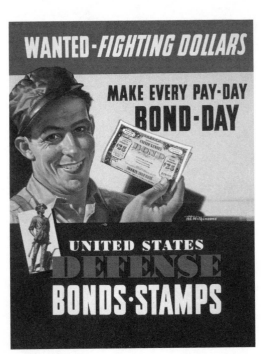

On the Home Front, whether farmer, housewife, or laborer, purchasing war bonds was a patriotic duty

paid for it. The next thing I ordered was a new combine. This was right after the end of the war, 1945 or 1946.

John tells how farmers escaped certain restrictions. He also remembers that personal contacts were invaluable in obtaining a product in short supply, like a new car, and the permit required to buy it.

The remarkable thing was that as a farmer, you were number-one priority. If I had a tire that went bad I could go to town and I could get the tire. . . . It changed certain things, because you had to make do in some respects. But in other respects it was no hardship for me, because as a farmer you were entitled to things. For instance, I got a new automobile in 1942. . . . When the war first started they had a few automobiles. I had a car that had a hundred thousand miles on it, which doesn't sound too great today, but at that time that was really miles. Besides that I was on the township board, which doesn't mean that much, but still a little extra. I was president of the local [grain] elevator, which doesn't mean much, but it's still a little bit. . . . I applied to the board, and I got a permit to buy a car.

The local Chevrolet dealer, Harvey, I knew him. He went to the same church. . . . Harvey and I'd done some business together. I'd bought some machinery from him. But I wasn't twisting any arms.

He had kind of a homely Chevrolet, a two-door, plain-Jane Chevrolet. So I went to him [on a Saturday] and said, "Harvey, I'd like to buy a car, but can you get anything different than that?" He said, "I'll see what I can do." On Tuesday I got a card in the mail saying, "your car will be ready Tuesday night." [When I went there] he had a green Chevrolet, torpedo shaped. . . . I couldn't have prayed for anything nicer.

Ervin Borkenhagen (b. 1918) farmed and worked as a blacksmith in Blue Earth County, in southern Minnesota. Married with one child in 1941, he was deferred for the entire war.

I DON'T THINK the war changed much for me, because you just went out and farmed and did the same thing. It never bothered us too much. . . . The farmers—They didn't dare to take too many farmers, because they had to have them out there farming.

My life was pretty normal. . . . I just farmed and done some blacksmith work and repaired machinery and stuff. There was a lot of work, actually, because they couldn't get the parts. . . . Like the planter that you put in the ground, we used to get a piece of strip iron and weld it back on the bottom to make it like new. There was a lot of stuff you had to get repaired because you couldn't get new. New, usually it was high priced as heck, and if they didn't have a ceiling on it, well. . . . A lot of guys got around that dumb ceiling anyway, under the table, one way or another.

They slapped a [price] ceiling on a lot of stuff. After the ceiling went on, the prices couldn't go skyrocketing. They had a ceiling on corn and oats. But it was a decent enough price. . . . Actually, the farmers did better during the war.

Price controls were placed on certain household goods, too, and when demand outstripped supply, lotteries might be held. Ervin remembers one lottery for a prized item, a gas refrigerator.

During the war we went to a sale because we wanted to buy a gas refrigerator. We didn't have electricity on the farm then yet. And they had a gas refrigerator on this sale. You had to put your name in a hat and draw because they had a ceiling on it. I think it was $137 for the refrigerator; I think that's about what it was. They said, "Well, we'll go until we get to the top price, and then that's it." If it goes higher, then they'd draw a lottery [of all those willing to pay the maximum price].

The auctioneer said, "Well, who's all going to stick in their names?" And he got the slips of paper out. And nobody said anything. So the auctioneer says, "Well, we'll just bid, and whoever gets to $137 first gets it. We don't have to pull any names." Well, they started out at $75, then $80, and then $90, and then I said, "$137." Some of the guys was a little peeved. [*laughs*]

[4]

War Experienced

Military Service in Europe and the Pacific

DURING WORLD WAR II, millions of men and women in locations around the globe were subjected to the emotionally intense, oftentimes horrifying experience of combat. Those who share their memories on these pages fought in many places: in Germany's bombed-out cities, in a submarine hundreds of feet under the ocean's surface, in the humid jungles of Burma, on the beaches of Normandy, on tropical islands across the Pacific, and in aircraft over Europe and Japan. The conditions they faced varied enormously, as did their individual experiences, as do their memories of that time.

There are both advantages and drawbacks to individual accounts of combat experiences. As noted in the introduction, memory is at times untrustworthy, even fallible. Additionally, time can alter how events and situations are remembered; memory, as Samuel Hynes comments in *The Soldiers' Tale,* is reflective and selective, "more self-consciously constructed than the immediate reports, an old self looking back at what the young self did" (xiv). Yet construction of the collective tale relies on these voices; indeed, it is the sum of these accounts that allows for a multidimensional whole. Perhaps nowhere is the personal story more important—yet also more complicated—than with combat. While some did not survive to record their experiences and while the psychological stresses associated with such situations make recollection difficult or undesirable for others, getting "on the ground" in a combat situation is the only way to understand the role of the soldier and the various impacts of warfare on his or her life.

In contrast to the larger canvas of narrative accounts, the purpose in this collection is to examine the individual brushstrokes, the participants. While these recollections often lack panorama, they provide something equally valuable: the perspective of one who was there, communicated through the individual voice, using words, phrases, and descriptions selected by that person, explaining how he acted or reacted, felt, and suffered. Here is the story of what happened; more precisely, here is the story of what happened to this soldier *personally*. What is recounted is less the story of *why* things happened and more the actual human experience.

One thing is clear: those who were involved in or dispatched near the actual killing experienced a radically different war than those in rear-echelon jobs. Soldiers on the front line—those doing the killing and observing the dying—dealt with a different reality. Consistent themes also emerged, whether one served in Europe or in the Pacific: the development of animal instincts; long periods of boredom punctuated by moments of sheer terror; hatred for the enemy; an awareness of being transformed; and above all the power of certain events to evoke strong emotions more than fifty-five years after the fact.

It also bears considering whether these recollections reflect any particular Minnesota heritage. Responses to the subject of racism provided consistent evidence that growing up in this region instilled different values that evoked different emotions as one was confronted with prejudice in the South and elsewhere. After conversations with dozens of veterans across the region, however, it is clear that such is not the case with combat experience. The events recounted here—and how people recall them—are remarkably similar in content, feeling, and emotional response to those of a larger oral history literature on combat experience during World War II.

Voices from the European Theater

THE EUROPEAN WAR began on 1 September 1939 with Germany's attack on Poland. By the time the United States entered the war more than two years later, in December 1941, German forces had conquered much of Europe and had launched a war of annihilation against the Soviet Union.

The United States committed millions of men and women overseas, the majority of them to the conflict in Europe. Of the country's 407,000 military deaths during 1941–45, the largest number were suffered on the European continent. Direct U.S. involvement in the European war began with invasions of North Africa (1942) and Sicily and Italy (1943) and a bombing campaign of German military and industrial targets (1942–45). The American commitment gradually intensified, culminating with landings in southern France and Normandy (1944). For Americans, the ground war that lasted from mid-1944 until war's end in May 1945 covered Western Europe and Germany itself; the fighting was on the beaches, through the countryside, and in towns and cities. America's popular image of World War II is often of this western European ground war, which involved more U.S. military personnel than any other theater of the war. By the time Germany surrendered, American forces had advanced into central Germany as far as the Elbe River, across south-central Europe into Czechoslovakia, and south through Bavaria and Austria.

The men whose combat experiences are presented below participated in this European war, some on the ground, others in the air. Their recollections offer evidence with which one can construct an image of what this war was like and begin to understand its impacts, many of which have lasted for decades.

✦ ✦ ✦

Frederick Branham grew up in Scanlon, near Cloquet. He worked at Cloquet's largest paper mill until being drafted into the army in November 1944 at age eighteen.

IT'S A VERY BRUTAL business being in the infantry. It's very brutal. . . . Because, believe me . . . man isn't made to *do* this kind of thing. It's certainly no place for eighteen-, nineteen-year-old kids.

Right after the Battle of the Bulge [in December 1944], they were short of infantry . . . and we all knew it. Our basic training [at Camp Robinson, Arkansas] was cut short. We were supposed to have seventeen weeks, but we got fourteen weeks.

At the beginning of February 1945, Frederick shipped overseas with units of the army's 70th Infantry Division. He remembers that their very youth allowed the soldiers to accept what was being thrust upon them. Frederick's unit was engaged in some heavy fighting near the French-German border in March and April 1945, and Frederick fought there until being felled by illness in late April. Combat as experienced differed greatly from how this young soldier had imagined it; he recalls that it changed the way he approached his daily existence.

[After a while] we moved up and dug in on a hill, on the crest, on the downside. Not up where they could see a silhouette or anything. The Germans shelled us as soon as we got there. They knew we were there, so we had to dig foxholes in a hurry. We did get into them, and we stayed there for a few days. . . . We took a real beating there. . . . I knew two boys that were killed right beside me. One boy from Crookston, Minnesota. . . . I know we had quite a few wounded. We were just mauled. They shelled us, they machine-gunned us, everything.

Did an experience like this change me? Oh, yes, yes, yes. [*emphatically*] I told my wife here

Frederick Branham (left), back home in Cloquet, 1945

a short time ago that while I was up there I saw people being killed all around. I *never* thought I would go home. I made up my mind to that. Home. [*emotionally*] . . . It did change my life. I've not really been afraid of anything since. [I have] a fatalistic attitude, I guess. . . . There isn't a day goes by that I don't think of something. Not a one.

Tough situations also produced stress; not all men could handle it.

Oh, yes. We had a Sergeant Thompson. [He] almost cost me my life. We were in house-to-house fighting, and he and I were laying in a ditch together, side by side. You had to cross the cobblestone road or street, I guess it would be in [the town of] Forbach, and get into a house directly across from that. He was supposed to cover me, which means he would watch both ways and if the Germans started shooting he'd fire back at them. He didn't. . . . I was fortunate enough to get behind the low wall, which protected me. I couldn't figure out what happened, why he didn't fire. I thought maybe he'd gotten killed. . . . He was laying in the ditch. He didn't really have any touch with reality any more.

And we had one young replacement who came at the same time I did. I didn't know his name. He was working for a squad that got up on the tracks at Forbach, and he froze. I mean, he froze standing up. It's not uncommon to freeze laying down, but standing up you're *really* scared. Somebody finally knocked him down, or he would have been killed for sure by artillery. He just froze. I never saw him again.

Gerald Heaney was born in 1918 and raised in Goodhue, in southeastern Minnesota. He attended the College of St. Thomas in St. Paul and the University of Minnesota Law School, graduating in 1941. In 1942 he volunteered for the U.S. Army. He was an officer with the army's 2nd Ranger Battalion when that unit landed at Omaha Beach on D-Day, 6 June 1944. In an organized fashion, he details preparations for the invasion and what ultimately went wrong.

W E KNEW we were going to be part of the D-Day invasion. . . . We learned where we were going to land when we got to Southampton. The whole unit was told. Then we were confined. And we couldn't go out, couldn't write any letters or anything. There was some apprehension. Everybody was aware of the fact that there was a certain amount of danger involved. But I wouldn't say there was any essential change in the mood. These people were here—[as Rangers] they were all volunteers. They had volunteered to do this, and we were prepared to do it.

Our battalion consisted of about six hundred men, split up on these two ships. Three of the companies, A, B, and C, were to land on Omaha Beach, and three of the companies were to land on Pointe du Hoc, which was up the coast about five miles. I was part of Headquarters Company, and Headquarters Company was split between these two groups. I was to land with the A, B, and C group. I was in a boat with Company A.

The plan was that we were to land in the second wave, immediately behind elements of the 29th Infantry Division. You've probably seen the film *Saving Private Ryan?* That was [Company] C. I landed right alongside of them. The theory was that we would land in the second wave, and we'd be behind the 29th Division. Well, everything, anything that could go wrong, went wrong. First, the air force was supposed to bomb the beach. They dropped their bombs, but they were a mile inland. Secondly, the army had built huge barges, and on each of these barges were hundreds of mortars. The theory was that when we were about a thousand yards offshore, that they were to fire these mortars and that was to lay down a deadly fire on the beach. Unfortunately, they landed in the water about two hundred yards ahead of us. Thirdly, as I said, we were to land behind the 29th Infantry Division, but because of the intensity of the fire they drifted off to the left, so when we landed we were the first wave on the beach. Then the final problem was that we were supposed to be landed on the shore, but for some reason or other the explosive charges that had been placed on—if you saw *Saving Private Ryan* you saw those iron crosses—they hadn't been detonated. So when we approached them and our coxswain saw that he says, "That's as far as I go, lads." So we got off in the water.

When the conversation turns to the actual events of that morning, 6 June 1944, Gerald becomes more emotional in his recollections, and he talks about fear.

I'm in the boat, and the front end goes down, and Joe Rafferty, he's the captain of Company A [*emotionally*], he's the first man off the boat, and he's shot dead, and he goes off in front of the boat. So I told the men, "Over the side!" So we all went over the sides. And we're in the water, and we have these heavy packs on. And these packs became water soaked. I'm not sure what the others did, but I ditched my pack because I couldn't move. Some of the others did, and some of them . . . [*trails off*]. So we made our way in the water. [*pauses three seconds*] That was a short distance—maybe fifty, sixty feet from the edge of the water up to a seawall. We all hit the ground at the seawall. Most of them hit the ground, and the Germans had us zeroed in with mortars. *Boom! Boom! Boom!* We knew we couldn't stay there. So we leapt over the seawall across the road and started to make our way up the hill, where the German installations were.

I do know that at the end of the day—See it took us about, until about noon to get to the top of the hill, before we were all on the top of the hill and had those trenches and everything cleared off on top of the hill. Then we started to make our way into this little town of Vierville-sur-Mer. By the time we got there we had lost more than 60 percent of our people.

I would have to say, first of all, this was about the only time in the war that I really was not scared to death. . . . I think it was because, first of all, we didn't know what to expect. And secondly, we were so busy that we didn't have time to sit down and think about it. You didn't have time to think about it. If you were going to survive you had to make your . . . this is where the training came in. A lot of the officers were killed, so you had sergeants taking over platoons and companies. It was a question of a lot of individual leadership, down to squad leaders, corporals, and sergeants.

Gerald shares an interesting perspective on luck and survival.

The first time I knew, realized how difficult, how terrible it had been, was that night about eight o'clock. I took five of my men and walked down to the beach, because a lot of the people were just about out of ammunition. Some of them had guns that weren't working properly. So we went down to the beach to pick up what we could. I figured there would be stuff. They had gotten the wounded off the beach, but those people that had been killed were still lying on the beach, some on the beach, some halfway in the water. [*pauses three seconds*] Then you realized how difficult and how serious that had been. You just realized how lucky you were. To have survived.

You've got the Germans on top of the hill, and they're firing mortars, and you're firing your artillery and firing small arms. How do you know? You and I are going up together, and you get shot and I don't. There was not any skill on my part. It was just what was to be.

All night we were shelled. The next morning we had to take off to try and reach the people that were five miles up the road. It took us two days to get there, fighting all the way. You don't sit around and think about those things; you just do. You just do what you have to do.

Gerald Heaney stayed with the 2nd Rangers for the remainder of the war, surviving action in the Hürtgen Forest (November–December 1944), the German Ardennes offensive (December 1944–January 1945), and further engagements in Germany and Czechoslovakia.

◆　◆　◆

Joe Gomer, a fighter pilot with the segregated 332nd Fighter Group, was commissioned a second lieutenant and in early 1944 was posted overseas to Italy. He flew sixty-eight combat missions before rotating back to the United States at the end of 1944.

WE WERE BLACK [in the 332nd Fighter Group], top to bottom, from the commander on down. . . . The [segregated] system meant that we didn't get the advantage of the combat experience of the white pilots who had flown some of the aircraft. We just climbed in an aircraft and flew it.

[Once] I had a [German] Me-109 that hit me out of the sun. We were on a milk run; we hadn't even dropped our [wing-mounted] gas tanks. Just about ready to leave Yugoslavia, cross the Adriatic, and we flew the four-ship formation. The guy out here to my left was supposed to be covering me. But these two Me-109s dived out of the sun. I was totally exposed. I was the target. I was a sitting duck. . . . He shot pretty good, because I heard the explosions. When those shells hit they explode, you know. I didn't see any black puffs when I looked out at the wing. But there was a string of one-inch holes coming down the wing.

I still had my wing tanks on and gun switches off. . . . It's amazing how fast you can react. It's all instinct. You drop your tanks, turn into the aircraft. The second one didn't have a chance to shoot, but that swastika looked as big as a barn door as he went by. There wasn't enough time [for me to shoot]. . . . They just dived straight, and they were gone. Hit and run. I got back, but the plane never flew again. . . . You had to keep your neck on a swivel. And those white scarves that you see in the pictures, they're there to keep your neck from chafing as you moved it around.

Other than that, we had to worry about flak. If the Germans could track you for seventeen seconds they could put that first burst right up there. They were good. You varied your flight path if you knew you were in the area. . . . Strafing missions were the most distasteful of all, because the ground was blinking at you. I had the plane in front of me get hit, the plane behind me get hit.

Although Joe's plane was hit only once, the loss of other pilots, especially his three tentmates, to enemy action wore him down.

I think you kind of numbed yourself to it. Otherwise it would really get to you, you know. It was just something that happened. You can't do anything about it. After I lost all my tentmates and I was in the tent by myself, well, you do start thinking about it. It's like Russian roulette. They finally put a ground officer in [the tent] to keep me company. . . . But it preys on your mind after a while. How soon is it going to be me? My nerves were getting a little frayed about that time, and I asked to be rotated. . . . I came back in December [1944]. I had sixty-eight missions, and I had to ask for rotation. . . . But we had to wait until we got replacements. Which had to be black.

Warren Gerber was born and raised in St. Paul. He enlisted in the army in 1943, right after high school. After basic training, he joined the thousands of soldiers being sent to England to prepare for the invasion of France. Serving with the 4th Infantry Division, Warren landed on Utah Beach on D-Day+2, or 8 June 1944. His infantry unit quickly moved up to front-line positions.

THEY CAME AROUND and said, "You're moving up." It's dark, I have no idea what time it is, I have no idea which direction I'm going in, and I don't know how far it is that I'm supposed to be going. So we marched down the road, and we crossed the road along a hedgerow. . . .

As we're marching along, we see this soldier standing by the hedgerows. As you get closer we can tell by his helmet that he's an American soldier. Then you come a little closer, and you realize he's dead. Nobody had picked him up yet. Standing up there, right alongside of the hedgerow, just like he was waiting, looking out at something, or looking *for* something. I'm not trying to say I wasn't afraid or anything like that, but you just had to pay attention to where the fellow in front of you was going, and he had to figure out where the guy in front of him was going. You knew he was dead, and he was the first one that I saw. There were other ones that were the same way.

After almost a month of combat, Warren was picked to be part of a small group charged with seeking out and destroying German soldiers believed to be in the area.

[Late on the evening of 6 July] we were told . . . that an element of the German 6th Parachute Division was in the area. Our job was to engage, whatever you want to call it, and take no prisoners. Told to take no prisoners. There were six men, including myself, from my squad that were there. Equipment would be rifles with fixed bayonets, grenades, and knives. Everything else was to be left behind. . . . Again, it's dark, and you have no idea where you are or anything like that. We got up to a hedgerow, and as you looked out over the hedgerow it was a big area that was fairly flat. It was a swampy area

Warren Gerber,
Camp Blanding,
Florida, 1943

there, too. It must have been about six o'clock, or just before it was light, and they said, "We're going to move out." . . . All of a sudden, they got artillery homing on you. They waited until actually we were in the middle of that field before they put us under artillery fire.

They were also shooting white phosphorous. When this type of shell explodes, huge fountains of white phosphorus crystal chunks flew through the air. You know, phosphorous burns, so if you don't get it out, it's going to go through your clothing; it would go into your bone. They taught us in basic training that the only thing you could do was to hurry up and get it out. Either take your knife and pick it out, or stick it in water. I was not hit.

Then we got over moving again—there must have been eight or nine of us that were in a little ditch that ran up there. Pretty soon they said we were going to pull back. So everybody started to move back. The area of the hedgerow was about thirty yards away, so I waited for what I thought was my best chance. It was so quiet that I wondered, "Are they waiting for me to make a move or what?" Anyway, we took our chances, and I ran as fast as I could, and I got into the next hedgerow without any problem.

The next moment, Warren was felled by a German sniper's bullet. Warren's description—like that of many others wounded in combat—is one of astonishment, not of anger or fear, and he speaks about the experience in a matter-of-fact way.

I was just crouched down, talking to four or five of the soldiers that were there, none of whom were from my area. All of a sudden, it was like somebody would take a baseball bat and swing as hard as they could across your lower back. I can remember it: I kind of floated up—I didn't fly up, but just kind of went up—and then down.

The medic came over, and I said, "How is it?" And he said, "Not too bad. You'll be okay. We'll fix you up." They say that to all the wounded, I thought. I could not move my legs, no feeling. So they gave me a shot of morphine, and they moved me along a ditch, and they said the stretcher-bearers would be back—"You'll be all right." Somewhere in the vicinity of where I was laying there, along a hedgerow, under heavy leafy cover, was another soldier, and he was wounded. You could tell he was gurgling in his chest, so he must have been shot in his chest. He called—he was crying—he called for his mother. How old he was I have no idea; I couldn't see him, but you could hear him. Eventually, he didn't make any sound any more. He died there.

I don't know how long I lay there waiting for the stretcher-bearers to return. It may have been an instant, or it may have been hours. The stretcher-bearers came and got me on the stretcher, put me on the jeep, and took me to an aid station. There they told me what happened. An officer, he was a doctor, he looked at me and said, "What the hell are you doing here?" If you heard how he said it, you understood what he meant by it. Because I got a bullet from a sniper that went through the right side of my back, underneath the spine, and out the other side. A sniper bullet.

Warren spent more than eight months in hospitals in England and the United States before being discharged in June 1945. Given the option of returning to his unit or going home, he saw a clear choice.

I wanted to go home. I had no doubts in my mind that's what I wanted. There wasn't anything about being gung ho here.

Ed Haider (b. 1921) joined the army in 1942 and volunteered for the paratroopers. In July 1943 he parachuted into Sicily with the army's 82nd Airborne. Harassing the German rear positions, Ed and others were caught in several hand-to-hand combat situations. Relating memories of these encounters proves difficult for him.

ONE INCIDENT. There were four of us. Henry, Joe, myself, and Eddie. He's a boy that was from St. Paul. His name was Eddie. We were . . . it was just before, uh, we were fighting with bayonets. Very close [quarters]. That's the night I got my fingers cut [by a German bayonet]. . . . I never wanted to get that close to them, but we did. It was a distasteful thing. Very distasteful. Because that, that guy was somebody's son. Some mother's son. But it was him or you.

[Afterwards] you tried to form an image in your mind that that fellow was mean looking. That was something you just didn't want to think about any more. I've thought about that many times. Many times since then. All you can do now is pray. Pray that that guy went up [to heaven].

Eddie stuck this German with the bayonet, and when he pulled out his bayonet he hit the release button accidentally, and the bayonet stayed in the man when he dropped over. And that. . . . Eddie went berserk right there, from using that. He started to run across this field, and they trained an 88 artillery gun on him, and they shot him. He blew all to pieces.

In 1943, Mel Boggs was working as a plumber, married, and the father of a small child; nevertheless, he decided to enlist in the Air Corps. As the pilot of a B-24 Liberator bomber, Mel flew twenty-nine combat missions in Europe. He grappled with issues of faith, war, and his job, which sometimes was to bomb civilian targets far below.

MEAN, it was all part of the program. Nobody was happy to go out and kill people. Nobody was happy about having them come killing us. It didn't seem like religion entered into the program of what we did. We all knew it was wrong to go bomb a city and kill a bunch of people the same way it was that they came over and bombed us and killed us. The whole thing in war, there's nothing right about it. They don't make sense. . . .

I guess you feel that this is a part of doing what you should do or what should be done. I guess we felt as bad. . . . We weren't a bunch of warriors. We weren't interested in killing German women and children. That isn't what we thought about. When we bombed a target, it was always an industrial factory. Of course, people are down in that factory. Probably they got out of it when they knew we were coming. [*pauses three seconds*] I guess you can't let those kind of things worry you.

When I first went into the service we had a tough old officer there when we started our basic training, before we even got near an airplane. He said in no uncertain terms, "You're here for one thing: to learn to kill." That's what he told us. That kind of shook us up. And that's what it was about. I guess when we'd go to bomb an airfield or something, we didn't think we were bombing the people so much. And we're not. We were more interested in blowing up their airplanes than we were the people. If we had a choice, I think the United States . . . would have bombed places that didn't have people in it, if they could have. But that isn't the way war is.

Bill Devitt, a first lieutenant with the army's 83rd Infantry Division, saw combat in France, Luxembourg, and Belgium from August 1944 until January 1945. The chance of being wounded or killed was constantly present, but he recalls that he could not dwell on mortality.

I DON'T THINK I thought about it much, but I'm sure it affected me. You don't break down every time you see someone injured badly or have the top of his head blown off. Real trouble, people around you are in real trouble. I suppose I took it rather coldly. My combat experience was . . . limited, but I did see some people die. People I knew who died.

After I lasted through [the battle in the] Hürtgen Forest, which was a great part of my combat experience, after I got through that, I thought I was fairly impregnable—we walked in with maybe a hundred and ninety men and walked out with about forty. I knew you had to be cautious and be careful. I just thought I was lucky, and maybe I was going to live through it all pretty well. I learned otherwise later on.

I don't think survival had anything to do with skill. A philosophical thing. . . . Yes, I guess I thought I was lucky in the Hürtgen. I had close calls and got through it okay. I got nicked in the head once with a grenade. It didn't bother me at the time, but I think back now; I got nicked in my forehead—another inch to the left and it would have gotten an eye, and I could have lost an eye or something. I didn't think about it at the time. . . . We were busy thinking about other things, more important things, like how we'd get through the next day or the next hour. I didn't do a lot of philosophizing. I think if you did you'd go batty. I didn't intentionally *not* think about things. Maybe I was just a dumb kid with a lack of imagination; I don't know.

On 3 January 1945, Bill was badly wounded while on front-line duty in Belgium; he spent the next four months in hospitals in England.

✦   ✦   ✦

Henry Buczynski was born in 1917 and raised on a farm near Gilman. The youngest of ten children of Polish immigrant parents, he was drafted into the army in 1942 and trained as a cook. Henry served 1943–44 in a training unit at Camp Campbell, Kentucky, before being shipped to Germany in the war's final months. He viewed the war from a different vantage—that of the kitchen.

IT'S NOT VERY easy being an army cook, because it's just a little different than in civilian life. You go into a bigger scale when you're cooking for a hundred and sixty men. It isn't like cooking for two or three people. Over here you're probably going into a pound of meat, and over there [in Europe] you're going into fifteen pounds of meat. You have to consider so much. First they haul in food. They teach you, so much per person. If you're going four people to a pound, let's say, and if you have a hundred and sixty people, then you figure how much meat you have. That is the first step that you have to learn in service. A balanced diet, and make sure that the people have enough.

[I became a cook because] they asked me. When I was at home [on the farm], I had a little experience of it. . . . And then I was interviewed when I went into service, and what I'd like to do, and what field I'd like to go into, and if I had any special things I liked to do. I mentioned that I liked cooking and stuff like that, and that quick I was in that school.

I had short basic training because I was scheduled to go to school for cooks and bakers. That would take up my half a day. After the half a day of school I would go back in the kitchen and help out in the kitchen. That was my work as far as basic training was concerned. I would go out on marches, and I would go out on rifle squads and target shooting and stuff like that for effect, just to qualify. You have to qualify for all that stuff, regardless if I was a cook or mess sergeant or what. I still had to do that, so that I would have the qualification.

When you are close to the front line, you really have to cook what they give you. You couldn't sit out there and cook a roast beef or something like that. [*laughs*] There was a lot of dehydrated things. It all depends on where you were. If you were in the front lines, you wouldn't have any fresh vegetables or anything like that. It's mostly C rations, K rations, chocolate bars or candy bars, and stuff like that. In the field kitchen it's something when you've got shells going over you and bullets flying. You have to dig in. It's one of those things.

Many veterans discussed fear. Lawrence Brown of Minneapolis, who served in a segregated army ordnance company in North Africa and Italy, remembers the first air raid he endured, openly admitting he was scared to death.

WE STOPPED in the marshalling area in Algiers. We'd been out for nights and days, and we were stretching and scratching because we were all full of lice, from the straw. We heard these sirens going off. Someone hollers, "Air raid! Air raid! Air raid!" Air raid? What are you talking about? What's an air raid? You had *heard* about it, but. . . . These idiots get back in the cars, back in the railway cars. I'm smarter than that. But I still don't know where to go. I heard the bombs coming down. Could hear them whining. I ran this way for a while, then I ran that way for a while, then I ran that way for a while. And then one hit the ground, and I hit the ground. I started digging with my hands, trying to dig a hole. Like a perfect animal. All the animal instinct came out and I—I think, I hope I'm explaining to you how these things just happen, and you haven't any way to prepare yourself for it. I was scared the whole damn time. Yes, I was so scared—people talk about hair standing on end—I could feel my hair doing that. But after a while you get used to it. . . . It was a part of life.

A rifleman in the infantry, Augustine Martinez of St. Paul shipped out from New York in January 1945, headed to France. His memories of the months he spent in combat in Germany are of being scared and of the constant stream of new faces.

I THINK IT WAS nine days after we left New York when we got there. Took us nine days to get to Le Havre. When we got there they had those semi-trucks, those open trucks, semi-trucks. . . . There must have been sixty-five in one truck. Just like sardines, one next to the other one. . . . All bunched in like that until we got to the camp. We went to a camp. . . . Then it was a muddy field or something.

We must have stayed there . . . oh, to get organized . . . oh, I'd say about two weeks. About two weeks. That's about it. Then they got us all prepared. . . . I was scared going up there. I was scared, hungry, and cold. You don't believe it, but it's the truth. We were all young and green. We started out and started working. . . . Bullets all over the place. Flares all over. They were throwing them from way out there. So when they throw a flare, you don't run. You stay right there. Freeze, or they'll shoot you right there. A lot of guys were shot running. They were shot.

You know what happened during the war? The first thing, the first battle, like that? We went in a great big house. Everyone was running like hell. Run scared. I was scared. Into the house. You know how many GIs were in that basement right there? There must have been about fifty, sixty GIs, just curled up like that. Scared. Scared as ever. And hungry and cold. . . . All of a sudden there comes the sergeant. "What the hell are you doing here? Get out of here! Come on! Out! Out!" We go around front. Snipers all over, shooting at us. That's when we used our rifles. Shooting at them over there and running up this way. You could see them. Running this way, up in the house there. That's when I used my rifle the first time. . . . Some, they came over to surrender, and some, they are going to shoot you, and you have to shoot back. So you shoot them. . . . That's all.

Here's another thing. We had a lot of close friends. Buddies. Like brothers. As we go overseas in the battles . . . killing each other. Killing. Every other day we get new guys. All the time, new guys. Two, three, five guys. All the time they're new. We don't know who they are anymore. So from there on they disappear. The ones I knew, they were gone. Left it to the Lord that I was alive. I came back with no scratch. [Some of my friends,] they got killed. Then replace them. Replace them. Replace them. We don't know anybody.

As Allied forces moved across western Germany in spring 1945, towns were taken and soldiers came into contact with German civilians. Many of them were afraid, too.

They just stayed inside, that's all. It seemed like they respected us. We'd never hurt them. The women, we never hurt them. Just stayed inside, that's all. We go downstairs and see what they got. Search the house. . . . We didn't destroy anything like that. . . . Look for rifles and things, what they have. They had glasses. Beautiful things, big chandeliers, linen and all that, clothes. You didn't monkey around with anything like that. We didn't care about that stuff. I got a pack of German money. I got a whole bunch of it. I got a lot of it from Germany. I kept that.

Another time, a woman had a big box, in her house. I went in and searched for guns, and I was in that box. They were full of medals. Beautiful medals. Military medals, from her husband, from way back, World War I. . . . I kept them for two or three weeks. I finally sold them to my buddy. . . . Just to get rid of him. [He wanted them] bad. I wanted them bad, too. . . . I could get a fortune today for those medals.

Frank Soboleski grew up on a farm near International Falls. After finishing high school in 1943, he enlisted in the army and, following basic training, volunteered for the paratroopers. With the 101st Airborne, he shipped out to England in 1944, joining thousands awaiting the invasion of Europe. Tensions were high as the day drew near.

YOU COULD FEEL the electricity in the air. Everybody was walking on their toes. "It's going to happen; that's what we're here for. Let's go! Why aren't we going? The weather's lousy. It's cloudy and there's fog! Why are we still here!?" [*impatient sounding; agitated*] Everybody was ready to go. We just about went crazy. There was fights all the time. Any minor interruption, you'd get a poke in the nose. Real tense.

I was in a lot of fights. Over nothing. [*pauses three seconds*] Just *nothing*. Some guy'd brush you or something like that, or his cap was on crooked, "What kind of a soldier are you? Straighten it up." [*speaks quickly again, recreating the sense of agitation*] You saw a lot of that. Everybody did.

Units of the 101st Airborne landed in Normandy as part of the D-Day invasion in June 1944; Frank joined the unit in September as it fought through the German-occupied Netherlands.

It was about the first week in September. I landed in Holland, [by the city of] Nijmegen. The unit was already there. They kept us in reserve for when it was . . . was really rough, to drop in help. . . . That's when we came in.

They kept everything secret all the time, so that the wrong hands didn't get a hold of it. . . . They alerted us, gave us our last supper, and all that good stuff. [*pauses five seconds*] Well, there was a certain element of fear, and anticipation. "I've been waiting for this; let's go. Why are we dragging our feet? That's what we're here for." [*tense, anxious tone*] That's the feelings that had been generated among the ones that were held in reserve.

The jump into the Netherlands [was] a peaceful jump, beautiful jump. Where I landed there was no opposition—I landed in a cow pie. It was a pasture, where there were black cows with white stripes on them. I'll never forget that: a big white stripe right down the middle of the cow. No opposition whatsoever.

I had a .45[-caliber] Thompson submachine gun, was well fortified with hand grenades, had a musette bag full of ammunition and two units of K rations. Enough for two meals. . . . No extra clothes, no sleeping bag, none of that. . . . Supplies for two days.

I don't remember [how many guys altogether made the jump], but there was a lot of them. We had these crickets [that made a clicking sound]. It was broad daylight, and we were walking around in the wrong position. You didn't need the cricket. You'd see people coming from all over that had landed. It wasn't even a combat situation; it was like the Fourth of July. We all met in the orchard. It was an orchard. Well, it's a hell of a word to use, but it was a letdown. I expected all hell and brimstone and fire and all the rest of it. But it didn't take long, and then we were into it.

You could hear it the whole time when we landed; you could hear artillery, you could hear machine guns, you could hear everything. But we were in like an isolated pocket, just fortunate. . . . A lot of people never made it to the ground—they got hung up in church steeples, in trees, and they got riddled all to hell. That's luck on my part, just sitting on my shoulder again. There weren't that many of us that were in there; there were probably forty people that landed, maybe four or five sticks, twelve people to a stick, that landed right where I was. The rest of them landed where they came—they got all blown to hell. Other planes.

The first thing, it was bullets, mud, artillery, trees shattered, just all around you, all of a sudden. As though [the Germans] anticipated the replacements. And they were ready for us. That's what we stepped into. That peaceful cow pasture situation didn't last very long. It was within minutes. They saw us land; they saw us come down, and they were waiting when we came up to where the people were that we were sent to assist and replace.

Frank believes the instincts of a hunter helped keep him alive; he remembers one young recruit who did not seem to have those same instincts, and it cost him his life.

The next place [we were, in mid-January 1945,] was Haguenau [a city in eastern France, twenty miles north of Strasbourg]. It was a constant movement; they were retreating, and they always left resistance. It was more treacherous than the actual war, when they were shooting at you, and you *expected* behind every building, behind every outhouse a gun, somebody with a hand grenade, there's a machine gun in the window at the top of the church, or something like that. All the time . . . every little town we'd come to.

We'd just got a whole handful of brand new recruits. And this kid [Patrick Neal], it was his first trip; he was on the job about fifteen minutes. I said, "Neal, do you want to go that way, and I'll go this way." Well, I ducked behind this building, and then get behind that, and there's a rock pile, [*claps hands*] real quick, you know, and you get out. You don't get a chance to get shot. Just like a skinny rabbit. I never did get shot, but I heard a shot, and I saw a puff of smoke coming out of the window. And then another shot. I just backed up, and I lobbed a hand grenade in there, and pretty soon the top of the building blew all to hell. There was a German. . . . He was like that [*points, like holding a gun*], so I had to rake him [with automatic weapon fire], because there was some more of them in there.

And then when we took that and came to the end of the town, there was no more buildings, there was no more people. Then we went back, because Neal was missing. He had a blue bullet hole right here [*points to center of forehead*], between his eyes and his forehead. He was on the job fifteen minutes. . . . I felt like I was responsible for him, because he was a brand new recruit; he was in my platoon. And he didn't make it. [*pauses three seconds*]

But later on, when I looked at it, it was just like, I'm over here, and he went where there was nothing to hide behind. When he came around the corner of the building and realized that, I wouldn't have gone there. When I saw that wide open and no place to dart behind when they're shooting at you, to get behind some cover, get behind a good one and see where [the German soldier] is. That kid never had that chance. [*pauses three seconds*]

Most of that comes from when you're a kid, and you're chasing wild game. If they can see you out in the open, they're not going to be there when you get where they were. That'll be it—that's where they *were*. But you can go behind these bushes, get upwind from them—that's the way it was over there. I felt my life as a hunter and a trapper had a lot to do with my survival. Because you'd be walking in the woods with a rifle, and an animal's smart; they're on their home ground. Just like the Germans—they were there before we were. They were well settled, dug in, waiting for us to come. It's the same thing, you just hear a flicker of something; you just freeze and get down and go around and find them. All that came to my mind when I was over there. That flashed back from when I was a kid, hunting rabbits and then deer. You've got to think like they do, in their world.

The callousness of war produced abuses on both sides, including mistreatment of German soldiers who had surrendered.

Especially with my unit [it happened], because so many of them had friends that were killed. It happened more than people realized. It happened in our outfit almost all the time. Most of them were "take no prisoners." It was part of the war. It wasn't reported . . . it was just, "Look at that—there's casualties of war." The real truth of it never came out. We didn't do it with civilians, just the opposition, the ones that were shooting at us ten minutes before that. [*pauses three seconds*] I saw it.

This one guy, he killed eighteen of them once when he was supposed to take them back. They didn't have any ammunition. I remember him; I didn't like him for that reason. I think when a person has his hands up, he gave up. You shouldn't murder them. [*pauses three seconds*] But he did. Because his brother had just been killed, in Italy or something, and he'd just got word of it. So there was no more prisoners from him. Nobody would let him escort prisoners to the rear, because he killed them.

Another time, we came to a burned-out basement, and there was puffs of smoke coming out of there before. And when I got up there, there were seven dead Germans and three GIs loading up their guns. They just massacred them in that basement. . . . They had that little .30-caliber gun that they jumped with, with a folding stock. He said, "These god-damned guns won't even kill these Krauts." He just gave them all fifteen rounds [that the gun held], and he stood there and grinned at them. He put in another clip and finished them off. . . .

[I thought] much less [of a guy who did that]. They're human beings: they are there for what they think is right, and when they realize it isn't right, they give up. You shouldn't kill them—you should respect his rights as a human being, that he gave up. . . . Let him live. That's the way I looked at it. I never murdered anybody.

Alan Woolworth at
the close of the
war, spring 1945,
near Dortmund,
Germany, with his
M1919A4 .30-caliber
machine gun

Alan Woolworth spent his childhood in Clear Lake, South Dakota; he joined the army in 1943, some months after finishing high school. In fall 1944, as a member of a machine-gun crew with the 79th Infantry Division, he was sent to a front-line position in France. Alan saw action until the end of the European war in May 1945.

COMBAT IS pretty exciting. . . . You live in a very heightened state. Your senses are all very alert. There's a lot of action going on around you—there's yelling, there's noises, there's odors, explosions, bullets zipping by, people dropping, and stuff like that. It is very exciting, I assure you. It's hard to describe that. It's a thrill. An acceleration type of thing. You see, so much of combat is, sure, you're in a foxhole with a buddy. You eat K rations and smoke cigarettes. You haven't shaved for a month, and you're dirty. You're tired and wet. The time that you're actually under fire is relatively quite a bit less.

I remember one time we attacked on the Ruhr River [in Germany]. We attacked a German position, where they had been at least. At night. The assistant gunner was carrying the machine gun. It was pretty heavy. I was running alongside him with a belt of ammunition in my hands, feeding it in while he was shooting it. Our men, maybe a platoon of us, shooting at this house, positions there, the out buildings, yelling and whooping it up. I suppose partly to encourage ourselves, partly to intimidate the enemy. I can remember how vivid that was—the night lit up by the flashes of the machine gun and the other things. . . . I suspect it's the adrenaline rush mostly.

Alan remembers that the army worked to dehumanize the enemy. Other factors also helped make him more calloused.

We used a lot of training films in the basic training and unit training. Basically, what any government does is to dehumanize the enemy. They're the Krauts, the Huns, the enemy. It's your duty to kill them, to reduce them, to destroy their capability to fight.

I think a lot of us did have some constraints about it, but you have to remember that . . . when you saw friends being killed and wounded and things like that, it made you wish for a callous heart. I think toward the end of this . . . one of the rather shocking things was that we realized that we were becoming more professional, like the Germans. . . . You could see that pretty clearly.

My twin brother Arlan was killed in July of 1944, [fighting the Germans] in Italy. He was in a unit at the Anzio beachhead. . . . I got a letter from my mother telling me about it. . . . It was a blow. For twins we had considerably different interests. I was bookish; he was more an outdoors type. Loved farming and being out of doors, that type of thing. . . . It took a long time to get over it.

[After I got the news] I'd say I was focused on just the daily routine. [*pauses five seconds*] Getting back to shooting. . . . As I say, after a while you develop something, an animosity toward the Germans. I mean as a group. You realize that you had to reduce them, to destroy their capability to fight, and you didn't feel any emotion about it. It was like shooting a rabbit or a duck or something.

With this steely resolve, killing became easier.

Oh yes, sure. [I came out from the basement of a house where I had gone during some shelling.] Another man in my unit came up. We were standing there on a low hill and I happened—We were smoking cigarettes or something, just looking down about a hundred yards or maybe little more. A lower piece of land, to a river or something. There was a column of Germans, Jerries, about maybe fifteen or twenty of them, running single file toward a bunker. I yelled, "Look at the Krauts!" and got my rifle. We all did. We were shooting at them, dropping them. The German civilians were behind us. They had just come out of their bunker, out of the cellar where they were. They were screaming and holding their heads during the firing. Extremely upset about this.

You know, gee whiz, one big factor in this is that all across France and western Germany, when we were always attacking and we took our lumps, many of us were killed and wounded. . . . About three times as many men cycled through the division as we normally would have had. It was a great kind of a relief. We relished the opportunity to finally get a chance to be on equal terms with them. They were at somewhat of a disadvantage. We were on an equal plane. We could shoot *them* for a change.

Voices from the Pacific Theater

JAPAN'S December 1941 attack on Pearl Harbor thrust the United States into the Pacific war. Seeking to gain a controlling position across Southeast Asia and the Pacific, in the months that followed Japanese forces attacked and occupied British-controlled Hong Kong, Malaya, Singapore, and parts of Burma; the Philippines and several of the Aleutian Islands, both U.S. possessions; and most of the Netherlands East Indies (present-day Indonesia). American forces began to halt this advance at the Battle of the Coral Sea, off northeastern Australia (May 1942); they defeated the Japanese at Midway (June 1942) and also during the six-month battle for Guadalcanal, in the Solomon Islands, which concluded in January 1943; and they forced the last Japanese forces to withdraw from the Aleutians in July 1943.

From this point American forces, with Allied support, went on the offensive, gradually reducing Japan's area of control and moving closer to the home islands. The China-Burma-India theater was formed in spring 1942, and varying numbers of American forces fought there through the end of the war. In the Southwest Pacific, Japanese forces were defeated or neutralized during 1943–44, allowing the invasion of the Philippines to begin in late 1944. In the Central Pacific, isolated island strongholds were attacked one by one beginning in late 1943. From this region, a number of epic battles etched themselves into the American consciousness—Tarawa, in the Gilbert Islands (November 1943); Saipan and Guam, in the Mariana

Islands (July 1944); Iwo Jima (February-March 1945); and Okinawa (April-June 1945). Accounts of suicidal resistance and banzai charges confirmed for many that the Japanese were a fanatical, perhaps less-than-human opponent. Military planners, front-line troops, and the American public all feared the casualties projected for the invasion of Japan, scheduled to begin in late 1945. Japan's surrender in September of that year made invasion unnecessary.

ONE IMPORTANT consideration with regard to the American experience in the Pacific war is the role played by racial hatreds and national stereotypes. American society had applied negative racial stereotypes to the Chinese who in the mid- to late-nineteenth century began coming to the United States in large numbers, defining them as dirty, backward, unintelligent, and treacherous; as Japanese immigrants arrived around the turn of the twentieth century, their similar appearance made these traits easily transferable.

Such attitudes changed little in the intervening decades, even though Japan was on the Allied side during World War I. As Japan's military aggression and atrocities in China were reported during the 1930s, Americans became convinced that the Japanese were a ruthless people, fanatical warriors devoted to an emperor and lacking any moral code. The "sneak attack" on Pearl Harbor confirmed this negative image, and events during the Pacific war merely intensified American feelings. Japanese conduct toward civilians in occupied territories or treatment of Allied prisoners of war strengthened an image of cruelty; widely circulated reports of battlefield deceptions, such as feigning surrender, validated the stereotype of treachery; and a willingness to fight to the death, as well as the kamikaze attacks of the war's final years, seemed proof of an irrational fanaticism.

It is not surprising that this enemy was dehumanized in newspaper reporting, political cartoons, and Hollywood films. From the unintelligent figure with buckteeth and thick glasses to more vicious portrayals of monkeys or vermin with Japanese characteristics, such images represented American beliefs about this enemy. Such an enemy, it was easy to conclude, deserved to be destroyed on the battlefield, its cities burned to the ground. Indeed, from the service personnel who speak here emerged a consistently negative portrayal of the Japanese, illustrating the deeply held and pervasive nature of these particular feelings. On this matter, those from Minnesota were right in step with the nation as a whole.

✦ ✦ ✦

Art Pejsa (b. 1923) entered active duty with the Army Air Corps in 1943 and earned his wings the following year. In 1945, as a B-29 Superfortress bomber pilot stationed on the Pacific island of Tinian, he completed fifteen combat missions over Japan. The Japanese were to him ardent opponents, and he greatly feared falling into their hands as a prisoner.

B-29 Superfortress pilot Art Pejsa, Karaghpur, India, 1944

THEY WERE determined fanatics. Absolutely. They'd come diving right through the formation. . . . They were absolutely fanatical. We knew that. [When I was flying from the base on] Tinian, I encountered a couple of the terrible kamikazes. Twice they came right at us. At the last second I dumped the stick down and he just went over the top. . . . We'd see explosions here and one over there where they rammed our B-29s. Two different times I came close to buying it.

We just wanted them to quit so we could go home. That's all—we just wanted to go home. . . . If we had to kill every Japanese to go home, we might have to do that, because they were fanatics. . . . We might have to kill every Japanese. They were defending their Mikado, their god, to the last man. They advertised over and over again that they will be meeting us on the beaches with pitchforks and with scythes, and you'd have to kill every one of them if we killed their Mikado, their king, their god. That was our perception. They meant it.

[Many American air crews were] slaughtered when they hit the ground. The two people that I know that survived being shot down happened to end up near [Japanese] army people, army officers and army personnel who protected them, took them to prison camps. The population, normal people, hated us. We were such devil figures, I guess is the word. We had been demonized so bad in the public mind.

If we were shot down . . . as a matter of fact, [during a mission] over Sendai, [when my plane was damaged,] I knew that we just had to get out over the water. Get out over the water and get far enough away so we can ditch. At least we had hope that we could get picked up maybe by a [U.S.] submarine. We were radioing our position, and each time there were submarines out there who did pick up a few crews. So that was our only hope. *Never* over land. I was never going to go down over land. I was heading for water because we knew it was the end [to go down over Japan]. It was the end.

Herman Hinrichs (b. 1921) was a navy enlisted man who survived Pearl Harbor and the sinking of the USS *Oklahoma*. He spent 1942–45 in the Pacific as a machinist's mate on the battleship *Massachusetts*, but he never forgot 7 December 1941. He admits a bitterness toward the Japanese that remains even now, more than sixty years later.

[THE JAPANESE,] they were always sneaky. Let me put it this way: we were *not at war* when they attacked us. [*angry tone*] I lost everything I owned in life when the *Oklahoma* went down [at Pearl Harbor]. I hated the Japs because of Pearl Harbor. I had a real hatred for them. I was hoping I could kill every one you ever seen. . . . I had a personal grudge.

Japan never gave us one penny for our personal losses. . . . I got a couple of friends of mine who went through the Death March [at Bataan, Philippines, in 1942]. How come they're not compensated? Japan went and compensated the prostitutes that they had taken from Korea and those places. . . . I don't feel sorry for any Jap, to this day. . . . The way I feel with Japanese people—I don't think I would have ever felt the way I do if it hadn't been for [Pearl Harbor]. I have real strong feelings that way; I have no love for them.

Cloquet native Bob Drannen volunteered for the Marine Corps after high school and was shipped out to the Pacific in 1944. He remembers learning about the inhumanity of the Japanese and what treatment to expect from them.

THERE WAS a lot of discussion [about the Japanese]. Most of the discussion wasn't good. A good example of this is when I got through training, just before we were going overseas. We got shipped to San Diego. Our head sergeant told me, he said, "Don't smile too much when you're over there." I've got this gold in my front tooth, see? [*smiles to show front teeth*] I got my teeth kicked out in high school. It was there, he said, "That's the first thing the Japanese are going to look for, and take and knock your teeth out." There was a warning about it. Very definitely, yes.

In basic training [we learned] not to trust them. We were told this constantly. Don't trust them, because they will do anything to get you. They never cared for human life, where the Americans did. I think that was the most important thing: you just don't trust them.

Jacob Gondeck grew up in rural Benton County and enlisted in the navy in 1942, after high school. He served as a corpsman during the battle of Okinawa (1945); his job was to collect wounded from front-line field hospitals, help transport them to waiting aircraft, and accompany them on flights to Guam. What he saw on Okinawa produced a hatred that endured long after the war ended.

YOU WANT TO know the truth? I didn't know anything about the Japanese, only from what we heard by word of mouth, you know. The guys that had come back from Tarawa and Okinawa and that, they told stories. But you know, I was a person that I always wanted to see both sides. . . . I didn't know anything until I got to Okinawa, and we went out in the fields. When I saw, actually with my own eyes, how they chopped our own kind up—the corpsmen—chopped their arms and legs off and their heads . . . I had an instant *revulsion* and an instant *hatred* of the Japanese that I can't get out of my system to this day. Since I'm a Catholic I have to forgive before I die, but not until my deathbed. Not until then. . . . [The Japanese] were so stupid as an army to do what they did, because it just got everybody's hatred in full bloom. [*louder*] They wanted to *kill* them, see? That was the *stupidity* of war. Jesus!

The son of Serbian immigrant parents, Nick Zobenica was born and raised in Coleraine, on the Iron Range. He enlisted in the Marine Corps in November 1942, at age eighteen, and saw action at the invasion of Guam (1944), in the Marianas, and during the bloody battle for Okinawa (1945). His vivid description of the fighting on Okinawa illustrates the effects of depersonalizing the enemy.

YOU'D BE surprised how calloused you get. I remember in northern Okinawa I was at the point, and I saw a Jap laying there. He had rigor mortis and everything. He was killed. Dead maybe two or three days. There were a lot of bugs on him and everything. I didn't want to touch him. Every marine that went by him went [*makes shooting noise*] and gave him another one. He must have had so many slugs in him by the time we finished walking by there. You just get so calloused and so sick of them.

Another time there when we were in northern Okinawa, we had these flamethrowers go in there. The Japanese would come out of those caves with their skin and clothes and everything burning. And they're coming out of there, trying to put themselves out, and [*shooting noises*] we just nailed them as they were coming out. We'd pick them off. We just, it was like an amusement park. It was fun killing them like that. You get hardened. You just, you have no sense of, no sympathies at all.

And yet there were exceptions. Stationed with Allied forces in Burma during 1944–45, Toshio Abe of the U.S. Army did translation work and also served in front-line areas, interrogating Japanese prisoners of war. Provided a rare first-hand opportunity to interact with and speak to captured soldiers, he reached a different conclusion about the Japanese enemy.

THE SITUATION WAS, we had teams of ten people, ten guys. . . . They would send us out in pairs. One guy is usually more proficient in language than the other guy. He would do most of the translation of documents. The lesser guy would interrogate prisoners. If he needed help, he'd ask his partner. That's the way you worked, in pairs.

When we were at Camp Savage [in Minnesota], they gave us the mental makeup of the Japanese soldier who is, you know, totally devoted to the emperor at any cost. They were willing to give up their lives, which was probably true during the early part of the war.

This is my personal impression of the Japanese soldiers: they thought they were invincible. Especially their attitudes toward Americans, I thought, was that they looked on Americans with disdain, because they felt that the Americans lived a soft life in the U.S. and out there, especially in the jungles of Burma, there was no supply. The bottom line in my opinion of the Japanese, and why they lost the war, was they underestimated their enemy. As the war progressed in favor of the Allies, the Americans, particularly in Burma, the Japanese found out that maybe they underestimated the enemy, and consequently they started losing the war. They started losing people.

Their replacements were younger people. The younger people weren't all that devoted to the emperor. They were thinking maybe they wanted to live through this instead of dying for the emperor. In my interrogation, some of these younger guys couldn't care less about winning the war. They wanted to get home. . . . They were resigned to their fate, and they weren't about to die for their emperor. That's the impression I got from some of these guys I talked to.

The guys we talked to, a lot of them were wounded. They were in tough shape. We'd try to comfort them. Sure they were our enemies, but the American troops handled prisoners very well. Humane. Tried to comfort them. In those days you'd give them a cigarette. We weren't aggressive, and I think they appreciated that, especially in fighting out there in Burma. They were fighting the weather, too, and the terrain, jungles and all that stuff. Sometimes I got the impression they were glad to be captured. [*laughs*]

The following recollections—a representative sample of combat experiences in the Pacific—put forth many of the themes evident in the stories shared by veterans of the European war: hatred, boredom, terror, fear, a hardening of the heart, and the transforming nature of combat.

In February 1945, navy torpedo bomber pilot Leon Frankel was assigned to Air Group Nine, which flew missions from the aircraft carriers *Lexington* and *Yorktown.* He flew twenty-five combat missions in the Pacific, including some at Iwo Jima and Okinawa. Some of Leon's strongest memories are of his first combat mission, a carrier-based strike at a mainland Japanese target. He describes a feeling of sensory overload, recalling that the whole scene had a surrealistic quality about it.

O UR TARGET was the Nakajima Aircraft Factory at Ota, Japan, which is about eighty-five miles northwest of Tokyo. . . . We crossed over Japan. I saw Mount Fuji in the distance. Sort of looked

Navy pilot Leon Frankel (front row, second from left) at Pensacola Naval Air Station, Florida, 1944

like California; it was beautiful and green. We'd been at sea for a long time, and this was the first time I'd ever seen. . . . It was kind of exciting. . . .

We led the mission; we led the strike. As we headed in toward our target, we got jumped by about forty or fifty [Japanese] fighters. I saw my first airplane being shot down. Then our fighters got behind the Japanese fighter there, and I see smoke streaming off the Japanese fighter, and they went right past me. I'm looking out, and I was like a guy seeing a deer for the first time. [*excited tone*] I'm just fascinated by the whole thing. Flak is exploding all around us. They were shooting; they had anti-aircraft guns protecting this factory. The flak had multicolored explosions . . . so there were red and blue and green and yellow explosions all over.

It was almost surreal. Actually it was just like it wasn't happening; it was like I'm watching a movie. This is *not* taking place. It's almost three-dimensional. It's not taking place against me or anything. I'm outside of this action and saying, "Oh my god, if they're all like this, I'm not going to make it!"

Dick Baumann grew up in St. Paul Park; he enlisted in the U.S. Navy in 1942, at age nineteen. He volunteered for the Submarine Service and in 1943 joined the USS *Greenling* (SS-213), then stationed in the Pacific. Dick remained on *Greenling* until 1945, a crewmember on four war patrols throughout the Pacific. In 1943, he was at Midway Island, waiting for a permanent assignment.

I WAS PART of a relief crew. A relief crew's job is, when a submarine comes in off of a patrol run, the crew leaves the boat for two weeks, and the relief crew comes aboard and repairs all the various equipment that isn't working 100 percent. Maybe one or two would join the sub when it went back out, depending on the needs of the crew. If they need a torpedo man, or an engineman, or an electrician, they would pick them out of the relief crew. It just depended on the needs of the crew at that time.

I was there about three months before I caught my first. One of the boats I was going to be assigned to, a friend of mine caught it, and he went down on it. So I was very fortunate. I could have been on that same submarine. I think about that every time I look at his books—I have several books that he gave me to keep for him. I still have them in my basement down here, with his name in them. Every once in a while I look at those books, and I think, "Hey, I was pretty lucky." . . . I guess when you're twenty-one or twenty-two years old you don't think too much about it. But I look back now and think that I was pretty lucky sometimes.

Dick remembers that life onboard a submarine could be tedious.

Everyday life on a submarine was actually boring sometimes, because until you got to your station—which was a designated area out in the ocean maybe two miles square—it was very boring. The same thing night after night, day after day. But then if you got into hostilities things moved quite rapidly. There was no happy medium, I don't think.

The everyday life was not too interesting. You're moving to and from station, which took probably a week or ten days, depending what station you were assigned. Onboard, you would do a lot of reading and play a lot of cards. On the other hand, you had four hours of work—you'd stand a watch—and then eight hours off. A lot of times, those eight hours off, they'd turn all the lights on back in the sleeping compartments, and you would clean the ship. You'd clean it, and make it presentable for an inspection, even under way, to the captain and the officers. Just to keep it clean. Various things you could do while the submarine was running, you would do them. Electrical work maintenance, preventive maintenance. . . . I was electrician, and our job was to keep all the various electrical equipment running and maintain it.

Close quarters inspired a different relationship between officers and enlisted men.

The restrictions and regulations on submarines are so different from surface ships, larger ships like cruisers and carriers. . . . You had to wear whites and blues topside, and we would not go topside if we were in port if we had to wear our blues and whites. All we lived in were cutoff jeans and sandals below decks. . . . There was no real distinction between being an officer and an enlisted man. You respected them, and you said "sir," but other than that, they were like one of the crew. . . . We had a couple of officers who *didn't* have the respect of the crew. They didn't last long.

St. Paul native Reynold Dittrich (b. 1925) was also in the Submarine Service, completing three war patrols during 1944–45 as an electrician's mate on the USS *Aspro* (SS-309). He has distinct memories of cramped quarters, minimal personal space, and constant noise.

WHEN I GOT there to Pearl Harbor, I had carried this hammock and mattress and seabag all the way from New London, Connecticut. When I went aboard the *Aspro* the chief of the boat . . . said, "Get rid of that junk. We ain't got no room for that stuff. You just take your underwear and your blues and a set of whites, and get rid of the rest of it." You could have a picture album—which I didn't have right away but I did have later—you could have that if you could find a place for it.

I was really pretty lucky. I slept in the after torpedo room. There was more room back there than up in the after battery room, where thirty-six guys slept. In the aft torpedo room there were only fifteen of us. And we were spread out, because the bunks were fastened to the torpedo skids. It was pretty nice back there.

You didn't have *any* space. You had this bunk that slid underneath the torpedo. You just pulled it out when you went to bed. You put your blues and your whites underneath your mattress and kept them pressed that way. You had a locker about fifteen or eighteen inches square. That held everything else you owned. You kept your underwear. You could wear dungarees—they call them jeans nowadays—and some shirts. There was no more room for anything else. That's it.

There was always noise. You couldn't get away from that. But I was very lucky. I just lay down and go to sleep. . . . It's funny. We were electricians; we were always involved with the engines and the generators and the motors. They used to say, "Watch the electrician when he's sleeping, when the boat changes speed. He'll move in his bunk when an engine starts or an engine stops." Well, it's true. We lived by those engines running, you know.

Born in 1921 and raised in Maiden Rock, Wisconsin, Keith Hansen joined the U.S. Navy in 1943 and by 1944 was serving in the Pacific as an officer onboard the USS *LSM-80*, a small landing craft with a crew of fifty-eight used primarily for cargo transport and island invasions. Life became routine; one challenge was to stave off boredom on long journeys across vast spaces.

U NDER WAY, in a long stretch from, say, the Philippines to the Hawaiian Islands, every day was just like the other, unless you got bad weather. Otherwise, you just ground mile after mile. Every mile looked like the next one. It was monotonous. That's where you were lucky if you were an ardent reader, because we were supplied very well with books. A reader or a card player—that's the way you'd pass the time.

On a little ship like that, as an officer you have to do censoring— an obnoxious job, censoring people's mail. The outgoing mail. It was carried to kind of ridiculous degrees, because there wasn't anything in all of the time that would have mattered. But we had to go through it. I hated reading other people's letters. Then we'd black, cut stuff out. That was one job I had that I didn't like. Then of course you had a four-hour watch, you had a log to write up. I used to get up to do star sites, to do navigation; you had to get up at daybreak to do that. It was just an accumulation of jobs.

Guys would draw some pay in order to play cards. They'd get cleaned out at the card game, and they'd go and draw some pay at the next chance. There were some terrible guys at gambling; they were always getting victimized. I used to play poker, pretty heavy stakes. There'd be another ship, we'd tie up with them and get a game going. Sometimes the game—One time things were quiet, and the game last from seven o'clock in the evening until noon the next day. Overall I came out pretty good on poker. But as far as drawing money just for recreation, they'd usually draw it just to have a card game or something.

There were never any hard feelings about card games in my group. You figured, okay, you lose it, get some more later. People didn't worry about money too much then. Now, a few years later, when you'd come back and started living civilian life, I'm sure that getting laced for a couple hundred dollars would be kind of bad. But back then you didn't think anything of it.

Boredom during long periods at sea was an issue for enlisted men, too. Herman Hinrichs remembers that alcohol consumption was one escape from the monotony of everyday life. Although alcohol was not allowed aboard ship, enlisted men found numerous ways to get around the restriction and seemed unconcerned about possible punishment.

WE'D STEAL BEER aboard ship [when we could]. We'd get it up in the machine shop, take a CO_2 fire extinguisher, and cool it down that way. Although we made brandy and everything else aboard ship. We made apricot brandy; we made raisin jack. The thing is, you steal a couple cases of apricots, the canned stuff, and then you have a good bootlegger from down Tennessee, and then he'd go to work! [*laughs*] One time, there was this guy whose name was McGee, he was from Tennessee; he was an old bootlegger. He didn't have anything to make the stuff in, so he took these buckets, these galvanized scrub pails, and he made it in there. Then we had to hide it, so nobody would know. . . . Later we brought it down, and we looked at it, and it had eaten the galvanizing off the side of the one bucket. [*laughs*] . . . We got one guy to try it, and he passed out, and we didn't know if he was going to die or what. When he came to, then we started drinking it, because we knew it wouldn't kill us. Then he wanted more, and we told him he'd had his share. [*laughs*]

We drank a lot of alcohol, too, 180 proof. Then we'd use that old grapefruit juice, you know, because you had to cut it. Oh, would you get stone drunk on that. Oh, god, that was vicious. [*laughs*] You wanted to die.

You know, sometimes we'd get carried away, because some of us figured we were out there until we got killed. So the officers would come, and they'd want to raise hell with you. And they'd sometimes say, "You know, you're looking at Mare Island." That was the naval prison right in the base [near San Francisco]. We'd say, "Go ahead,

Frank Valentini (riding) grew up in Chisholm, on the Iron Range. From 1943 to 1945 he was stationed with the Army Air Corps at a remote duty station near Kunming, in southwest China. "We would take about six months out in the field, then maybe a month back on the main base. . . . We lived off the land. We kept on the move a lot, so that eliminated the boredom. When we were in the Himalaya Mountains we had pack animals that would carry my radio and the food. . . . Dysentery was prevalent, and stomach problems. I didn't get normal until I hit the States."

send me there—no one to shoot at you there." They'd take off. I mean, what are you going to threaten me with?

Other men described a desire to be part of the action, to avoid boredom or inactivity. Nick Zobenica makes clear why he joined the Marine Corps—he sought combat. U.S. Marines invaded Guam on 21 July 1944, meeting entrenched Japanese forces. More than one thousand marines and ten thousand Japanese died before the island was secured in early August. Nick remembers the noise and chaos as the invasion began in the early morning hours.

WE RENDEZVOUSED [in landing boats] about two miles out. We went right by these cruisers and battlewagons shelling the beach. We had a number of ships off shore. A lot of ships. You have no idea what that's like going past the bow of a battlewagon, when he's got a broadside going. Those cannon looked like big telephone poles out of canoes. When they let go the broadside you can actually see that ship move backwards, from the recoil. From our planes strafing, and that napalm, and our battlewagons, it was just. . . . And the noise—you couldn't believe it. You couldn't hear *anything*. It was just [*explosion noise*] massive.

Other landing boats, there were hundreds wounded and killed. If you took a direct hit, you were done. . . . The Japanese hit six or seven of them. You could see just the bodies blowing up. . . . When the shells would hit the water that concussion felt like you were getting electrocuted. Your knees would kind of numb up. Just the shells hitting the water near us, it just about paralyzes your knees. It just feels like, like you're getting an electric shock.

When we went towards shore, we got hit about a hundred yards out by this big gun, and it knocked our right track off. So we had to swim to shore. . . . We come into the beach, and you've got machine-gun fire. They cut loose with these machine guns, and one of our destroyers came back and fired [*makes shooting noise*]. You could see the Japanese bodies flying in the air. Holy cripe!

Marine casualties were heavy on Guam, and within hours Nick was one of them. He recalls being wounded by grenade shrapnel, and, like Warren Gerber, who was hit by a German sniper in France, Nick describes that moment in a rather detached fashion, as if it had happened to someone else.

We landed about six twenty in the morning, and I got hit about eleven o'clock in the morning. So I was there fewer than six hours. We got in about a thousand yards just before I got hit on Guam there. There were twenty-two dead or wounded out of thirty-six of our platoon in about fifteen minutes.

Suddenly I saw these two grenades land here by my feet . . . so I got right in the middle of them. I put my helmet on. . . . I couldn't move. They were going off. I didn't want to get up, because once I got up, they were going to nail me. . . . I don't know why I didn't get hurt worse, because they blew my cartridge belt off . . . and blew my helmet off.

When I got hit, there was a Sergeant Mike Dunbar there. He was from California. I say his name every night before I go to bed, in my prayers. Anyhow, he picked me up and was taking me to the beach. He was dragging me, really, because my whole side was paralyzed. I couldn't see with one eye. I never had control of my eye because of that wound in the face. Dunbar was hauling me down to the beach and a sniper cut loose and hit him. Dead.

When I was laying there then, I couldn't move. I thought awwww! [*painful sound*] I couldn't see. My face was bleeding. I could kind of see the blood squirting out of my gut. Every time I would breathe blood would squirt up. I was scared. I was just, you know, I was just kind of thinking, why did this have to happen? I thought I was lucky I was living. I was thinking about this side [of my body, where I was wounded]. I wondered how bad that is. I was evacuated to a ship [where they had medical facilities]. They bring you down in that ship and get down those steps, and, oh . . . [*trails off*]. Seeing the guys coming in without an arm, without a leg. Crying and screaming. Just unbelievable.

Nick spent time in the hospital recovering from his wounds but was able to rejoin his unit for the invasion of Okinawa on 1 April 1945. This costly Pacific battle lasted for almost three months and left more than 12,000 U.S. and 95,000 Japanese military personnel dead. Moreover, as Nick makes clear, the brutal fighting day after day could push men past the breaking point. Eventually, his view of death and killing became fairly detached.

There were hundreds of dead Japanese laying around, but we knew we had to bivouac [at this certain spot]. So we got in parties of two, and we'd take these shoulder straps and tie them around their ankles and pull them away from the coral rock [where they were laying dead]. Once we got them on the flat we would have this Sherman tank, this medium tank, with a blade, put them all in one big pile. Then my buddy, by the name of Lieberman, he run up and down the bodies with fuel oil, and we burned them all. You should have seen that fire. Anyhow, [a friend of mine in the unit] says, "Isn't that too bad. All that meat is going to waste."

[Another time, in the north of Okinawa,] there were Japs piled up, I'm telling you, I'm not exaggerating—for two square blocks there wasn't a place where you could walk unless you walked on

Ed Sovik of Northfield was a fighter pilot with the Marine Corps, flying missions in 1944 from the Pacific islands of Kwajalein, Eniwetok, and Saipan. Here he stands in front of his plane, an F4U Corsair. He tried to explain a fighter pilot's view of aerial combat: "[T]here is something in this whole business of aviation where you think of what you're doing more like a game than like a battle. . . . It's a life and death game . . . of who would kill whom. . . . When we shot down Japanese airplanes we won the game."

bodies. . . . They must have been marching through there or something. And then what [our guys] did, they took flamethrowers, and they burned them all. They were all smoking. Their clothes were burning and everything. . . . The stench, it's not as bad, though, as you think. It's a sweet smell when flesh is burning. I thought it would stink, a stench, but it wasn't; it's a sweet smell. When we piled them up that time with that Sherman tank we could smell them, but they weren't sickening. When they decomposed, that's when they stink. But when they're burning, they don't.

Such brutal undertakings were not limited to Okinawa. Army paratrooper Henry T. Capiz describes his combat experiences in the jungles of the Philippines, providing further evidence of a savagery that differentiated the Pacific conflict from the European war.

AT THE END of the day we would stop, because the Japanese owned the night. We'd stop, and we'd dig in. My first foxhole I had to dig right next to a dead Japanese soldier. Still laying there with his guts hanging out. I went over there and threw dirt on him.

Then I dug my hole. He had just come out of one of the pillboxes when he was hit. So I went over and threw dirt on him as much as I could.

That night you could hear all kinds of noises. You didn't know what they were. The jungle has a lot of noises. You never know if the Japanese are signaling each other or it's just birds or what. Anyhow, the next morning I woke up, and here the soldier had popped out of the dirt. He had just swollen up, is what happened. He uncovered himself. What we used to do, because they started decaying right away in that hot sun—it was summer and tropical—we'd tie communication wire around their ankles and drag them off into a pile, and then a bulldozer would come along and dig a hole and bulldoze them in.

You know, having worked at Swift [meatpacking house], I saw a lot of blood. I was working up to my ankles in blood sometimes. So blood and carcasses and all that didn't bother me at all. So actually, it didn't bother me too much except that they were human beings. . . . Some of the guys would get in there and pry their gold teeth out.

Like Nick Zobenica, Larry Strand of Minneapolis also volunteered for the U.S. Marine Corps, joining in late 1942. In November 1943, as a scout-sniper with the Second Marine Division, Larry participated in the invasion of Tarawa Atoll, in the Gilbert Islands, which for the United States was one of the war's costliest actions. His internalization of Pacific combat experience contrasts significantly with Nick's recollections.

THEY DROPPED US in the Higgins [landing] boats and then took us over to another larger ship and dropped the scout-snipers off and left us there ready to go if we have to. So we were there until the third day [of the invasion]. Late that third day they brought us in.

I remember the first thing I saw when I got off the Higgins boat was a guy, and this plays in my memory forever. The guy had been sitting down on the beach for some reason, sitting on a stone or something. And his whole body was blown away from here up. [*motions to waist*] And to see a stomach starting to bloat from the heat. . . .

This is the first real thing that I had seen that really got to me. He was American. Back on ship before we left, we left late, they were bringing casualties on the ship, and they were dropping them off overboard in their body bags. There was a flag draped over the body bag, so this was a burial at sea. There were a number of these.

Waiting on the ship after the landing had started, wondering if or when he would be needed ashore, generated a physical reaction.

I was nervous as heck, and that was when I discovered I had eighty boils on me. I went to the corpsman and showed him, and he said, "Sorry." [*laughs*] He wasn't going to put me in sickbay. That wasn't why I went to see him. I just wanted some help with the pain of those damn things. They hurt; they were boils. They would raise up, just like that [*extends hand and raises it slightly, to indicate swelling*]. And if you puncture it, then you let all that pus out, and it wouldn't hurt any more. And that's what happened: my gun belt and stuff just punctured all those boils, and I don't even remember them any more. Once they had been punctured, the pain was basically gone, and I was able to keep going.

I'm sure I felt [a sense of nervousness]. But you know, I've always been ashamed of being nervous, but I can't help it. That's the way I was. When I think back before we made the landing, before I left ship, here's some guys playing poker down there, and just having a heck of a time. [*laughs*] . . . I think I lived inside myself for a while there and didn't discuss it with anybody.

The Second Marine Division returned to Hawaii to rest, to add replacement troops for the Tarawa casualties, and to prepare for the next inevitable Pacific island invasion. While on Hawaii, Larry developed a serious skin problem, a condition that steadily worsened.

[After I left Tarawa] I never thought about it any more. . . . Never thought about it, and, still, when I was on the Hawaiian Islands . . . on R and R . . . that's when my skin trouble started. I had no reason to think about it as being nerve-racking or anything.

When I got the skin trouble on the inside of my arm, the corpsmen didn't know what to do with it, so they sent me to an army hospital in Hilo, hoping they could clear it up rather quickly so I could get back on duty. . . . I was in the army hospital there for thirty days. . . . It got so bad they finally put me in a private room, and they didn't know what to do with me. It just wouldn't stop. It wasn't painful; it just itched. At night I would scratch it, and I would scratch everything right off. Heavy pieces of skin right off down to the watery skin. They called it chronic eczema. . . . They had me in sitz baths to soften up the abrasions on my skin a little bit. In thirty days they put me on a hospital ship. [It was] down my arms. I didn't have it on my back because I couldn't reach back there and scratch. I had it all over.

When I got out of the warm climate and got up in the state of Washington, then it just started gradually healing, and I did more bathing. . . . But eventually [in December 1944] I got discharged. The doctor called me in, and he went over my paperwork, and he said, "How would you like to go home?" I said, "I'd love it!" So I went home. But still I felt a little bit, [*pauses three seconds*] what do I want to say? My buddies were landing on Saipan, and they were probably going to go on to Iwo Jima. I don't know. I wasn't sure. I thought about that a lot. You know, "Why me? How come I was given this break?"

When I was discharged . . . I started stuttering, and to this day I don't know why. But I stuttered for a couple of years, and in the beginning, I couldn't even go up to a drugstore and ask for a package of gum. I couldn't get it out. I would just struggle, struggle, struggle, and they would finally understand me. And at that time one of the people at Minneapolis Moline [where I worked] wanted to get me some disability because of that, but I never did. That wasn't why I was stuttering. I certainly wasn't stuttering on purpose, just to get some kind of disability. But he thought I deserved it, because he thought it was war related. And I think it was—it was war related in that I was coming from one environment to another environment, and I couldn't handle it. I handled it, but something up here [*points to head*] said something else, in my head.

Earl Nolte was born on a farm near Fairmont, in southern Minnesota. He graduated from Fairmont High School in 1942, worked briefly for the local telephone
company, and enlisted in the army in 1943. When he arrived in the Pacific in 1944,
he was made a machine gunner and assigned to the 1st Cavalry. Earl was
wounded during the March 1944 fighting on Manus, in the Admiralty Islands, and
spent time convalescing before rejoining his unit for the invasion of Leyte, in
the Philippines, on 20 October 1944. On the beach during the landing, Earl was
hit five times by Japanese machine-gun fire. Nevertheless, he still managed to
eliminate a heavily armed Japanese position. In doing so he risked his life and
likely saved the lives of others in his company, brave actions for which he was
awarded the Silver Star. Almost sixty years later, his memories of that day are
partial glimpses, their recollection a struggle.

I GOT HIT right on the beach, almost as soon as we landed. They had
a machine gun on the side of the beach[, and I was hit five times].
I got hit on the beach. [*pauses three seconds*] The last thing I remember is one of my good buddies laying beside me. He got hit in the
stomach. His stomach was . . . [*trails off*]. I was hurt on my left side,
and he was over on that side, and he grabbed that arm. His grip was
so strong that it pretty much took the pain away. He didn't want to
die. He had me promise to go and see his parents. . . . That's the last
I remember. I didn't come to until three days after, on the ship.

Evacuated off Leyte that day, Earl was returned to the United States and spent
six months recuperating in hospitals before being discharged in May 1945. Concerns about his postwar future began almost immediately.

When I came to on the ship, the surgery was all over and everything
by that time. Then it took me another day or so to find out that [my
buddy who had been wounded with me] had died. That was hard on
me. We were good buddies.

I was in hospitals from October 1944 until I got out in May 1945.
The second time [I was wounded, at Leyte,] I had no idea how I was
going to come out, whether I was going to walk again or what I was
going to be able to do. Whether I could go back to the phone company
to work, or what. I didn't know how serious these wounds were.

Earl Nolte (center front) with members of the army's 1st Cavalry unit, New Guinea, December 1943

One part was very reassuring, [that for me the war was over]. I felt good about that, that I wouldn't have to go back again. But there were thoughts of, "What am I going to do?" That was a big question mark in my mind.

I tried to think about what this is going to mean [for my life], but it was hard to visualize. . . . At that time I hadn't had any rehabilitation or anything. I did wonder, "What am I going to do?" I can't climb poles or anything like that. That might keep me from being taken back. The only thing is, when you went in service and you were working for a company like the telephone company and you came back from service, they had to take you back with no ifs, ands, or buts. They had to take you back; that was reassuring. But what could I do?

Dick Baumann's sub *Greenling* left on its twelfth Pacific war patrol in December 1944. For the young submariner, this patrol was a memorable one.

W E SIGHTED a seventeen-ship convoy on the surface early in the morning just by lookouts. We just had surfaced, and we saw this smoke. We went forward and found out that it was a seventeen-ship convoy. We dove again, but unknown to us, they had us in their radar. So the minute we got ready to fire torpedoes, they started dropping depth charges. . . . It started about eight thirty in the morning, and it finished about five or six o'clock at night. All day long. Everyone and everything is very quiet. Nothing is running—you shut down every noise maker aboard ship. You tiptoe around, you don't run around, you don't talk out loud, you whisper. You don't make any noises whatsoever. Of course you're doing a lot of praying, too. You looked around and did a lot of praying for yourself. . . .

The lights on a sub are all hung with rubber cords. So instead of a light bulb being screwed right in, it's hung by a rubber cord and then a socket. So when you do get a depth charge, they won't break the light bulbs. Otherwise they'll snap them right off. Or your coffee cups—I've seen those smashed sitting on the deck, just go to pieces from the concussion.

They caved us in pretty badly. We surfaced that night about nine thirty or ten o'clock. We had four hot runs, meaning the torpedoes were running in the tubes in the after torpedo room due to the pounding we took. To make a long story short, we got knocked over, out of the war.

We did get depth-charge brandy aboard ship, if you got pounded pretty good. It was brandy, a hundred proof, and it was a tenth of a pint, a little miniature. They'd pass them out to those that wanted it, after a depth charge was done. That was sanctioned by the navy. The skipper had it. Sometimes we'd pray for a good depth charge, when we wanted a drink. [*laughs*]

Dick recalls one occasion when the *Greenling* picked up two survivors from a Japanese ship.

We had sunk a small merchant ship with our deck gun. We set it ablaze, and it sank. We picked up two Japanese people out of the water and brought them back for intelligence. Brought them onboard the boat.

We shot quite a few before [we picked these two up]. It's not very nice looking back on it. . . . The ship sank on the bow, and the stern was in the water, and I heard somebody say something, and all of a sudden this machine gun let go, and this guy was just raking the whole stern with these Japanese guys on it. They'd have died anyway; they were too far away from land. And the [captain] says, "I didn't. . . ." "Sorry, sir, I misunderstood you," he said.

We had them up in the forward torpedo room, handcuffed to the bunks. . . . But as the days wore on, we gave them more and more freedom. We were coming into Saipan, and there's a corridor that's a certain width and certain latitude and longitude. If you stay in that corridor on the surface, then our own planes would not bomb us. Except this one didn't get the word. He came in very low—we were on the surface, of course—and he opened his bomb bay doors, and the old man said, "Dive!" and we dove the boat in a hurry.

This Japanese fellow thought we were being depth charged. So he tried beating on the lockers of the mess hall, so he'd be heard if it was a [Japanese] ship up there. He didn't know we were on the surface yet. . . . Well, that didn't last long, because one of the cooks knocked him out right then and there. But that shows he was willing to die for his country yet, by giving our position away. . . . We were fortunate he didn't try to sink the boat some other way. If he was knowledgeable, he probably would have.

Born and raised in St. Paul, Lyle Pasket was a seventeen-year-old sailor in June 1945, newly stationed onboard the cruiser USS *Indianapolis*. In mid-July, the *Indianapolis* left on a top-secret mission, transporting crucial parts for the first atomic bomb from the U.S. mainland to Tinian Island in the South Pacific. After successfully completing this mission, the *Indianapolis* sailed for the Philippines; under way, just after midnight on 30 July 1945, the ship was torpedoed by a Japanese submarine and sank in just twelve minutes.

I HAD JUST got on topside when the first explosion hit. The ship went on her side, and we crawled on our hands and knees to the opposite side and laid against the bulkhead back there. People were screaming; it was all confused. We knew something had hit us, but . . . we kind of figured, the old timers kind of figured, it was torpedoes.

Where I was, now, we crawled on our hands and knees while the ship was listing, because we didn't hear, "Abandon ship," and there was a lot of hollering. So we crawled on our hands and knees on the opposite side and waited for the ship to keel over. . . . When the ship *went* on her side, we knew then we had to get off. So then we jumped in the dark then and took off. I was scared. . . . We couldn't see out there, because it was pitch black. . . . A lot of them even crawled on the keel, the bottom of the ship, got hit by the screws and stuff like that. A lot of them got hit by the screws.

The first thing when I got in the water, the first thing I remember was telling myself, "Get out of here! Don't get caught in the suction. Get away." So I did take off, and I got about a block out. There was about seventy-five of us out there. So we all formed a circle. . . . There was a chief in charge of us. You couldn't tell a chief, or an officer, because everyone was black faced, stuff like that. But this chief took charge of us. The first thing we did, we all prayed.

We knew we were in trouble, but we didn't think it would be this long. Because right away, the first thing that came out was, "We were supposed to be in the Philippines on Tuesday, so they'll find us missing, and they'll come and get us by then."

During the daytime, we found a floating net. So we unraveled it and put the wounded inside the net. Then those of us that weren't, we stayed on the outside. In the supplies of the net, we found a can of malted milk tablets. They were rescue equipment. Malted milk, you know, is nourishment, stuff like that. I did have a malted milk tablet on Monday, and that was all I had to eat the rest of the week. So then we all got in line and got our tablet, then went back in a line again. The water keg was busted.

The daytime was hot; the nighttime was cold. You would urinate at nighttime, and warm water, you wish you could hang on to that. . . . Guys stabbing each other—that happened out there. They went berserk, started stabbing. So there's only one way to stop it. You really had to [kill them]. Seventeen years old, it's the first time seeing death like that.

Monday afternoon, the sharks. You heard someone scream real loud. The sharks were all around us then. So we started treading water, kicking. It seemed like the sharks were smart; they stayed outside the perimeter most of the time. Then when these fellows hallucinated and stuff like that, they thought they'd seen this and that over there, you know. We tried hauling back into a group, but that was taxing our strength. So we just had to let them go. . . . Some seemed to slip beneath the water. They would never come back; but we could hear them scream, and you know the sharks got them. . . . They were chewing up quite a bit. . . . I remember them swimming right off from me and even underneath me, but they didn't attack. But they did take a lot of fellows. [*emotionally*] . . . I mean, it was just that way, going all the time. I don't think I slept up until Wednesday. But I don't remember nothing Wednesday night.

More than three days passed before an American air crew sighted some survivors floating in the Pacific; by this time, more than 500 sailors had succumbed to thirst, exhaustion, and shark attack. Lyle was one of just 317 men rescued from one of the United States' worst naval tragedies.

After 107 hours I was picked up by the destroyer *Ralph Talbot*, DD-390. . . . They asked if we could climb the ladder. "Sure, sure, sure," we said. But they had to come and get us. . . . Our bodies, when they lifted us out of the water, the skin just peeled right off of us. That's when our skin started coming off. It was salt-water ulcers. They're like a boil. . . . They're round spots; they were all over our bodies.

A crewmember of the ship, he was assigned to us, and he took us to his bunk, stripped us of our clothes, whatever clothes we had on. He gave us a hot bath, sponged us off. He gave us fresh clothes, and then they stood by us and offered water every so often, a whiskey glass full of water. I slept most of the time.

Along with other *Indianapolis* survivors, Lyle was transferred to another ship and transported to a navy medical facility on the Pacific island of Peleliu.

There was a field hospital there. They had all us survivors, had all of us quarantined. They wouldn't let no strangers come and talk to us.

It was hush-hush. [*laughs*] We were all wounded, 100 percent wounded. Some could walk yet. I couldn't. From the water. My pants rubbed my skin right down to the bone, behind the knees.

As far as the life in the water, I don't think that at Peleliu we ever talked about it. We just couldn't do it. They just couldn't talk about it. I don't know why. I can't even recollect talking about it. It wasn't painful. I think we were just tired, physically and mentally worn down.

Lyle's recovery took more than six months. He spent several weeks at a naval hospital on Guam; then he was transferred to facilities at the Great Lakes Naval Training Center in Chicago. Questions arose in his mind, questions that persisted for decades.

I let it go by the wayside all these years, until. . . . Oh, I may have brought it up once and awhile, or something like that. But there were things in my mind that I still couldn't comprehend. I still can't. "Why me?" That's the big question, "Why me?" I was a small kid, I was inexperienced, and stuff like that. Where did I get the strength from? I know the Lord was with me, but [*pauses three seconds*] it's one of those things. "Why?"

I still haven't processed that question yet. [*pauses five seconds*] To me, it's a mystery yet. I have, when I was passed out [in the water], my hallucination, it's in my mind, very vividly. . . . There I was at the door of the good old Lord's heaven. And I was walking on this path, going up to where the sunlight was, and there was a white picket fence, a red barn over there, and this man sitting there milking a goat. He says, "Go back; you're not wanted." And you know—this is God's truth, as I am sitting here—that's when I came to, and two hours later I was rescued, spotted. Now, you'll have to figure that out yourself. To me, the Lord did it. But I couldn't talk, I still can't talk about that without. . . . [*emotionally*]

You never stop thinking about it. You think every day about it. Things come up that remind you of it. [Years ago, three other *Indianapolis* survivors] and I, we all got together once a month and had lunch. We started letting loose, and stuff like that. It was hard. Some things I won't tell them about. Some things I couldn't tell them about.

Some who were rescued had a difficult time afterward. Lyle feels he was helped by conversations he had while at Great Lakes.

We had a couple guys that lost their mind. That went [*pauses five seconds*] mental. They committed suicide, a couple of them did. One thing I can be thankful for, when I was at Great Lakes, this one doctor, he says, "Gosh, you look tired. You need a rest. Go home." So I came home [to St. Paul] for the weekend, or something like that. Then I find out his brother was killed aboard ship, and, after talking to him a couple of times, sitting down in his office there, and I'll never forget, he said, "Tell me all about it, would you?" I tried, you know, sitting there. And after a few more times sitting there, it started to come out a little bit. . . . I think that helped me a heck of a lot. It did, very much so. Because I realized what happened then. I didn't keep it within me that tight. Lot of things I would tell right away, but a lot of things I wouldn't, wouldn't mention.

As military planners turned their attention to the invasion of Japan, the U.S. Treasury encouraged civilians to buy more war bonds

Bob Michelsen (b. 1925) of Minneapolis volunteered for the Army Air Corps in
1943 and was trained as a waist gunner on the B-29 Superfortress heavy bomber.
By April 1945 he was part of a B-29 crew stationed on the Pacific island of Guam,
from which missions were launched against mainland Japanese targets, military as well as civilian. Bob describes a nighttime incendiary raid over Tokyo.

OVER JAPAN it was at night, and all you could see was the black-
ness in front of you, and if you were going to a larger city, the
red burning buildings in front of you and below you. It was an eerie
feeling, because you just hoped you'd get over the target and come out.

We knew that Tokyo was burning. There was a wall of heat coming up from the city. We tried to avoid it, but we took it straight on,
and so we went up, with a thermal, we went up four thousand feet
and immediately down four thousand feet. We tried to take thermals
straight on, because otherwise your airplane is flipped upside down,
and you've got a real problem. You don't know, in this heat and
smoke, which is up and which is down. . . .

You'd smell the smoke. I think it was smoke; it was like a burning building. A burning building has a peculiar odor—the charred
wood—and many of those buildings, at least the smaller homes,
were made of wood. And we wondered, are we just burning up
homes or burning up people, too?

I think every time we went over a burning city we did think, at
least I did, of what was going on, on the ground. You didn't dwell on
it, though, but you did feel some compassion for that. And yet your
job was to drop those bombs where you were told to drop them.

On the night of 25–26 May 1945, Bob's crew was part of an incendiary raid on
Tokyo involving more than five hundred B-29 bombers. His plane was hit by Japa-
nese anti-aircraft fire, and the crew was forced to bail out over the burning city.
Bob knew he would be captured.

I went out the rear bomb bay. . . . I just stepped off like you'd step
off a diving board. You hit the wind; you can feel the wind right
away. It wasn't that dark. I looked at the ground. It was a windy
night, and the parachute was moving with the wind; it was back and

forth. I tried to control that. One searchlight had picked me up after I jumped, but that went out almost instantly. I tried to control the parachute a little so I'd go straight down, [*pauses three seconds*] and I remember glancing at the ground as the ground actually came up closer to me, and there were people there. I'm sure they could [see me coming].

Also there was a railroad track, and I landed just to the side of the rails. How big the crowd was around me I do not know, but there was quite a number of people. And there were other, what looked to me at that time like soldiers, home guard or whatever you want to call them, with rifles and bayonets. . . . I hit the quick release before I hit the ground, because I didn't want that parachute to come down on top of me. On the ground I glanced around, and I could see that these, what I thought at the time were soldiers, with their rifles and bayonets, they were pointed at the crowd and not at me. It didn't come into my mind that quick, but I thought at the time that the Japanese wanted prisoners to interrogate and that these men with rifles and bayonets were protecting me from the crowd. [*pauses three seconds*] But for them, I was dead.

Right away my hands were tied beyond my back, immediately, blindfold and a rope around my neck. I was just hoping I'd stay alive. I don't know how far it was; it seemed to me like it was probably two hundred yards or so. But a gauntlet formed on each side. As I was dragged to wherever we were going, it was like an Indian gauntlet, people on each side, just hitting me, swinging whatever they had at me. There was no order to stop it, because it kept on for as long as we were moving. I couldn't understand them, but I could hear them. . . . A couple of times I, I remember going to my knees a number of times, and how long I was on my knees I do not know.

I was conscious then, and I was tied to a post of some kind, and I surmised that it was close to a building because I could hear doors opening and closing. There was no light, but I could hear the door opening and closing. . . . Every time the door opened and closed I'd get beaten a little bit. [*pauses three seconds*] I say a little bit—it was more than that. Thing I remember about daylight, looking down at the ground and I said, my god, I pissed in my pants. But as it grew lighter, I said, geez, that's not urine, that's blood. And most of it came from my head. I did get a little shrapnel in my leg—I didn't even know it until later—but most of it came from my head.

But back to the night: it's dark, and you could hear airplanes flying over. Once in a while you could hear everybody cheer, because you knew an airplane got hit then. In the morning I heard a vehicle drive up, it sounded to me like a motorcycle, and I was placed in a trailer attached to the motorcycle, face up, on my back. My hands are still tied behind my back, and my legs are tied now, and I'm placed on my back in this vehicle. And a canvas put over the top of me. We begin to go somewhere, and about what I assumed was every block—I don't know how many feet—they would stop and give people the pleasure of beating on you. And then they'd start again, and go a little while longer, and stop, and you'd get beat again.

At one of the stops, while I was getting beat on, I could feel that another person was put into this same trailer and the canvas put back on top of us. Then the same—you go a ways, you stop, you get beat, and stop, get beat. During this process I heard the grunts and the groans and everything, and they sounded familiar, and I knew it was the left gunner from our crew. So underneath this canvas he maneuvered and I maneuvered so that, although our hands were tied, we could still touch each other and hold hands. And I've thought about that a great deal. Holding hands—you know, the connotations of it are, are such, but I think that a person in fear of his life needs a friend, and I think that was it.

Bob remained a "special prisoner" of the Japanese until the end of the Pacific war in August 1945. Held at a secret police facility in Tokyo with other captured American airmen, he endured a starvation diet and repeated interrogations.

[5]

War's Impacts

The Human Side

WORLD WAR II forced men and women, whether civilians or veterans, to confront a wide assortment of situations and to make necessary adjustments. Two very different perspectives have already been presented: first, the memories of those who remained on the Home Front, living and working as civilians, and second, those of service personnel who were exposed to combat situations. Their experiences were worlds apart, yielding diverse concerns and daily routines.

In this chapter, the focus turns from working lives and combat reality to what might be termed the human side of war. By discussing the value of correspondence and the role of faith, men and women from all walks of life share their memories about who and what was important to them and why. Finally, service veterans from the medical field talk frankly about the horrific costs of modern war and their roles in the healing process.

Staying in Touch: Letters to and from Home

IN AN ERA without e-mail or readily available long-distance telephone service, people kept in touch by writing letters. As evidenced in literally scores of interviews, servicemen and -women liked getting mail and, more importantly, viewed it as an important link to what they had left behind. Home-front civilians, too, looked forward to receiving word from those who were away; for them it was less about "hearing the news" and much more a means of maintaining human contact, however tenuous. By far the strongest and most meaningful memories of writing and receiving letters were shared by women; some men did not recall writing at all, even to family members, and for those who did, the experience generally lacked the emotion conveyed by women.

Other interesting details emerged as military personnel and civilians recounted their experiences. Long periods apart, at a relatively young age, led to the breakup of relationships: "Dear John" letters were a reality. Servicemen and civilians alike admitted to sending and receiving these messages. One Pacific theater sailor recalled consoling more than one shipmate whose wife or girlfriend had strayed from or decided to end the relationship. For several in uniform, there were memories of helping illiterate others write out a letter; one soldier bravely acknowledged that he was the one who required such help. By far the most difficult writing duty fell to the chaplains, however; they composed the letters sent to family members when a soldier had been killed.

Some on the Home Front remembered sharing news and feelings openly, wanting to keep recipients as well informed as possible; others practiced a form of self-censorship, holding back potentially disturbing news so the reader would not worry about something over which he or she had little control. There were memories of letters filled with banalities or of the post's arrival being the highlight of the day. Some civilians described writing letters as a wartime duty, others as a welcome relief from the stresses of work and family responsibilities. Whatever the memory, rare was the man or woman for whom written contact was insignificant.

✦ ✦ ✦

Guadalupe Velasquez (b. 1923) was living with his mother and sisters and working at a slaughterhouse in South St. Paul when he was drafted into the army in January 1944. As an engine fireman with the 732nd Railway Operations Battalion, he served in Europe in 1944–45. For Guadalupe, receiving mail from his family was something to look forward to.

I USED TO WRITE two of my sisters and a couple of friends that I knew here. Sometimes you wouldn't get a letter, say, for a couple of weeks. So by the time you got your mail, you'd probably have four, five, six letters there. They were very important to me because, well, they didn't say much. They didn't say much of anything. Mostly hello, how are you doing? And whatever was going on [at home]. All that. But I would keep them on me as long as I could, and whenever I had a chance I would take them out and read them over and over. Just like I was talking to that person. Really, you know, you really enjoyed those letters. It was so important to get mail. Very important.

Veda Ponikvar of Chisholm was an officer in the Navy WAVES. Far from home in Washington, DC, she appreciated every bit of mail she received.

M OST OF THE LETTERS I got were written by my mother. I was always real, real thrilled when I got a letter from my father. I knew that my father worked in the mine and that he'd come home very tired and get some sleep and go right back to work. I recognized that. And yet he took the time to write.

I think getting mail from home strengthened the bond, and there was a feeling of everything was going to be all right. It was a feeling of security. Both my father and mother, when they would write, they would talk about going to church and talking to different people and getting together. . . . It was a wonderful tie.

Emmett Yanez (b. 1920) of the army's 82nd Airborne shipped out to North Africa in 1943; before his departure he got married while home in St. Paul on leave. Both he and his new wife adjusted to the long-distance relationship, but not without difficulty.

I DON'T KNOW what made me get married. I was going to be away. We had decided to get married, so I came home, and I had about five days or something. And when I left, before I got shipped out, Natalie went down there to see me. . . . I was very surprised. Very happy that she did.

She used to write a lot. She used to send me gifts. Cookies and stuff like that. The mail came. They delivered to me a whole bag full of goodies and different things. Scarves, towels. I just couldn't think why she would send stuff like that, but she did. . . . I couldn't use it. I was on the front lines. All the eating stuff I passed around. We were off on the front, we were on point when this happened, and that night we got attacked.

When I wrote I tried not to mention anything that was going on. She was very young. I was five years older than she was. She was eighteen. I just wrote the right stuff for her, that I loved her very much, I missed her, and not to worry. I was trying to take care of myself. Stuff like that.

Florence Andersen Glasner lived in a small mining community near Hibbing. After marrying a serviceman in 1943, during the war years she worked in the tool shop of a large iron ore mine. Writing letters was a way to reach local men in the service and also her husband, Tony, then in Europe.

THERE WERE a lot of us that wrote to a lot of the fellows that were in the service right from our community. I wrote to many of them. . . . They were all kids from our location. I would tell them mostly about what was going on that was with people that they knew. We all knew the same people in our little location. Some of it was gossip. Then you'd always try and put something in that was a little humorous, so that maybe they could get a little chuckle. And tell them we were praying for them. . . . I think a lot of people sent cookies. I sent cookies. I didn't know any better. [*laughs*]

I wanted to write, but then I had the feeling that a person *should* do it in case they weren't getting any letters. A lot of them, their mothers and fathers were foreigners and probably couldn't write English.

I wrote [to my husband Tony] every week. My sisters were all married, and he knew all of them and my nephews and nieces, so I would write about them. What my mother and dad were doing, and what I was doing. [*pauses three seconds*] I don't think he was happy that I was working with a bunch of men.

During 1941–43, Velda Beck lived with her parents on a rented farm outside of Palisade. She, too, responded to the call to write letters to young men serving in the military; she clearly recalls one she received in return.

WE HAD A LOT of dear friends that were a little older than me that we kept in touch with. I started writing letters and this one young, young man—I think I probably had a crush on him when I was about ten years old—his name was Whitey. He always said, "You save a dance for me!" Then I get this letter saying, "I'm sorry, Velda, I won't be able to dance with you, because my legs were just all shot up."

Elaine Bunde Gerber graduated from a St. Paul high school in 1943 and then worked in the bookkeeping division for First National Bank. During the war she had three brothers in the service as well as her fiancé, Warren Gerber, and she wrote and received frequent letters. Other family members also wrote to various loved ones.

IT WAS WHEN I got home from work that mail would be there. I would go over to Warren's folks' house maybe once a week, and I'd call his mother almost every day, because she had to know if I got a letter and what Warren had to say. I'd call from work, because I could go in the mailroom and use the phone. I would ask her if she had heard from him, and if they didn't get a letter, then I'd tell them what I knew. Then I'd find out if I had a letter when I got home.

My sister-in-law was living at our house then, too, with our little nephew. So we both wrote at night. She wrote to her husband, Bob, and I wrote to Warren. My sister, Ruth, would write to my brother because she didn't have a boyfriend at the time. She was writing to him all the time.

When you write every day, you write about some of the things in the day, but you don't want to make him think that you're having a great time without him! [*laughs*] You want to let him know how much you miss him and how much you love him. That's what they wait for. I would tell him about work, what we did at work, because he knew a lot of the girls at work. What you did that day. It was just kind of like a diary. What you did in the daytime.

Warren was good about writing. He couldn't write every day, but as often as he could. Then when he was injured, was shot, we didn't get any letters, but I still wrote every day, hoping that he was getting a letter. Not until he was [in] England did he get the whole bag of mail with all my letters in it. When he was in the hospital I heard from him all the time. [It was difficult not knowing what was going on,] especially when he said [he] was just "nicked" in the side.

Elaine's older brother was a bomber pilot serving with the Army Air Corps in Europe. In mid-1944 his plane was shot down over Germany. Elaine and her family waited anxiously for news, which eventually arrived via telegram.

When my brother Herb was first missing in action, we didn't know where he was, if he was killed or not, until they came with a telegram. They delivered that personally; they didn't call you up or anything. And of course, then the next time they came, with a second telegram, then you really thought, "Oh-oh. Here comes the word." We had a driveway that the garage was way in the back. I can still remember them walking up the driveway. We wondered, "Now what?" Naturally you think the worst.

My mother was home, of course; she was always home. So when the second telegram said that he was a prisoner, well we were so happy because at least we knew he was alive. I think [the man delivering the telegram] thought, "What's the matter with these people?" But he didn't realize that the first we'd heard was that he was missing in action.

Doris Shea Strand lived with her parents and worked in the main offices of Minneapolis Moline. Also a volunteer for the Minneapolis Girls Service Organization, she felt that writing to servicemen was another way to contribute. Through her letters, Doris met a young marine, Errol Fox. Their mail friendship led to a 1944 wedding.

A GROUP OF seven marines who were stationed in San Diego wrote to a Los Angeles paper . . . saying that they were lonesome and wanted to write to someone. They hoped that some young ladies or girls could write to them. My girlfriend's aunt clipped it out and sent it back to us in Minneapolis. So, we thought, oh, boy, we'll do this. . . . At that point Errol Fox started to write to me. We corresponded for a couple years, just very generic.

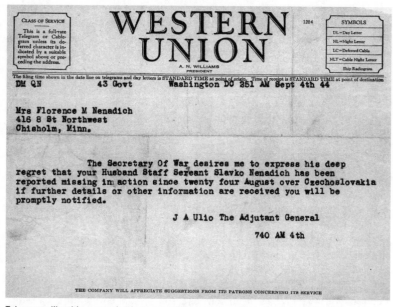

Telegrams like this one arrived at many Minnesota homes during the war. For Florence Nenadich of Chisholm, anxious weeks followed before she finally received confirmation that her husband, Sam, was alive, held as a POW in Germany.

Then I didn't hear from him for a long time. I assumed that he was dead or just didn't care to write any more. My mother still encouraged me to write to him. "You don't know what he's going through. You just write a few more letters."

Anyhow, in June of 1944 our family was having a quick supper so we could go to a wake for a family friend, and the phone rang, and a young man was asking me to a party. I insisted I didn't go with anybody I didn't know, so I hung up. . . . On the fourth call he finally identified himself as Errol Fox, and I about fainted. At that point he said he was coming over, and all of a sudden we didn't care about going to the wake for Mr. Perry. [laughs] The whole family wanted to see who this joker was.

We saw this car go by with this fellow in a marine dress uniform, his blues. He drove right by the house, and my daddy goes out on the curb and flags him down like he had a spinster in here he had to get rid of! [laughs] I was so embarrassed. Anyhow, he came in, and we got acquainted. That was June fourth. On June sixteenth I got a diamond, and in December of that year we were married in San Diego.

Edmond Broberg (b. 1921), a farmer in Swift County, Minnesota, had several family members serving overseas. He remembers exchanging letters with them but notes that it was difficult to get any real information about the war.

WE GOT SOME news, too, in the letters we got . . . [from] my brother and cousin. Lowell was in the medics. He was over in Italy. Bernie was in Germany and all over—Northern Africa, France, Normandy. He was in quite a few places. You'd try to ask them a question, and they'd try to answer it, but it wasn't very good. . . . If they did write something, it was crossed out anyway. Didn't go through. All wiped out.

Marie Cavanagh (b. 1921) was married and the mother of two when her husband, Jim, was drafted into the navy in May 1944. Her cousin moved into their family house, and the women tried to keep contact with their military husbands. Marie wondered whether writing and receiving post was worth the trouble.

I CAN REMEMBER at night, every single night, we sat and wrote letters to our husbands, which, if I had to do it again, I wouldn't. I suppose we felt we were staying in touch. [But] it really was hard to find things to write about. I can remember I never wanted to write things to him that were difficult. It was always about the kids. . . . There were lots of things to write about, about the kids. And the weather. I remember every time we wrote, we wrote about the weather, which, who cares, really?

I had a feeling that I didn't want him to worry. One time, we had an old furnace that used oil, and at the time oil was rationed. I ran out of ration stamps. I needed more, so I had to go downtown; I can't even remember where. They did give me more oil, and I can remember I never wrote that to him. Then when I would get letters from him, there were so many portions that were cut out.

Marie Cavanagh with husband Jim and children, St. Paul, summer 1944

But for most, the contact represented something positive. Mel and Aileen Boggs, married for several years before Mel entered the Air Corps in 1943, share memories of frequent correspondence and an openness in what they wrote to each other. Bomber pilot Mel, stationed during 1944–45 in England, remembers almost daily communication with Aileen, home with their small son. There is a touch of melancholy in his recollection, but he adds that being far away was just a fact of life.

W E STAYED in touch by mail. That's about the only way. If you got a letter within a week, that was really good. . . . That's the same way [Aileen] would hear from me. She'd know I was alive a week ago, but whether I was today or not, she'd never know.

I wrote every day. I wrote every day that I could. I mean, if I was there. Sometimes we'd get weathered out or something, and I wouldn't. And she wrote to me every day. [I wrote] pretty much what we were doing. What we did that day. We couldn't say we were going to bomb Berlin tomorrow, or something like that. We could tell them what we did, like went to town, and went and saw a movie. We had a special dinner at the officers club. Something like that. I don't think Aileen knew exactly where I was. "Somewhere in England." That's all we could put.

I was pretty much aware of what was going on [here at home], because she wrote to me every day. She wrote to me, and she could tell me just about everything. She'd send me pictures. See, we had a little one. When I left we had an eleven-month-old baby. I was home for his . . . the first birthday I was home for was his fourth birthday. [*smiles*] It bothered me, but that's the way life was. . . . I was one of a million guys that were doing it. We were going through the same thing.

Misery loves company, I suppose. We'd cry on each other's shoulders and tell our troubles to each other. Of course our crew got to be . . . we were like brothers. Particularly my copilot and I; we were very close.

In a separate interview, Aileen tells much the same story. She also tried to keep track of Mel's missions as a bomber pilot.

I wrote every day. I told him everything. There wasn't anything I didn't tell him. I don't remember that we were ever short of money or had anything wrong in the house. I don't remember any big bad stuff that I had to tell him. I think we pretty well knew each other, and we didn't hold things back.

One interesting thing: when Mel wrote, he couldn't say, "I flew a mission today." That was illegal to do something like that. So we set it up ahead of time if he said "Dearest Aileen," that meant he flew a mission that day. But he couldn't say where. We had that code set up before he left.

What happened was, it was in the paper every day, when a mission—What the Eighth Air Force did. I would clip—Every day I would clip out the mission, where it was and everything, and then I'd save it, and then when he sent me a letter that said the date—he'd have the date up there, and he'd say "Dearest Aileen"—then I would look and take that clipping that was that day and put it in a scrapbook. So when he came home I had every mission.

Norty Lund (b. 1925) was a navy medical corpsman in 1944–45, stationed in the Pacific on the remote island of Peleliu. He left a steady girlfriend when he shipped overseas, but he eventually received a letter telling him the relationship was over. Thousands of miles away, Norty could do nothing but read and reread the letter.

S HE WROTE ME the "Dear John" when I was over there. Here was the thing—we were both very young. But we were both very serious when I went over. But you know, when you're a young girl like that and a good-looking young girl, and you've got some clown sitting out there in the middle of nowhere, you know, that's. . . . So anyway, this guy came along, and I guess they had drafted him, but he had something wrong with his feet . . . so they discharged him. So anyway, he went after her. I don't know why he didn't go after somebody else. That ended there.

I felt terrible. I read it I'll bet you fifty times, a hundred times. But it was so much to the point: "Don't write me anymore. If you do write I will put your letter in an envelope and mail it right back to you." That's pretty. . . . There was nothing I could do. I was just sitting there. I kind of thought something was going on, and I had written her, and I said, "Why don't you just give me a chance when I get home? Let's see if we can get this thing sorted out." But she didn't even read that letter.

So I came back [in late 1945]. It was a very traumatic thing, because she completely rejected me. That was the first place I stopped when we came back. I drove the car, and I stopped at her place, and she wouldn't even hardly see me. That was the end of that. Then I decided I was going to stay in the navy, because there was nothing back here that I really was interested in.

Navy enlisted man Walter T. Larson survived Pearl Harbor on the battleship USS *Nevada* and then served in the Pacific from 1943–45 on the USS *LCI-455*, a landing craft used in a supporting role during island invasions. He remembers mail less for its importance to him and more for the effect it had on others.

I WASN'T MUCH OF A letter writer at that time. I'd get a letter from my folks, and then I would write back. I supposed I'd write a letter every couple three weeks. But our mail wasn't like it is today; it might take a month for our mail to get back home, or to get a letter from back home a month, maybe longer than that. That was the only way we had to communicate. . . . Everybody, when they had mail call, when you got a letter usually you went off by yourself and read it.

I remember several of the guys that went on liberty or went on leave and got married when they were on leave, and they'd get a "Dear John" letter after a while. It was kind of hard for some of those guys. You'd try to help them out by talking to them. I know several of the guys that got "Dear John" letters on the *LCI-455*. I kind of acted like a chaplain, I suppose, to a couple of the young ones who got married, who then found out when they were out to sea for about a year that their wives were pregnant. That was pretty hard on them.

Not all those who wanted to write were necessarily able to do so: some were unable to read and write and needed help putting their thoughts on paper. During 1944, navy enlisted man Russell Reetz (b. 1916) of St. Paul was stationed at a rear-echelon post on a small island by Bougainville, in the Solomon Islands. There one of his duties was to help a young illiterate sailor with his correspondence.

THE LAST THREE or four months, they gave me a fellow that was from the mountains in Tennessee or something. He couldn't read or write, so I used to write letters for him. And then I'd read his mail to him. He could read a little bit, but some of the words he couldn't say. I don't think he felt embarrassed by that. We got along real well. He was a good guy, a youngster; he was probably eighteen or nineteen. I don't know [how he got in the service]. Of course, back then they would take about anybody, I guess.

Augustine Martinez left behind his wife and two children when he was drafted in 1944. While he was with the army in Germany in 1945, fellow soldiers helped him compose letters to his family in Minnesota.

EVERYBODY WAS writing letters when they got a little chance here and there. I didn't write very much. Very little, once in a while. [*pauses three seconds*] Well, I can't write very much. Some of the guys used to write letters for me. Some I can do, and the rest they can do for me. I would copy, and the rest they can do for me. They helped me out. That's it.

To chaplains fell a most unpleasant task: the personal notification of next-of-kin about a serviceman's death. Navy chaplain Fritjof "Fritz" Lokensgard served almost two years in the Pacific, during which he at times had to write letters to surviving family members.

WRITING LETTERS to parents when their son had been killed, that was tough. The only approach is direct. You can't hesitate or beat around the bush. You have to come right out. There were times when I would write the letter after they'd already known about it, after they'd been notified officially. If you knew that they had been officially notified, it made a difference. Once in a while [when I was stationed stateside], I was requested to go and visit so-and-so in a neighboring city or something. Just to give encouragement, offer support, anything that might be done to ease it.

Faith: What Place for a God?

RELIGION AND FAITH represent another human side of war experience. Across differences in background, level of service, and opinions about the war, similar themes emerge. One group of men and women remembers their faith as something that they relied on and that often grew stronger. Others, seeing a lack of compassion or losing companions or loved ones to war, questioned their beliefs or the presence of a god.

Members of one group—military chaplains—dealt with questions of faith as part of their duties. With U.S. entry into the war, the military embarked on an aggressive campaign to expand the size of the chaplain corps, believing that the millions of young men entering service would need encouragement and spiritual accompaniment as they were taken far from home and subjected to the hardships of combat. Chaplains represented three faith groups—Jewish, Protestant, and Roman Catholic—and were assigned by a ratio reflective of soldier populations. Chaplains were all volunteers—as ordained ministers they were automatically deferred from military service—and all men—women served only as chaplain's assistants and performed limited duties. Although such service was voluntary, chaplains needed to be endorsed by their denomination and underwent a military review process. Special chaplain schools run by the army and the navy offered orientation to the military, instruction in first aid, and physical training.

The duties of military chaplains were in many respects similar to those undertaken in their civilian lives: preaching and conducting worship services, counseling and encouraging the troubled, providing comfort to the injured and dying. They also administered last rites, oversaw burials, and, as noted above, wrote letters to surviving family members. But there were differences: enlisted men could approach them with a wide assortment of personal problems. Though chaplains were commissioned officers, enlisted men could, and frequently did, complain to them about superiors, without fear of punishment. More significant differences from their civilian lives included facing battlefield conditions and the possibility of being taken as POWs. Chaplains went wherever the troops did, including into situations where they would be under fire. By July 1945 almost 11,000 chaplains were on active duty with either the army or the navy; 188 of these men died in uniform, 73 of them killed in action.

✦ ✦ ✦

Fritjof "Fritz" Lokensgard was born in 1911 in the farming community of Hanley Falls, the youngest of eleven children of Norwegian immigrant parents. After graduating from St. Olaf College in 1933, he decided on a career in the ministry; he completed studies at Luther Seminary in St. Paul and was ordained in 1937. Married and the father of three small children when the United States entered the war, at age thirty-one Fritz nevertheless decided to offer his services to the navy.

M Y OFFICIAL TITLE was Protestant Chaplain. I felt that as chaplain I was doing my duty to these men as individuals and also to my church. I felt, too, that I was making some contribution for the good of our country. Patriotism was a very important thing. I never regretted having gone in, although there were times when I wished I were a lot closer to home.

Fritz's first duty station was at the hospital at Great Lakes Naval Training Center, near Chicago.

We had about nine hundred patients in the hospital. We would go through the wards every day, and quite often a man would stop us. Otherwise they'd greet us and be glad to see us. Or they'd say, "Are you busy, Padre? Can I talk to you?" "Sure."

The main duty was to conduct services and Bible classes and visit every patient, every new patient that came in. There were two Protestant chaplains and one Catholic chaplain, and the three of us were kept pretty busy with nine hundred men. . . . Of course our office was always open. People came into our office with their problems. . . . They looked upon you as a sort of father figure, especially some of the young guys. And we had many that were just seventeen, eighteen years old.

I found out that my main usefulness as a chaplain came not from the big services where there were maybe several hundred men but where there was one-on-one, because then I got to speak to individuals. Sometimes I spent the entire night with a patient who was really having problems.

Visiting with convalescing sailors and marines was a large part of a chaplain's duties at Great Lakes, but there were other issues to deal with, including some patients who had psychological problems.

We did have a ward at the hospital called the psycho ward. Quite often I would go down there. Men would ask to see the chaplains. So we would always go and see them. Some of the men didn't want to see us, but for those who did we were available. I had some quite lengthy talks there.

I remember the first time I went, the sailor in charge of the security there let me in, at the end of this ward, and the door clicked behind me. Here I was alone in this room with a sailor, who was lying on a bed. There was just the mattress on the floor. I had no idea what I was in for. The main thing I did was listen. Listen to him. I don't think anybody had done that for a long time. And he appreciated that.

Homosexuality was cause for discharge from military service. Chaplain Lokensgard recounts an instance of five sailors caught in a difficult situation.

One day at Great Lakes five young men came to my office. They were being discharged, and they were unhappy. They had all admitted being homosexual and thought they would get a medical discharge. Now they were really mad because, instead of that, they were getting an undesirable discharge. That's quite a difference. It meant that they got no benefits, ever.

The thought in my mind was that somebody had told them this was a good way to get out of the service. But at this point they couldn't say, "We made this up." But some of them *had* made it up, in the belief they could get a medical discharge. They thought I could intercede for them. I said, "You've told your story. Are you going to change it? Who will believe you this time?" . . . They had come this far, and there was nothing now I could do about it. They were done for.

During 1944–45, Fritz was stationed in the Southwest Pacific at a naval aircraft depot on Ponam, in the Admiralty Islands.

There were different types of problems [out there in the Pacific]. Men worrying about their families. Or maybe somebody being ill at home. All sorts of family affairs. Some of the letters from home that the boys let me read were unbelievable. . . . People at home would write and tell them about how sick they'd been, or they were losing their job, or somebody had been mean to them, or done this and that.

Sometimes they would get a letter from the mother. At one point I had the feeling that the worst enemy of the young fellows in the navy was a mother back home. The ones who were not supportive, who were complaining or telling terrible things that were happening at home.

I did write a few letters to mothers when a fellow would come with a letter that was just so far out that it was ridiculous. I'd just tell them that they're not helping things at all by writing about these matters. . . . I just suggested to them, don't tell your son in the service all your troubles. Keep them to yourself; he's got enough to worry about. Things that they could have kept to themselves.

By and large, I had fewer problems with the men overseas than I did when we were here in the States. Here we had more problems with the men. Here they had their families either to contend with or to interfere, and over there, there was nothing that could be done about that. You made the best of it.

Fritz spent some months after V-J Day at a Coast Guard facility in New York City.

I remember one night in New York, I had to report the death of a young boy in a jeep accident down in Puerto Rico. That was tough. . . . I went to see the parents personally. They did not know [the news before I arrived]. . . .

They were at a theater. The elevator boy [at their apartment building] asked me when I arrived, "Is something wrong?" I said, "The parents of James Caplan, do they live here?" "Yes. They'll be here soon." So I waited.

They came off the elevator . . . and went up to their room. I gave them time to get their coats off, [then] I rang the bell. I said, "I'm sorry to interrupt. I saw you down in the lobby, but I thought I would give you a few minutes." The mother said, "Come in. Is it about Jim?" I said, "Yes." They both sat down, and I just told them that I had had a telegram saying that he had been killed. He was their only child, their only son. . . . I read some scripture, a couple of the Psalms. They were in no hurry for me to leave. They wanted to talk. The war was over, but death was not taking a holiday. That was tough.

Navy chaplain Bernt Opsal aboard the USS *Burleigh*, 1945

Born in 1919 and raised in New Jersey, Bernt Opsal came to St. Paul in 1941 to attend Luther Seminary. When he graduated and was ordained a minister four years later, in January 1945, Bernt volunteered for service as a chaplain with the U.S. Navy. Chaplain Opsal's first duty station, in late spring 1945, was at a navy personnel depot in San Bruno, California. By this time, U.S. forces were engaged in the bloody fighting on Okinawa, and military and civilian planners were preparing for the invasion of the Japanese home islands, expected to begin before the end of the year. Millions of men would be involved, and hundreds of thousands of casualties were projected. Some navy personnel sought to avoid being sent out to the Pacific—for legitimate reasons or because they perhaps feared what they would encounter there. Bernt's primary duty at San Bruno, as part of a chaplain team, was to interview enlisted men who were seeking emergency leaves or discharges and judge whether or not their cases warranted action. Thousands of men passed through this facility every month; each had a story.

M Y MAIN DUTY was to interview the men who came in. These are mostly enlisted men. Somewhere along the line they had indicated they wanted to go home. They felt they should be returned home, and not sent out [to the Pacific].

You'd want to help. The poor guy, if he had a legitimate excuse, he could go home and wouldn't be expected to go overseas at that time. . . . We had to verify every story through the Red Cross. If their stories *weren't* approved, the next stop was [the navy base at] Treasure Island, by San Francisco. They would go there and then be sent out.

There were so many stories they gave me. They'd come in, "Chaplain, here's my story." Many were black and white. They might come in and say that their brother was hurt in an automobile accident. I know I had a case like that. His brother was hurt in an automobile accident, and so that was easy to verify. You could get that verified by the Red Cross. They found out what hospital his brother was at.

One guy said his grandmother was dying and he wanted to go home for the funeral. He said he was very close to his grandmother. It was legitimate; he got home. The Red Cross could verify that, too.

Each chaplain interviewed thirty men a day. If you talk to thirty men a day for a few weeks you develop a sense of—Well, you could sense whether they were sincere or not. And, of course, they still had to verify their story. I'd say, "If you can't get this verified. . . ." Some of them, when they heard this, they said, "Excuse me, Chaplain," and they'd leave. Or, "Chaplain, I'm changing my mind." So in that case no message was sent back, and the case was closed.

After we interviewed them, some of them, it turns out, were legitimate. Others we found out were just faking it.

Delbert Kuehl was born in 1917 on a farm outside of Alexandria. After attending Bethel College and the University of Minnesota in preparation for a career in the ministry, he was ordained in 1942. In July he enlisted in the U.S. Army as a chaplain. At the conclusion of the four-week chaplain-training course, Kuehl volunteered to join a paratroop unit. He slowly built a close relationship with the troops in the 82nd Airborne; during training he often traveled, jumped, and lived with them.

THE REASON I did that is to be with the men. I found out that when I went through what they went through, they seemed to really appreciate it. We went out on bivouac, for example. We'd go out in the field like real simulated combat. We'd lay on the ground all night. I didn't have to go out there, but I'd always go out there with them. I'd be with them all night long on the ground with them. Eat when they ate, or when they didn't have food. And they began to really appreciate that. They said, "Chaplain, you don't have to be here." Went on twenty-five-mile hikes. I didn't *have* to make the twenty-five-mile hike with full pack, but I went with them.

Delbert served more than two years overseas as regimental chaplain with the 82nd Airborne, in front-line duty at the invasion of Sicily (1943), Anzio (1944), the Netherlands (1944), the Battle of the Bulge (1944–45), and Germany (1945). He describes in some detail how he understood his role as chaplain and what these duties required of him on a daily basis, under difficult conditions.

The day-to-day job of a chaplain was varied of course. I would try to help the troops as much as I could. Encourage them. Whenever we could we'd have a service. It wouldn't always be on Sunday. We'd get a little group together and meet. In some old bombed-out building or wherever we could, under the trees. I would try to get food up to them when I could. And so many were wounded, and I would spend time with the wounded and take care of the wounded and help the wounded get back to where they could get medical care. I did a lot of that. Encourage the fellows who were . . . some were almost ready to break under combat. Be with them and encourage them. Many different areas a chaplain could help.

The service we held, they'd be called interdenominational. People from the whole panorama, from more free-type Baptist to the Episcopalian. Anybody could come. With the paratroopers I would not go into deep detail or have a message that's pretty hard to understand. I would give a very simple message, like the sower went forth to sow and the seed fell on the various grounds, something they could understand, and then bring the application. They really appreciated a simple message that was not difficult to understand.

We didn't have very long for messages. And we had to be very careful getting groups of men together in combat. I remember one time, in the Battle of the Bulge, we were gathered around in a timbered area and a shell hit right nearby. So we had to be very careful that we didn't have groups together. You had to disperse, so if artillery came in maybe one or two might get killed but not twenty-five or thirty. So we had to be very careful on that. But I found that, as I had the time with the men and we would spend time having a message from the Bible . . . I found that there was a tremendous comfort to the men.

In early 1943, units of the 82nd Airborne shipped over to North Africa in preparation for the Allied invasion of Sicily. Airborne units were among the first troops that landed, in July 1943. Chaplain Kuehl jumped with the first wave.

We trained pretty diligently in the desert, and then we got word that we were going to be making a midnight jump [into Sicily]. . . . We were jumping at midnight, and I decided to jump with F Company. I tried to go with different companies at different times. We were in the C-47 [transport aircraft], about sixteen, eighteen men in a plane, and I was the only officer in our plane. Before we loaded the planes the colonel spoke to us. [Among other things] he said, "Now the chaplain has a chance to speak with you." There was a great big cactus plant there. I told anybody that wanted to, to come and gather around there, in the sand of North Africa. And quite a large group gathered around the cactus plant. . . . I said, "Now, I think we all have a certain amount of fear of facing the enemy. That's natural. But some of you probably have a greater fear. If you don't make it tonight you'll stand before God, and maybe you're not ready to do that." I said, "You don't have to have that fear. . . . If any of you want to stay behind a bit and pray together we'll do that." And quite a large group did.

By late summer 1944, Allied troops were advancing toward Germany. In September, Chaplain Kuehl voluntarily joined the troops making the dangerous crossing of the Waal River in the Netherlands. On the riverbank under heavy enemy fire he cared for the wounded and helped carry numerous men to safety. For his actions that day he received the Silver Star, this nation's second-highest award for valor.

When we crossed the Waal River in Holland, we lost 50 percent of our men in that crossing. We started with twenty-six boats, and I think eleven or twelve made it across, and there were wounded and dead in all of those boats. So it was very tragic. I crossed with the initial assault wave. Somebody said, "You're crazy," because I was regimental chaplain and I didn't have to. I thought, boy, if they ever need me, they're going to need me now. So I decided I'd cross with the assault wave.

After we were across [and the Germans continued to fire at our position], I leaned over a man that had three bullet holes in his stomach, and it's just heartbreaking to see these men, brave men. I was trying to help him, and then a mortar shell evidently hit behind me. What hit me was a piece of shrapnel. I fell right on top of him. He said, "Oh, Chaplain, they get you too?" I thought, here's a man with three bullet holes in him, and he's concerned about me. But I was able there on that bank of the river and in the boats to help save the lives of a number of men because I carried a big [medical] aid kit. So I

Reverend Fred Miller of Minneapolis was a Lutheran chaplain. He served with the army's 3rd Armored Division in Europe during 1944–45, coming ashore in France three weeks after the D-Day invasion. Conditions were spare: "I did have one or two graveside funerals there in France. . . . Graves registration would be right there, because we didn't even have any caskets. The bodies were very often in wooden boxes, or sometimes even just in blankets or tarps."

worked in that capacity also. . . . Later, when the colonel came over and we had already taken the area, he came over and saw me and said, "What in the hell are you doing here, Chaplain?" "Sir," I said, "the men are here."

Throughout two years of combat, death and killing were always present.

I spent a lot of time ministering to dying men. When you see your buddies that you trained with and worked with and was with, to see them die is heartbreaking. . . . My heart went out to them. I tried to comfort as many as I could. That's why I was on the front line, to help them. Help them physically as much as I could, and comfort them as much as I could. It's very, very difficult.

As to what you say to a man you know is likely to die, I guess it depends on what they believe. I can never tell a man, "You're going to heaven just because you're dying," because that isn't the truth. . . . I would try to help them spiritually if I could. But to somebody who doesn't believe, who is agnostic, I could comfort them in their physical need, but I could not lie to them spiritually.

The question of killing is not an easy one to answer. We know that it's wrong to kill if you have hatred against an individual, someone that you know individually. But when you have the situation we faced in World War II, where you have a man like Hitler killing millions of innocent Jews and others—and we saw a concentration camp, we took a small concentration camp in Germany—I could see that we *had* to take action against that kind of a dictator.

Now the Bible says, "He who takes up the sword will perish by the sword." What does that mean? Hitler and others have taken up the sword and killed millions of people. Who is going to stop him? God says the man who takes up the sword will perish with the sword. That means somebody has to take up the sword against him. . . . Where there are these atrocities, we're expected to try to take a stand against it. . . . The tragedy of war is that there are innocent ones on both sides. Humanity is godless overall in many ways, and that's what causes wars. It's a very difficult question to answer.

Aside from chaplains, civilians and veterans alike were often willing to speak openly about the role of religion and faith in their lives. Opinions and beliefs varied widely: for some, faith, prayer, and their church provided a pillar of strength; for others, war yielded terror and tragedy, forcing an appraisal or reappraisal of faith and the role of a god. Easy answers were rare.

Civilian Maybelle Broberg (b. 1925) of Kerkhoven recalls the impact of the war on life at her small-town church.

WE HAD A flag in church with stars on, representing each fellow that was in the service. When they were going to leave, it was just like a funeral. The men sat up front with their families. Everybody was crying; it was sad. We didn't know if they would be back or not. Give them a New Testament, and they were in your prayers.

Bob Michelsen of Minneapolis, member of a B-29 Superfortress bomber crew, was shot down over Tokyo in May 1945 and imprisoned until the end of the war by the Japanese Kempetai secret police. The effects of more than three months of harsh imprisonment, of maltreatment and a starvation diet, affected Bob long after the physical scars were healed. He wondered about the role of a god.

I REMEMBER BEING at home one night in early 1946, and there's a bed that I could have slept in, but it was too soft; I slept on the floor. I was used to sleeping on a wooden floor. And I was on this floor, thinking about everything that had happened and wondering, and the thought came to me, "Why *am* I alive, when friends of mine are obviously dead?" I thought, "How can I [*pauses three seconds*], how can I join my friends?" And there was only one way, and I remembered that gun I had left behind. So I briefly entertained suicide, to join my friends, and it actually was, to join my friends . . . the thought did enter my head.

The thought, "Why *am* I alive?" That is a very difficult question, because some people say, "God has saved you." Well, why didn't he save the others? So you get these questions, and "No, you're alive because you are going to do something great." Well, you are dead because you do *nothing* great? So all of these questions. . . . I think that it's just a matter of good fortune, and that's all I can attribute it to. I cannot say religion, or my own will, or my own pride, or anything else. Good fortune. I don't want to say chance—good fortune. [*pauses three seconds*] So for months and months, maybe years, that was my reaction at home, to all that episode. That was my main reaction.

Lavinia Stone Murray's husband, James, spent three years in the army; she lived with her in-laws in St. Paul, cared for her daughter, and worked. Separation was hard; Lavinia found the support offered by her church, Pilgrim Baptist of St. Paul, to be crucial during this time.

WE HAD A good minister that really kept us up-to-date on everything. And the church was really the thing that brought us through. I know I looked forward to going to church every Sunday. We had a good choir and a good minister. I felt like if I would just go to church on Sunday, I could make it through the week. That's the way I lived.

[Church was important] through prayer and the service. The message. We had faith. It gave *us* faith. Hope and faith that the Lord would bring us through, and He did.

Lots of us women, everybody around my age, their husbands had gone. . . . We had church clubs. Sometimes it was in our homes. Then sometimes we'd get together for somebody's birthday or something, and then mostly it was all women. We used to party. But it was just all women. Getting together [with other people that were sharing the same experience], that's one of the things that kept us going.

Different ones would speak of if their husband was—about where they were. We were all looking forward to our husbands coming home. We didn't really focus too much on our husbands. We would play games and talk and do things like that. . . . Most of us, those that are still living, are still friends.

Maurice Raether of Duluth attended church regularly with his wife and children. He questions how one can reconcile faith with the presence of war.

WELL, YOU wonder. Now I'm of German descent, from out there in Wisconsin. So a lot of our people, Germans, were in the service during the war, too. They were brother fighting brother, you know. We wondered about that. The preacher in *your* church is praying for an early victory, and the preacher in the *other* church is praying for an early victory. [*laughs*] I mean, where does it add up? I can't say I have much good to say for war, but what are you going to do? The good book says there's always been war and there always will be war.

Minneapolis native Paul Peterson, who endured months during 1944–45 as a prisoner of war, describes a spiritual accompaniment he felt during his experience as a German captive.

DURING THE long walk after we were captured, they moved us back out of harm's way, so to speak, to a little town in Germany. We walked at night. And it was snowing. Trees overarching the roads. The roads were very narrow, very small. But I felt—I've never said this to very many people because I don't know if people really understand it, and I'm not sure I understand it—but I had the feeling that I was being carried on that march. That it was more than my strength that was getting me through that.

And when we got to the town they warehoused us; the group that I was with, we were housed in a bombed-out convent. The roof had been blown off, and we were on the second floor, open to the stars. Some of the guys in the outfit took their boots off—to their great chagrin, because the next morning they couldn't get them back on again because their feet were swollen. My feet weren't swollen. I was comfortable. Maybe that was because I was in good physical condition. If you want to leave it at that kind of plebian, mundane level, okay. [*pauses three seconds*] I don't think so. I think that I had then, and have had in that experience, a sense of being accompanied. That's the experience that I had pretty much through that whole thing.

In his mid-forties, Paul changed careers and entered the ministry.

Lawrence Brown, also of Minneapolis, served 1942–45 in North Africa and Italy.
He is cynical about religion and those who claimed it would save them.

I'M A RELIGIOUS GUY, I think. We've got to have religion or we'd kill
each other. Everybody. But I have trouble with religion. You gotta
watch who's around you and what they're doing. And all these guys
that were so pious on the Sabbath were scoundrels. Ninety-nine percent scoundrels. Then it became humorous to me because we were on
the ship going over [to North Africa], and when you got these alerts
that there's a possibility of something going to happen, all these
Christians were praying and singing. It was so funny because my
buddy and I were saying, "Hey you guys, you better take swimming
lessons." None of them could swim, those guys. "We'll teach you to
swim because if this boat starts sinking, your butt's going to be out
there in the water. You better know how to swim." But they were
singing the old spirituals. I got a good education off people singing,
"Ain't no danger, danger, danger in these waters." And then when the
waves got more choppy the tempo of the song would get speeded up,
and [*sings faster*] "Ain't no danger, danger, danger. . . ." And I was
sitting there, and one guy almost shot me. He wanted to shoot me
because I was being kind of jovial about this.

   I just knew I wasn't going to make it back. That guy that said he
knew he was going to make it, he was lying or he was crazy. You see
guys dying around you. Now if you think that you're immune, these
are the guys who bother me. They don't want to think past their
noses. They're so steeped in religion that they believe that the person
they believe in is going to protect them. What about this other guy,
who believes the same way they do? I'm not that stupid. I have a
respect for a supreme being, but I say, here's what I say, all the reli-
gions in the world and all the people who have supposedly gone to
Valhalla or wherever, heaven or whatever it is, somebody should have
escaped and come back and said, hey, those guys are *lying,* or, man,
hurry up, you cannot *get* a better place! There's got to be a bit of logic
in this thing because this thing is too complex.

I saw a guy, I saw a guy's grave there in Sicily. The guy who was right before me in Fort Snelling [when I was being inducted] was holding up a cross. He got killed there in Sicily, and that was his grave. That's when reality set in.

Healing: Nurses and Medics

COMPASSION, care, and human emotion were at the center of everyday life for service personnel working in the medical field, specifically nurses and medics (known in the Navy and Marine Corps as corpsmen). These women and men, some stationed at or near the front lines, worked directly with the sick, wounded, and dying. They were confronted, sometimes daily, with the many physical and psychological casualties of war, and they worked to provide comfort and, when possible, to repair the damages.

The scale and scope of World War II produced vast numbers of casualties. Not only was the wounded toll for combatant nations in the millions, the terribly destructive weapons systems caused wounds and injuries unlike those seen in earlier conflicts. Complications from what were sometimes shattering wounds included blood loss and severe shock. Other soldiers were psychological casualties.

Care began with first aid provided on the battlefield by medics and corpsmen. Hastily trained in the basics of physiology and medicine, these men (nurses were not members of combat units) served on the front line in dangerous situations, often under fire. Moving from one wounded marine or soldier to the next with a small medical bag, their job was to provide immediate, at times lifesaving help. Exposed and in the open, medics and corpsmen were themselves casualties at correspondingly high rates. Off the front lines, treatment continued with various levels of rear-echelon hospital stations—hospital ships and evacuation and field hospitals—that could handle more serious problems with their more complex technology. Long-term care facilities such as general hospital units treated difficult wounds and assisted with recuperation and readjustment. These more permanent structures were located far from the front, many in the United States.

Women in uniform made a profound impact in the medical field. Of the more than 300,000 that served in the five U.S. military auxiliaries during World War II, 76,000 joined the Army and Navy Nurse Corps. Nurses worked alongside male medical personnel in every theater of the war. In the Pacific, for example, army and navy nurses served on offshore hospital ships at numerous invasions, including Okinawa and Iwo Jima, but also in evacuation and general hospitals in Hawaii, Australia, New Zealand, and various other locations. They dealt with battle casualties and injuries, their work complicated by tropical diseases such as malaria, dengue fever, and beriberi. In Europe nurses also moved with the fronts: they were present at North Africa and Italy and, following the landings in June 1944 in France, joined medical units in that country as well as later in Luxembourg, Belgium, and Germany. They remained in the region after the war, treating the final casualties as well as prisoners released from German camps.

✦ ✦ ✦

Martha Ryan (b. 1922) grew up in the small Minnesota towns of Lydia and Webster. She graduated from nursing school in 1943 and enlisted in the U.S. Army in March 1944. Late that year she was transferred to the 119th Evacuation Hospital and shipped to Europe. The unit moved to France in early 1945, and Martha spent the remainder of the war at locations in Belgium and Germany. Her primary duty was in the recovery room of a first-echelon hospital facility, where combat casualties were operated on and others were stabilized for shipment to rear-area hospitals.

THERE WAS ONLY one of you. We had two nurses assigned, and we worked twelve-hour shifts. You worked very hard trying to get everything done. There was always so much to do that you couldn't do. Corpsmen were trying very much to be helpful. However, they hadn't had the training. They weren't through nurses training.

The young men, they were all angry that it had happened to

them. But maybe relief that they were being taken care of. You couldn't spend enough time with them, really.

Almost all types of casualties [arrived at our hospital]. There were burns, but they couldn't do much besides put dressing on them. The amputees stick in my mind mostly. But we also had stomachs that had been shot. We tried to stabilize them enough to send them back to a general hospital. Amputees—they usually had to be removed. This was one of the most difficult things. We were all very young people, and to have to tell the patient when [he] was waking up, and he wondered, and he would look, and you had to tell him, "We had to take it off."

A young man that I had to tell that we had to take off his leg stuck with me, because he was such a young boy. [In a situation like that], you just have to tell them. You hold his hand and you have to tell him. . . . I don't remember that he said anything, except the look on his face was horrible. . . . But you couldn't do anything about it.

Martha shared photographs she took in late April or early May 1945 near the small German town of Gardelegen, where there had been a concentration camp facility. Some prisoners had been killed just prior to the Americans' arrival.

By this time we had already heard about the concentration camps. The tremendous loss of life that had been going on, that we just couldn't quite believe, and this was sort of . . . it was so close to us. It didn't seem real.

It made us sick when we were told that these people were killed a matter of a day before our American troops arrived. . . . We went to the building a short time later that they had been held in. A wooden barn. We could see the claw marks where they had with their fingernails scratched on the wood trying to break through, to get out from the inside. I think they'd been shot. . . . [The local German civilians] had to furnish a clean, white sheet to wrap each body in.

Lottie Shultz was born in Germany in 1920, emigrated to the United States with her parents in the mid-1920s, and grew up near St. Peter. After she finished nurses training in 1942, her German-born father pressured her to join the American military.

M Y FATHER was wondering why I didn't go into the service. He tried, and he couldn't get in. . . . He wanted to get into—not any front-line duty or anything like that—in like the Seabees. But he wasn't successful. I don't know; he was too old, I think. He was in World War I in Germany for a short time. In the German Army, though.

[It bothered him that he couldn't get in,] because he really pushed to get *me* in. There was some talk, rumors about drafting nurses. So I finally thought, oh well. . . . I wouldn't have *had* to go. . . . He pushed. Definitely pushed. . . . Practically pushed me out the door. . . . So I decided, okay, I'm *going*. [*determined sounding*] That's it. I got my stuff packed, what I was going to take, and left one morning. Got on the train and took off.

Lottie enlisted in the U.S. Army in January 1944. Later that year she was sent to England and posted to the 187th General Hospital Unit at Tidworth. While she cared for many seriously wounded men at Tidworth, including some who died, one of Lottie's clearest memories is of men who feared a return to their families and loved ones.

Lottie Shultz (standing, left) and other staff of the 187th General Hospital, Tidworth, England, 1944

Some of the fellows that were wounded and had been at the front lines were just on cloud nine to think they were going back to the States. Of course, the amputees, and we had a couple of blind patients, they weren't too gung ho about going home. They didn't know how their friends or relatives would accept them. That was pretty tough for them. We could tell they'd just as soon stay there.

Army sergeant Lawrence Brown of Minneapolis described the same sentiments, but from a patient's perspective. In February 1945, he was badly injured
in a truck accident near the city of Foggia, Italy.

I WAS GOING to see my brother, Harold[, a pilot with the 332nd
Fighter Group, stationed nearby], and they bombed this bridge out.
It was dusk. You've got little dinky lights; you don't have big bright
lights. We shouldn't have gone down where they had blown the
bridge up, but we went where the bridge was supposed to be, and it
just, the truck went over the bridge. There were twelve of us in the
damn thing. Four got killed and four got the crap scared out of them.
Then four of us were really, really injured because the truck fell on
us. We were pinned. One of the guys that died was under my legs.
My legs were on top of him, and I was pinned. Part of the truck had
a big steel bar that had me pinned in, and there was water in the
creek, and I had to put rocks under my right side, under my head,
to keep from drowning. But the water was so cold that I didn't bleed
to death. They had to go get some big machinery to pull this truck
off of me.

Transported to a field hospital and then a general hospital, Lawrence describes
what Lottie Shultz identifies—a feeling that he did not want to return home a
broken man.

When I was lying there in the hospital, I didn't know much. I was
still goofy. I had a cracked head, and my brother, when he came to
see me, he says the first thing I said to him was, "Brush my teeth." I
was goofy for a while. I got a fractured skull and a concussion of my
eye and cuts all over my face. And then I had this steel bar that had
impaled me, and I had a wound in my back about six, seven inches
long. Of course there was a lot of debris in there because I had been
on the bed of this river or creek or whatever it was. They were picking stuff out of me for a long time. And the severed nerve in my right
arm. My right arm was paralyzed for a long, long time. I felt that I
didn't want to go home because I was paralyzed. I didn't have time

to dwell on the fact that I might have permanent damage. I just didn't want to get home and let the people I know see me as an invalid. I wasn't going to do that.

Otto Schmaltz (b. 1922) was drafted into the U.S. Army in May 1943. He received advanced training as a medic, shipped to England, and was assigned to the 31st Medical Company. On 6 June 1944, Otto participated in the Allied invasion of France, landing on Utah Beach.

FROM OUR hospital ship . . . we jumped off the ship, and we went down the cargo nets into the Higgins boats. Higgins boats were bouncing up and down [in the water], about six to eight feet in the air. We waited until they got up, and then we went down into, jumped down into the boat. I had to be one of the first ones out of the boat, so I got to go up by where they dropped the front end of the boat.

At Utah Beach . . . I landed and—first of all, the guy didn't bring the boat in far enough, and I jumped off the gate into water up to my neck. . . . I landed and the water was up to my neck, and I just waded ashore. I waded ashore, one half a step at a time, foot over foot, and got to where I was exposed pretty good. Then we still hadn't drawn any fire of any kind, but we had all kinds of dead bodies, dead bodies that were lying in the water. . . . I was just pushing them out the way so that I could get myself on dry shore.

Every guy, regardless of size, carried about seventy-five to one hundred pounds of equipment on his back. . . . When these people that were smaller of stature than myself dropped off of these Higgins boats, they landed in water over their head. . . . The only thing that saved me was the fact that I was six foot four inches tall. I could touch the sand . . . with my feet, my toes. And then also the fact that I was a medic and not a combat person. I didn't have any ammunition to carry. I had no guns, I had no ammunition, I had no grenades. All I had was medical packs, which are very light and compact. . . . These men lying in the water were not killed by hostile fire or shell fire or nothing. . . . Most of them were drowned.

For several months after D-Day, Otto's unit was attached to the 4th Infantry Division in combat situations in France, in the hedgerows of Normandy. He remembers clearly the wounds made by the Germans' illegal use of wooden bullets.

Hedgerow fighting. We were just making headway maybe one city block a day. The Germans were using wooden bullets at that time, just for hedgerow fighting. See, a wooden bullet does not have the distance that a regular metal bullet has. These wooden bullets were designed especially for this hedgerow fighting . . . the casing is metal, but the projectile is wood. . . . It's actually designed so when it hits you, it goes in and splinters. The Germans were not allowed to use these wooden bullets by the terms of the Geneva Convention; they were barred. But they used a lot of them, many, many, many of them.

These were the worst kinds of wounds that we had to treat; they are just terrible, they're terrible. When it goes into you it immediately splinters and ruptures vessels, and the only way you can do anything with it is to stuff a big wad of gauze or cotton into the hole and plug it up as tight as you can plug it. Then get the stretcher and have them haul him back to where they can take it out. And then you've got to remember, like in our case, all these people—Showers were unheard of. You slept in dirty clothes, you slept with sweaty bodies, you slept in dirt. Our uniforms are dirty, you're dusty, dirty. . . . You're just one

Army medic Otto Schmaltz, who photographed civilians he met during the American advance through western France, poses with three farm boys, 1944

filthy pig. When you get hit with anything, shrapnel especially is bad, because it pushed all that dirt and crap and all that slimy crap into your body. This is what causes quick infection and quick bleeding.

Catherine Lemmer Brueggeman grew up in Grand Rapids, Minnesota, and Somerset, Wisconsin. She graduated from nursing school in 1943 and in January 1944 enlisted in the U.S. Army. In October she arrived in France and was assigned to the 240th General Hospital Unit in the city of Nancy. Casualties were high, especially during the German Ardennes Offensive (December 1944–January 1945), hours were long, and stress was part of everyday life. Managing that stress was at times a challenge.

I DON'T THINK you could call it hardening; I think it was the fact that you have to detach yourself, emotionally, from what you are doing. You work at it, but you also look at, you try to zero in just on the medical problem and the physical problem of what you have to do for this person, and you cannot really let yourself get emotionally attached, because that does something for your own ability to keep coping. It's a very fine line, but you are busy enough and you just do it. It's exhausting and after a while you feel . . . you have to. . . .

[T]he doctors and the other nurses, we all handled it. Every once in a while somebody would kind of break down, but then the others were very supportive. Oh, once in a while somebody'd go back to the main hospital or something. And there were times when somebody would just run out of the hospital and out to the tent, or wherever we were stationed, and go wandering off and somebody'd go after them, talk to that person. They'd say, "I just can't. I can't handle this anymore. I can't see another person in this condition. I just feel like committing suicide." Well, then that was an indication that this person had taken all the trauma that he or she could take.

I think I felt sympathetic, because I could see where they were coming from, and I just was thankful that I *was* so able to cope. I didn't put that person down; I didn't see them as not being efficient or able to cope, because people have different levels of coping, too.

I think there were times when I kind of came close, but I don't think it ever got to the point where. . . . I mean, at the end of some days, we'd sometimes work twenty, thirty hours [nonstop], and so, you would wonder, how much more of this can I do? But then all the people around you were doing the same thing, and you *did* cope. You weren't alone in it. And I think that's what helped.

After the war in Europe ended in May 1945, Catherine was stationed at a small hospital facility set up to treat Allied ex-POWs. The month she spent there remains the strongest memory from her wartime service.

I went to a unit, a small hospital; it was in France, right on the border between France and Germany; it was like a field hospital. And what we were getting were the ones that were being liberated from those German concentration camps. They were POWs. Allied POWs.

That is something I'll never forget. We were getting these people, and you've seen movies and stuff about that, that's exactly what they looked like. They'd come in looking like skeletons. They'd have had an injured foot and [the Germans would] take their leg off at the hip joint or a whole arm off for a hand injury. They were, they looked like skeletons, they actually did look like skeletons, and they would be dying for something to eat. They were living on just vegetables, you know, like a vegetable soup that was just water and vegetables; there was nothing else in there. And, oh, they were dying for ice cream and milk and stuff like that, and it took them a while before their stomachs could handle that. You can't take that right away. They gradually had to bring everything back to normal again.

So it was like having a bunch of skeletons there, treating them, getting their stomachs back to working again, giving them some food, getting some, you know, flesh back on their bones again. And they were so weak; they couldn't do anything. And besides that they were so abused. So we really worked at getting their strength back and everything, so that they could stand the trip home [to the United States or whatever country they came from]; that was the goal. Stabilize them and get them healthy and strong enough so they could stand the trip back home. That was probably the most devastating thing I did there, I mean the thing that stays with me.

This was way above and beyond the casualties of war. It was destruction of human beings for no reason at all; it was senseless cruelty and it's . . . some of the things that they would tell you that had been done to them when they were in these concentration camps. And you could see the physical abuse. . . .

It's something that you have to just look at that person as a human being that needs a lot of help right now, and that's all you see. You don't see their abused, neglected, mistreated body; you're looking at the person that needs your help right away. . . . And you can do that. After a while it just becomes part of you.

Catherine Brueggeman in 1944, before shipping out to England

Martin Steinbach (b. 1919) of Loman served in North Africa and Europe with the 41st Field Artillery. Toward the end of the war, he saw the inside of one of the German camps.

NEAR MUNICH we hit a bad deal there. There was a big concentration camp, one where they burned all the bodies. They had flatcars in there with people piled on them like pulpwood, about two or three feet high. There were bodies laying on there, just like pulpwood. They would throw them in the incinerator and burn them up.

There was guys laying on the ground, dying. Some of them, you might as well say they were dead, but they were still alive. They were starved to death. That's what it amounted to.

Emmett Yanez, a paratrooper in the army's 82nd Airborne, participated in the liberation of one of these camps. He struggled to find the words to describe what he saw.

CONCENTRATION CAMPS. We saw those people. Oh, man. Nothing but bones. It just . . . [*trails off*]. How could one human being do that to another? . . . And the people that could walk were all just walking skeletons. You just kind of felt sorry for them. There's nothing really you can do when they get to that condition.

I saw boxcars full of bodies in the one area that we came into. Big, long, dried up. They had big open pits where they had all the bodies in there. It was terrible. . . . It just made you sick.

Climate, diseases, and a different type of enemy combined to make combat experience in the Pacific especially horrific. The medical personnel who served there discussed these topics in some detail, but the images that remain strongest in their minds more than five decades later are those of human suffering and loss.

In June 1943, immediately following high school, Ken Firnstahl of Minneapolis was drafted into the U.S. Navy. After basic training he was schooled as a medical corpsman, and in December 1943 he was posted to Aiea Heights Naval Hospital, Hawaii, where he served until late 1945. Ken's various duties included dealing with seriously wounded military personnel from all over the Pacific theater.

I WAS THERE right in the midst of it. All the troops coming in all wounded and shot, arms off, legs off, everything. . . . Amputees. Guys with their heads crushed. TB cases. . . . We had one ward with everybody with their rear end shot off. And one room with all the legs shot off, one room with all the arms shot off. . . . Stinking, rotting flesh. The odor. I couldn't eat for a few days, for about a week and a half [when I first got there. I was] shocked at first. It really was a shock.

I grew a little numb from it. And you'd say, well, this is war and they're coming in. They're shot to pieces. We had to fix them up. Get them fixed up. Get them some plasma, get them some this. Do this. Get them some morphine. Check on this. Ask them how they're feeling, how are you doing? I would always try to be cheerful.

I would say you get used to it, and in another way you *don't* get used to all these guys getting all shot to pieces, but you finally adjust to it, and you go ahead and do your job. When the troops would come in heavy, you'd work almost around the clock. Then you'd get a little rest and then you just, you seemed to adjust to it. You didn't go off in a corner and say, "I can't take this anymore." I didn't notice anybody that gave up and couldn't do it anymore.

I think what it did is, it made a man out of you. I used to be eighteen, but suddenly you were forty years old. You were a man, and you became a man pretty quick. You had to. You weren't sitting giggling and saying, "I'm not going to do this," or anything. You went ahead.

One of the ways Ken dealt with the stress of hospital corpsman duty was to put his thoughts and emotions into words, by writing poems.

For three years being there it probably wasn't that often [that I would write poetry], but I would have night duty, guard duty at night. I just was a medic. . . . I would sit there at that desk, and there was an old Underwood typewriter. I didn't really remember how to type, but I started typing anyway. I typed this stuff out, and I'd mark out what I felt in

Ken Firnstahl with his father, Minneapolis, 1943

my heart, and I'd send it out. . . . I never felt I was a poet or anything, but I just, I just would write that stuff out. . . . I think it helped me a little bit. You could express yourself. It was kind of like a catharsis.

Ken wrote his first poem at Aiea Heights in 1944. He was nineteen years old.

> I have often tried to write a poem
> About a world of peace,
> About a sky that's always blue,
> Above a land where troubles cease.
>
> But then each time I'd start to write
> My pen would strive in vain.
> You see my heart is not in tune
> With words that are not plain.

I'd have to write of war and strife
Of things my eyes have seen.
A sky that's dark with gun smoke,
A land where hearts are lean.

I'd have to write of shattered dreams,
Of mothers who have lost their sons
A face with eyes that cannot see
The cries of little ones.

I'd rather write of love and spring.
A poem about the fall.
For if one must write of war and strife,
Best not to write at all.

Martin O. Weddington of St. Paul was called to military service in early 1945. Inducted into the navy, after basic training he was schooled as a corpsman and prepared for duty in the Pacific. Martin spent the latter part of 1945 working at a naval hospital in San Diego. Even though the war ended in August, America's Pacific theater casualties continued to arrive.

THERE AT San Diego we saw the results of war. . . . Ships came into San Diego. And aboard some of those ships were wounded military personnel. They were going to come into hospitals. And to go and to see these individuals, all different kinds, it made you aware of what you wound up not being exposed to. There were some guys that even in training, man, their stomach would. . . . They'd lose it.

Just like my mind right now is thinking of carrying individuals off of ships and just. . . . They had gotten fevers over there and everything, and coming back. Just in [*sighs*] awful shape. Others hurt. Different parts. I found, too, that actual blood, when you're trying to stop it, it can do things to you. I mean it can tear your emotions up, you know, because you're not doing it as fast and as complete as you want to. It's . . . well, you gotta get used to it. You just don't get used to it today, in one day.

As one of the first African American corpsmen, Martin recalls that sometimes race could be an issue.

Very rarely would you hear anything. You might hear of somebody, some remark being made. See, a lot of times, some people would not know what words might irritate a person, and they could use that word, and that would turn a person off. Because maybe where they grew up that word was common, and you probably wouldn't even think of it. For example: "Boy." Don't be calling me a boy—I'm a man! But down there in the South, "Hi boy." Boy. It was kind of a common thing to some people, but I'm from Minnesota. *Don't* call me boy.

Important medical work was also done by the women and men of the American Red Cross. Separate from the military, they nevertheless worked closely with doctors, nurses, and corpsmen/medics as they performed various duties.

Gertrude Esteros, born in 1914 to Finnish immigrant parents, grew up in the small northern Minnesota town of Saginaw. After graduating from the University of Minnesota, in 1942 Gertrude was teaching at a small college in Missouri when she decided to resign her position and join the Red Cross in June. After stateside training, she was assigned to the 37th Field Hospital unit and in late 1942 was sent to the South Pacific. For almost three years, until fall 1945, Gertrude had duty stations in New Guinea, at Port Moresby and Finschhafen, and in the Philippines, at Leyte and Panay Island. She did hospital field-service work, setting up and administering recreation centers for servicemen.

M Y JOB was the recreation for the ambulatory patients and, as much as possible, to make it possible for them to do it for themselves and to be doing things. Out of the group came the people who knew how to sing, who knew how to do things, who knew whatever—that's the recreation we would do. . . . My job was always one of finding some way of building and doing recreation.

Mostly we had, well, we had to scrounge. We had to learn to do with whatever we could. This went on through all of my time in the Southwest Pacific. If we learned that a plane had gone down somewhere and was crashed beyond use, or some other vehicles were

In March 1945, the Cloquet *Pine Knot* proudly noted one local connection to the war effort in the Philippines, Red Cross worker Gertrude Esteros

down, I would send people out to get salvage that could be used in a crafts program. We made all manner of things. We made rings that they sent home to their wives and girlfriends, and we did aluminum and Plexiglas. We built recreation centers with bomb crates for seats. We built lounge seats out of scrap army cots. All sorts of things.

Especially rewarding were the ample opportunities for interacting with patients.

Half of my time, and sometimes more than half, was with the ambulatory people. I spent the other half of my time on the wards in the hospital, with the people on the cots. That was a matter of visiting with patients. That was simply a matter of talking, a matter of visiting. . . . I went from bed to bed. I made a point of interacting with the men, and of course if I didn't get there I would be called. The men would let me know that I hadn't been there yet, that I hadn't gotten over there to that corner on that ward.

The men were so relieved that they were out of the thick of battle in a safe place on a cot and had a chance to talk with somebody. And of course with a Red Cross worker, a woman, they could talk about things that they never would talk about with a buddy, with another man. . . . I wasn't military. I wasn't official anything; I didn't have any rank. And I was a little older. You see, I was twenty-eight, twenty-nine, thirty years old, and most of these people were eighteen, nineteen. Others were twenty, twenty-one, twenty-two.

They were lonely of course. And they talked about their families. The saddest stories were the men whose wives had been, were unfaithful, who had given up the marriage and had married somebody else or gone out with somebody else. I began to think that there wasn't a single faithful woman left in the United States! [*laughs*] So I heard those stories. Oh, they talked about *everything*. They told about their dogs and their pets, and occasionally we'd have an intellectual conversation. We would talk about literature and opera. We just talked about whatever they wanted to talk about.

I was there. I had a job to do. I was a friend. And they responded to a friend as a friend. You can keep that, that distance, and yet you can be very close. You can have your arm around the guy, but there's a difference. You can be the sister. You can be the mother. You can be the nurse. You can be the something else.

At times, shortages of medical personnel forced Gertrude into patient-care duties. She recalls a few such episodes at Leyte, the Philippines, in 1945.

At the end of the war . . . we still had to clear up the hospital and take care of the ends of things. My first assignment in Leyte was at a cathedral hospital. . . . There were two hospitals combined. I was with the 37th Field Hospital, and we were joining the cathedral. My job was setting up a recreation area in a tent, just outside of the cathedral. I was dealing with ambulatory people, and the very ill, the severely ill were in the cathedral. [There were nurses there,] but when there was too much be done I was called into the cathedral wards. So I crossed the line, and I had to go into the cathedral where the very sick people were.

I was taking down the story of a young noncommissioned officer who was the last survivor, the only survivor, of his whole unit. He was desperate to tell the story so it could be told to the commanding officer. Tell what had happened to everybody. . . . He died just a couple of hours after I'd taken down his message. I also spent several nights with burn patients who were so desperately uncomfortable, and nobody had time to deal with them. I was there to give them liquid. Thirst is awful when you have been burned, when most of your body is burned. Even morphine doesn't help. You're just miserable.

Miserable. So there I was, just to be there. Just to be there. This one patient, he was gasping. We lost him. He died. But at least there was somebody there. I was there in several instances like that where the nurses were too busy with the surgery.

The most difficult thing for me was that I wasn't capable enough. I was sorry I didn't have more nursing experience. There were limits to what I could do. But then, there were limits to what anybody could do. I was in situations where nobody could have made a difference, other than that you make that human being feel a little more human while he's still living.

The end of the war brought certain changes that made Gertrude reconsider her position and her commitment to the work.

I went back from Panay to Leyte, to Tacloban, which is the capital of the island of Leyte. They kept assigning me different spots, you know, one thing finished then you get on to another thing. So here I was at another hospital. . . . There were replacement soldiers coming in, new recruits coming in to do various jobs that had to be done. The war was over, but they were coming to do different jobs. I was assigned and I was on a ward, and some of the men who came, they all had such fresh-looking faces. They still looked so good. I could hardly stand it.

And not only that, what were they in the hospital for? Venereal disease! They'd been messing around already. They'd messed around so that they were here. They had gone to prostitutes along the way and gotten themselves infected! This was new. [Men fighting in the South Pacific islands] didn't have the opportunity to—It wasn't available to them.

So there they were, and they were griping about the food and stuff, and I couldn't stand them! I looked at them, and I said, "Oh, you don't know anything! You don't *deserve* good food!" [*laughs*] I said to [my supervisors], that's why I don't want to remain in Red Cross service—because I don't want to have to deal with this kind of stuff. The Red Cross doesn't need my services anymore. I'm through.

Gertrude returned to the United States in November 1945 and resigned from the Red Cross.

✦ ✦ ✦

Jacob Gondeck was trained as a corpsman after his enlistment in the navy in December 1942. Part of his schooling involved spending time at a naval psychiatric facility, dealing with men for whom the strains of war had simply proved too much.

THEY SENT US . . . for six weeks of psychiatric training in the naval hospital in New Orleans. . . . For the six weeks we had two hours of classes, plus the rest of the time we worked on the wards. We had to know all the symptoms of schizophrenia, manic-depressives, inadequate personalities, and stuff. We got to know all the symptoms so that those that needed immediate treatment, they were kept in the wards, and those that were going to blow their lids and that, they were in straitjackets and lock wards. We had to have hands-on experience how to handle those people. . . .

[I]t made you so . . . you knew that there was two sides to war. One, the wounded by the ammo or the bullet, and the other the silent, what we called the silent. . . . These were all military. These were all mental cases, every one of them.

We went right into the lock wards. We put people in straitjackets, and those that were out of straitjackets, they were on our ward in beds and that. Some of them were comatose. We fed them, we bathed them, we gave them shots and everything like that. We sedated them. That was our routine.

In fact, I remember [this one guy], . . . he was about five foot four, stocky, and when he blew his top he just went along and knocked all the radios off the poor patients' [shelves]. By that time, it took four of us to get him down. In that state they have so much adrenaline going through their bodies they become twice as strong. It took four of us to get him in a straitjacket.

When the parents got there, then the psychiatrists . . . took them aside and told them. Gave them all the good news that he's going to come out of it. [*shakes head no*] We [saw] many, many parents in New Orleans that would come to visit there. The parents, some were in denial, especially fathers, you know, saying, "It can't happen to my son." But you know, it *did* happen. [*raises voice*] It *did* happen, see? And we used to get so *angry* at these fathers that looked down on their sons for being a weakling or something.

In March 1945, Jacob was assigned to Air Evacuation Group One on the island of Guam. He was a corpsman on evacuation flights during the heaviest fighting on Okinawa (April–June 1945), when naval transport aircraft carried seriously wounded combat troops from the front line to hospital facilities on Guam. Jacob's duty included collecting wounded from field hospitals, transporting them to the waiting aircraft, and caring for the wounded on the six-hour return flight.

When we got down on the ground the first time, then we saw all the carnage . . . I know [the first time,] I threw up. . . . Our first-aid stations were right next to the fighting, and then the field hospitals, where they did as much as they could. . . . Arms, legs that were close to the bodies, that were chopped up. Some cut off here from a bomb. You knew they were going to die. Wouldn't make it. [*sighs*] I don't know. [*pauses three seconds*] I mean, I cried when I thought of that.

Sometimes we had to help. . . . You were going out and putting the litters on the jeeps and stuff like that. Yes, you were working all the time once you got on the ground, too. . . . It depends on how many casualties came in while we were still on the ground. Grab the hemostat and then, you know . . . so we got to do all that stuff. Cut off the arteries and stuff. We always had these big safety pins, especially on, we called them belly wounds, or the stomach. Things, they burst, and sometimes you just didn't have the things on the field, and we just closed them up with safety pins. Until we got them back to the main station. That's where the doctor would quickly sew them up.

You know, the thing that overcame you is, "Am I good enough? Am I good enough to save these guys, get them back to Guam?" That was our thoughts. And, "Did I remember everything now?" All those little thoughts. . . . That was the whole thing in a nutshell. You didn't want to let that person down, that nurse down, or that doctor down, or whatever.

And I can remember so damn much noise. When you think about out on the base, and all the din. There was just constant, constant noise, but you kind of blocked it out after a while. It seemed like sometimes . . . during a heated battle, if we were there at that certain time, you could see all the things just popping at you.

Then we had to figure out whether we could get them for more treatment back to Guam. Those that you knew were going to die, the doc would say, because he would say, "I think this one is not going to make it." . . . Doctors made the decision. He would tell the nurse, "This one you can take." After a while we got pretty good at it. We kind of knew the ones that weren't going to, you know, [make it].

We tried to [keep them sedated on the flights], yes. Because, you know why? Then there weren't any yelling and the moaning and that. That's why we used a lot of the little morphine syrettes and stuff. Because a lot of them wouldn't probably wake up to reality actually until they got to Guam and the main hospital after a few days and realize, god, I have no legs or I have no arms.

The phosphorus-bomb wounded—that stuff would eat into your flesh—we kept those out, until it was a full planeload of just them. Because they were just . . . [*trails off*]. You know what it is, burning flesh? I'll never forget. . . . One of the guys [on a flight] had this thing over his eyes, see, and he took it off, and he yells, "I can't see!" And, jeez, I ran over there to put it on and [*pauses three seconds*] two black spots. God, did that hit you! When we got to Guam, and we opened the door and got that fresh air. . . . [*pauses three seconds*] Because it is *such* a stench inside.

Bill Amundson was a navy pilot with Air Evacuation Group One; he flew medical evacuation planes from Iwo Jima to Guam during March–May 1945.

WE MADE many, many trips in and out of Iwo Jima. Round trip [from Guam]. I don't recall how many stretchers we had in the plane, but there was a goodly quantity of wounded onboard each aircraft. We would load the wounded onboard and fly them back to Guam. That was our shuttle. We did that day after day after day.

That's the first experience I had of being in a battlefield situation. I wondered if the blood and the guts and the gore would bother me. . . . I soon found out that if it's my blood that's one thing, but if it's somebody else's blood [it's different]. . . . I had more compassion than anything.

By the time that we saw them they were fairly sedated. They were bandaged. There was a lot of blood and that sort of thing, but we didn't see any of the real raw stuff from the battlefield. Of course, we had people to load the stretchers onto the aircraft. These were people that were really in serious condition; those were the ones that we wanted to save. We saved a lot of lives.

Flying in close proximity to the front lines could be dangerous.

One time we were taking off, and because of the wind direction we had to take off across the Japanese lines. We were loaded with wounded. . . . I looked out the window, and I saw a hole in our wing. I don't remember hearing anything, but apparently some Japanese soldier had pointed his rifle up at us and put a hole through our wing.

They were forced to turn back and make an emergency landing on Iwo Jima.

Bill Amundson unloading a stretcher after landing on Iwo Jima, March 1945

The plane commander said it might have gone through a wing gas tank. We better go back, he said, because if we don't we may run out of fuel and have to ditch in the ocean and lose all these wounded that are onboard. It turned out that was a good decision, because indeed the bullet had gone through a wing tank.

After V-J Day in August 1945, Jacob Gondeck and a handful of other navy corps-men remained stationed on Guam; part of their duty during 1946 was returning to the United States numerous psychiatric cases, soldiers who had cracked under the mental strain of combat in the Pacific.

WHEN WE were in New Orleans for that training, we were talk-ing, and we said, "Why all this psychiatric training? Why are we working in the lock wards and all this?" . . . After the war, [on Guam, we] figured everything out. . . . All the mental kids, or the ones that got shell-shocked—that's a nice word for it. All those kids that lost their reality, put it that way. They were in, oh, god, all differ-ent phases of it. They started coming in, from all different places. See, you could keep those back in the hospital. They kept them sedated. From Saipan, Iwo Jima, Okinawa, whatever was left, they cleared them out. . . . [They sent them] all back to Guam.

They were brought from an ambulance. They brought them right from the hospitals, because that was the receiving area. Brought them, all these others, and then from there they were brought by ambulance to our planes. . . . From then it was *constant*. Day after day. . . .

We got many in the catatonic state. That catatonic stage is usually where the young guys lost everything because of the battle, the shell-ing, the constant . . . [*trails off*]. They just cracked up. . . . We kept them sedated from Guam all the way to Honolulu. That was almost twenty hours. . . . They were in straitjackets and in the stretchers. All sedated, so that we could get that far.

[One time,] this one guy got out of his straitjacket on the plane. So somebody goofed up somehow, maybe from Okinawa or wherever. They didn't give him his right dosage or something, and he almost opened the damn door of the plane! He would have went out, we know that for sure. And we would have had a hell of a time in the flight. Jesus! When he got up to the door we just, man . . . [*pauses three seconds*]. We carried towels in our back pockets. That was for this, if you ever got into a problem. You could not leave any marks on him, so you wrapped it around his neck like that [*puts hands to neck*]. And then you squeezed the thing . . . that towel cut off their wind . . . and the other [corpsman] held him until his knees buck-led. Then you got him back in the straitjacket.

The four of us [corpsmen assigned to this duty] were under oath that we would never speak of this [particular duty]. At that time we wondered why. But then, when we kind of figured out, when it got to be hundreds and thousands, oh, oh. [*sighs*] . . . They did *not want* the American mothers to know that their young boys cracked up. It was just *overwhelming*. We couldn't *believe* that that many kids cracked up. That was our feeling. Jesus, I said, this is as many as were wounded, [these] kids that had their flight from reality.

[6]

War's End

1945 as End and Beginning

I N MAY 1945, nearly six years after unleashing war on Europe with an attack on Poland, Germany surrendered unconditionally and Allied forces took control of the shattered country. The Pacific war dragged on, however, with no such end in sight. This increasingly violent theater of war—American casualties for the period mid-1944 to mid-1945 were greater than those the country had suffered during the entire war up until that point—seemed to be hurtling inescapably toward an American-led invasion of the Japanese home islands in late 1945. With images of Iwo Jima and Okinawa fresh in people's minds, there was a great sense of foreboding about the carnage expected from this final assault. The sudden end of the Pacific war in August 1945, following the destruction of two Japanese cities by atomic bombs, surprised civilians and military personnel alike.

National holidays were proclaimed. For the European war, V-E (Victory in Europe) Day was celebrated on 8 May. The end of the Pacific war came on 14 August, when Japan's leaders accepted surrender terms; the actual V-J Day, the day on which the surrender document was signed, came some weeks later, on 2 September. (Note:

Interviewees often mention V-J Day when it is clear from the context that they are referring to 14 August 1945, not 2 September 1945.)

War's end ushered in periods of recovery and adjustment. Personal experiences during this time could be radically different, as evidenced by those who recall happenings in Germany, Japan, and the United States.

War's End: Memories of V-E Day and V-J Day

"NOW WE CAN go home. We made it. We survived. That's all we wanted, was to go home. We didn't give a damn about the Japanese or anything." A reaction to announcements of war's end, these words of Pacific veteran Art Pejsa, a B-29 Superfortress pilot who flew more than twenty bombing missions during 1944–45 from bases in India and on Tinian Island, are simple, direct, and almost lacking in emotion. Among front-line combat veterans, he was not alone in expressing the thought that Japan's (or Germany's) surrender quite possibly saved his life and, further, would finally allow him to get on with a civilian existence. But as civilian and veteran voices make clear, a whole range of complex experiences and emotions accompanied the end of World War II.

Newspapers across the nation provided extensive coverage of the surrender days and the so-called "victory days," and Minnesota's dailies were no exception. Perhaps because Japan's surrender meant the end of all fighting, this event generated a higher output of print journalism. Prominent in local papers such as the Duluth *Herald* and *News-Tribune,* St. Paul *Dispatch* and *Pioneer Press,* and Minneapolis *Star* were headlines proclaiming "PEACE" or "Japs Surrender" or "WAR OVER" and photo essays on celebrations in those cities. Tens of thousands flocked to downtown locations like Superior Street in Duluth, Seventh and Wabasha in St. Paul, and Nicollet Avenue in Minneapolis, and smaller impromptu celebrations were held in city neighborhoods and smaller towns as well.

For many who recall this period, the end of the Pacific war left the strongest mark. Some describe the chaos and hectic activity, even violence, that accompanied announcement of the surrender as word spread during the early evening hours of 14 August—firsthand accounts from St. Paul and Minneapolis, but also from Minnesotans in Honolulu and San Francisco, are electric and full of excitement, even fear. All-night celebrations, many of them unplanned, took place in cities nationwide, but not everyone participated or even took notice; some admit to staying home. And many residents of smaller towns have memories of subdued celebrations or of none taking place at all. The contrast is striking.

Men and women in the military often viewed the end of hostilities in Europe and the Pacific in a manner that contrasts significantly with reactions from those back home. Most notable, and perhaps surprising at first glance, was the overwhelmingly quiet sense of relief felt by those in combat areas, their reactions generally lacking the outbursts seen in American Home Front cities. Particularly subdued in their responses were men in front-line units, especially those in Europe who after May faced the real possibility of being shipped to the Pacific for the invasion of Japan.

But beyond initial snapshot images of a day or an evening, regardless of where in the world it was spent, quite a number of people reflected at a deeper level about the larger meaning of the war's end. There were responses marked by emotion and thoughts of others, of loved ones, and how the conclusion of the war would affect them all. "One chapter had ended," a civilian resident of Minneapolis recounted, "and we all recognized that. But while we were happy about the war finally ending, it didn't take us long to get a bit nervous wondering about what was going to happen next."

◆   ◆   ◆

When the Pacific war ended, submariner Dick Baumann of the USS *Greenling* was in San Francisco. He vividly recalls how people reacted to the news.

I REMEMBER V-J Day. We were in Mare Island Navy Yard for an overhaul. We went up to San Francisco for the weekend. Well, unbeknownst to us, why, V-J Day happened. . . . The streets were so bad in San Francisco, so dangerous even to be on them. We were on Fifth and Market, and we went into our hotel room about nine-thirty or ten o'clock at night. The people that were really acting up were these kids that had never even seen a submarine or been out to sea. They were tearing the town apart. Civilians and military people. . . . They were the younger generation. We always thought, "Damn kids—acting up." We had just come back from catching hell, and we didn't appreciate all that.

So we got up in the morning and went to an early movie. We came out of the movie, and the shore patrol caught us right away and said, "What are you guys doing? Where are you from?" We told them, "Mare Island." "What are you doing way up here?" We didn't realize that they had put a limit on the distance you could travel from our base. They said, "Get back to your base as fast as you can." There'd been a restriction—they had to do that to control the people in San Francisco . . . the destructive behavior. . . . It was a mess.

Bernt Opsal, a navy chaplain stationed in the San Francisco area, was by chance in the city on the day the Japanese surrender was announced. Like Dick Baumann, he describes out-of-control revelry and chaos.

I WAS SENT just outside Market Street there, and there were two or three, I think at least three, sailors that saw me and came toward me. I was in uniform. And they said, "There's one. Let's take him." What they were doing is, they were tackling or scuffling with officers. . . . I don't know how prominent that was, but I experienced it. I don't know what they would have done with me.

On the streets, that was terrible. There were sailors there who were drunk. On Market Street they broke the windows of the liquor stores and walked in there and grabbed the whiskey bottles or whatever. People just went nuts. There was a statue on Market Street with a little platform that you went up. Some finally got up on top of it. They knocked the statue down off the platform, and some girl, civilian I think, went up there and presented what her dimensions were. Took off all her clothes. . . . Everybody could see.

I thought, "This is no place for me." So I headed for a church, where they were having a thanksgiving service for V-J Day. It was a service where they had singing and they had prayers of thanksgiving. It was very fine. . . . I wanted to be there for that. The mood was both [jubilation and relief], I think. We rejoiced that God answered prayers, that the war was over.

Excitement and rejoicing, though widespread in Minnesota's cities and towns, did not produce conditions like those in California. Representative memories of war's end in the Twin Cities come from three civilians and one serviceman. All recall in their own way some of the celebrating that took place.

After months of Pacific combat, Leon Frankel, officer and navy torpedo bomber pilot, was stateside in summer 1945, awaiting further training and redeployment. Just as he returned to St. Paul for a period of leave, the war against Japan suddenly ended. An important part of Leon's memory of Japan's surrender was his actual arrival at home. He had not seen his family in over two years.

I WALKED IN on my mother. She was in the kitchen. I'll never forget the look on her face, because I didn't let her know that I was going to be home that particular day. She just knew that I was in California, that I had called. I somehow hurriedly managed to get a flight out. Most of the time you had to take a train, which was like a five-day trip in those days. I managed to get a flight out and walked in, came through the back, through the kitchen door. She was bent over the stove doing something. I came up behind her and sort of grabbed her, and she turned around, and she almost passed out. [*with emotion*] I remember that.

Mildreth Nelson Olson (b. 1922) worked for an insurance company in St. Paul; she remembers chaos and excitement in the downtown streets that May day when Germany surrendered.

V-E DAY was a big day. We were at work, and we were downtown, and we all filed into the street. The downtown streets were jammed. There was a big celebration. I didn't get home very early that day, I remember that. You couldn't get a streetcar. It was one of the most packed times that I can remember downtown St. Paul. Especially because it was in the day, too. Everybody, they just forgot about work, forgot about everything.

In our neighborhood, Midway St. Paul, it was the same. Everybody was calling everybody up. Everybody was very, very happy. Celebrating, but it was a more relaxed feeling.

Mildreth Nelson and fiancé Osmund Olson, at the Nelson home in St. Paul, October 1945. They were married in January 1946.

That same month, her fiancé, Osmund Olson, a tail gunner on a B-17 bomber stationed in England, returned from overseas duty. Millie smiles as she recalls his arrival back in St. Paul.

OZZIE GOT back in August. I remember, he came home on a bus. And the bus station was right across, kitty-corner from where the Fire Marine Insurance Company building was. It was kind of in the middle of the afternoon. And my boss said I could go. So when I knew he was coming, I just tore off and went down and met the bus. I remember that the women were standing in the window watching. [*laughs*] I can remember that. That was . . . [*emotionally; voice trails off*].

He came on the bus, and of course I had no car, so we even had to go to my home on the streetcar. Got his luggage and went home.

St. Paul resident Lavinia Stone Murray had worked and raised her daughter after her husband, James, was drafted into the army in 1942.

I WAS HOME. It was my day off. Then the sirens came on and my mother-in-law was screaming, shouting. Happy shouts. And we went, she went running to the front porch, she was just shouting. I remember I went out. People were walking the streets. The little store on the corner, a lot of people running in and out buying beer. People were mostly shouting. They were so happy it was over.

Doris Shea Strand was living in Minneapolis with her parents as her marine husband Errol prepared to ship out from San Diego for the scheduled invasion of Japan.

I WAS BACK in Minneapolis. That was a wild celebration. I was pregnant at that time, but we all had to go downtown and help in the celebrating. It was just jubilation. The streets were full, and there was no traffic. Everybody was really so joyful and so relieved.

We were on Hennepin Avenue. It was just solid people on Hennepin. Just a lot of hooting and hollering and whatever. I went home early, because I was pregnant and I didn't want to be jostled around. It was a great day. The feeling that, now we can get on with our life.

The biggest relief was that Errol wouldn't have to go back overseas. He'd had one foot on the ship for about six months there. So I thought, at least we don't have to worry about that anymore. We'll still have a life. There was a sense of relief. It was good.

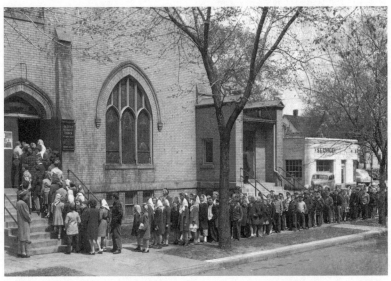

Cause for celebration: worshippers line up at Olivet Methodist Church in Minneapolis on V-E Day

Some small-town residents describe a similar amount of excitement. Lois Breitbarth, who lived on a Wheaton, Minnesota, farm with her parents, recalls the town responding to victory over Germany; V-E Day was somehow more important than Japan's capitulation three months later.

THERE WAS A lot of elation; the church bells rang and whistles blew. Of course in our little towns we didn't have as much as some of the bigger towns; they had the parades and things like that. And the churches, in our church anyhow, it was remembered in our prayers, and everybody was thankful. Thankful that the Lord had seen us through this.

The victory in Europe was celebrated more than the victory over Japan, you know, because that involved so many countries, and so many people in this area had ties to those people, to the people over there in Europe. We were glad that it was over. . . . Japan, sure we knew, but our ancestors weren't *from* Japan, you know; they were from Germany. That is probably the main reason.

Florence Andersen Glasner of Hibbing recalls vividly the end of the European war; her husband, Tony, was serving in the army in Europe.

I WAS VERY happy. I went to Chisholm and bought a bottle of whiskey. And my mother says, "Yes, I'll go with you." On the way I stopped at a woman's house whose husband was in the service, and I hollered, "I'm going to Chisholm to get a bottle. Come down to our house after." So I went and got that bottle and brought it home. My dad had a drink, and I called a couple of the neighbors over. We were very, very happy because these people had children, and their sons or husbands were gone.

In contrast to these many examples are the memories of other small-town and rural residents. At times, it seems as if they are describing other places and other times.

Lawrence Myking was a factory worker in Cloquet, married, and a father. Asked about his memories of 14 August 1945, he recalls the day as a fairly average one.

I WORKED THAT day, Tuesday, August fourteenth. I don't remember any celebration or anything special; I don't recall anything like that here [in Cloquet]. That [*pointing to pictures of downtown St. Paul on 14 August*] was more than we had here. [*pauses three seconds*] I never go to that kind of thing anyhow.

Priscilla Starn lived on a farm outside of Sleepy Eye and was a high school student in 1945. She recalls participating in her small town's spontaneous end-of-war celebrations. She adds that life did not change overnight.

WE HAD A parade down Main Street then in May, after V-E Day. V-J Day, too. The high school band marched, and I was in the band. . . . Everybody was happy. People were standing on the side watching. The mayor was down in the car. . . . But there wasn't much except the band. Same with V-J Day. It was over.

There were no changes yet at that time. Nothing changed in lifestyle. It was still hard. It was a hard life. Almost everybody I think felt relieved, just the fact that nobody was being killed and that things might get better.

An interesting contrast emerged when military personnel who were stationed abroad talked about the end of the war. Although they frequently mentioned a great sense of relief, it was unaccompanied by wild celebrations. Submariner Reynold Dittrich, a veteran of three war patrols in the Pacific in 1944–45, is an excellent representative voice. The end of the European war, he stated clearly and succinctly, meant little to him and to those around him.

THE WAR IN Europe never did concern any of us; we had no part in it. The Pacific—that's all it was about. We had no ties to Europe whatsoever.

But his sentiments were quite different a few months later: in August 1945, he was at sea on the USS *Aspro,* just completing a patrol, as the war ended.

We ended our last patrol the night the war was over. We were at Midway. When we got the news about the Japanese surrender, everybody got drunk. [*laughs*] Everybody was relieved. We were done. There was no more shooting.

Dick Mertz was an Air Corps radio instructor and technician stationed with a B-29 bomber unit on the Pacific island of Tinian.

About a week or ten days before the war actually ended, there was a rumor that got loose in the area that the war had ended. There was a wild celebration. People were firing guns and doing all kinds of wild stuff, celebrating the end of the war. Of course, the next day we realized the war wasn't over yet. [*laughs*] So we were prepared for it. So when the war actually ended, there wasn't nearly the exhilaration that there was ten days before when we thought it was over.

"V" for victory: a group of young employees gathers around the radio for news that the war with Japan is finally over

For me personally, the end of the war meant we were going home, and I guess I was very interested in getting off of that island. An island is tough to deal with, because you're only going to go seven miles one way and two and a half miles the other way.

Catherine Lemmer Brueggeman, an army nurse stationed in France with the 240th General Hospital unit, did a quick reality check when she first heard the news.

WE DIDN'T really know what was going on until it happened. . . . It was something that, it was like a miraculous thought, that people wanted to believe it, but they didn't know if they should or not. It seemed like it was something you'd been praying for and hoping for and waiting for, but once in view it was not real. Everybody was just elated. But still you had the feeling like, is this for sure, final? [*pauses three seconds*] But it was.

Bob Drannen of Cloquet was a member of the regimental weapons company of the Third Marine Regiment, 3rd Marine Division. In August 1945 he was stationed on the Pacific island of Guam, preparing with his unit for the upcoming invasion of Japan. He expected to be among the first ashore, and he knew what that meant.

V-J DAY was the happiest day of our life. We knew that a lot of us would never be living if we'd had to land on Japan. When that surrender happened, everyone was so happy. Officers and enlisted men were all buddy-buddy and everything. That was the greatest day. We had the whole day off. Do whatever you want to do. There was no high-ranking officer that was any better than a buck private. They'd shake hands and do this and do that. Everybody got joy up in their head.

Beyond the celebrating, Bob speaks of his fear of death or serious injury unexpectedly being lifted—a substantial change in outlook from one minute to the next.

What made me feel so good: I knew that I was going to be able to come home. I never knew before. If we'd had to land on Japan, you never knew if you were going to be shot up or if you were going to make it or not. . . . Being maimed, that was worse than being killed. I just can't see that. It's scary. That was my fear; it actually was. But I knew then that I could come home. That was just like black and white.

In August 1945, Red Cross worker Gertrude Esteros was stationed in the Philippines. She distinctly remembers the low-key response to the news that the war was finally over.

WAS IN Panay. I remember that, that evening. We heard it on the short-wave radio. It was suppertime. In the Southwest Pacific in the jungle, when you're near the equator—the Philippines are still near the equator—your difference from daylight to darkness is very sudden. We had started our supper at daylight, and then it was dark. And it gets velvety black dark. Of course there aren't any city lights when you're in a place like that, an encampment. We were hearing this stuff over the radio that was set up on a tree. On a coconut tree. A loudspeaker was up there, and we were hearing this. You know, it was very quiet. Very quiet. There was no sudden cheering. We just listened and said, "Oh, yes. So, it's over." But we didn't jump around. We didn't do any histrionics of any kind. Very low key.

Keith Hansen served with the navy as an officer aboard the landing craft USS *LSM-80.* His ship was en route somewhere in the Pacific when news of Japan's capitulation arrived.

CAN REMEMBER, I was on duty. We were on our way to . . . [*pauses three seconds*] I think we were heading back toward Hawaii. We were out at sea I know.

The news came through at night, where we were. It came through on the radio. The radioman of course was all excited, and he ran all over the ship. [*laughs*] I was officer of the deck. They went and got all the flare pistols, signal flares, and fired them up in the air. They shot up all kinds of stuff.

Personally, I was very relieved. And of course we were all looking to get back home. My oldest son was almost two years old before I saw him. So we were pretty happy.

For some, the results of the war's end were more prominent than what happened on that particular day. For example, navy aviation cadet Waldo Meier, stationed in Corpus Christi, Texas, was finally beginning to fly combat aircraft after almost two years of school and training. The end of the war meant the end of his training—immediately.

MORALE JUST dropped [among the trainee pilots]; the bottom just dropped right out of morale. Guys just said, "Let's just get out of here and go home." They gave us a week off with nothing to do. We didn't have to report except each morning at eight o'clock, we had to show up for muster, and then off the rest of the day. Then they told us we could sign up for release to inactive duty. I was just coming back from the flight line one day, and then here comes the announcement, "Now hear this, now hear this: the papers are at the squadron office." I was just right outside the door when the call came in. I walked in and said, "Where do I sign?" [*laughs*] I think I was the first one on that list, because he'd just put the mike down when I walked in. I signed up to get out. There were about two hundred in our group, I think it was, and seven guys stayed in. That's how the feelings had gone. The war is over. [*pauses three seconds*] Forget it.

Albert H. Quie was a navy aviation cadet in training at Pensacola, Florida, when the war ended in August 1945. Like Waldo Meier, his plans were changed from one day to the next. Al's reaction, however, was different.

I WAS TICKED OFF! Mad! Because I was so intent on getting into combat, that not to have the opportunity to do that was kind of . . . [*trails off*]. You look back on it now, and it was kind of dumb, but I was trained to go and do my job. When the two atomic bombs were used [on Hiroshima and Nagasaki], I knew that that was going to save an awful lot of lives of American soldiers, but still I'd sooner have gotten in there and done it myself. [*laughs*]

I got my wings a month later, but it surely was anticlimactic. . . . And the edge was off. To me it would be like going and training for some big athletic event, and then you found out the event wouldn't be held anymore, and you kept on training. You know? What for? The game was over.

Beyond these memories were many, many others, from both civilians and veterans. This section concludes with three experiences connected to the war: one humorous, one apprehensive, and one poignant. First, navy aviation cadet Waldo Meier remembers that, while the bars and merchants of Corpus Christi wisely closed their doors, some men were determined to celebrate.

WHAT THEY DID in Corpus Christi that day, they closed all the bars as soon as the Japanese surrender was announced. All the bars were closed. That night they even closed the retail stores; they all closed down. The only thing that was open was the movie theaters. There were some of those little ma-and-pa local markets that were open, but that was the only thing.

But they still had a victory parade, and I can still remember this one sailor, he had a quart of milk. Oh, he did some whooping and hollering, celebrating with a quart of milk. You couldn't buy liquor if you wanted to, so that was the best he could do! You've got this guy with a quart of milk, but, boy, was he celebrating!

Minneapolis-born Anna Tanaka Murakami lived through the war in Kure, Japan, raised by her aunt and uncle. In her memory, the end of the war produced no celebrations or hope for the future, only uncertainty and fear in a destroyed country.

WE KNEW WHEN Hiroshima was bombed [on 6 August 1945], that time we knew it was the end of the war, because after that the emperor decided to stop the war. The emperor came on the radio, the first time we heard his voice. We never saw him; I mean we saw him in pictures, but that's all. . . . When the emperor came on [in the aftermath of the two atomic bomb attacks], everybody was supposed to listen to the radio that day; they had all kind of notices up to listen to the radio. So we listened.

Then they said, all the young girls in the city should leave for the country, because all the soldiers [of the occupation troops] are coming in, and they haven't seen a woman for a long time. So young people should go. They warned us on the radio. "If you have someone in the country, leave for the country." Then you were supposed to have about ten days' supply of food and water in the house and don't open the door. Of course, in Kure, the first thing that came in was Australians. They wore the big hats, you know. [*laughs*]

Of course, Japanese are so small, [and] the Australian people were so big. Just looking at the people, it's very scary. First we were so scared, because, you know, [*pauses three seconds*] men. That's why we, I mean, I lived in the country. A month later they told us, "It's safe to come home again."

A crewmember on the USS *Ozark*, Manuel Aguirre piloted a small landing boat at the Pacific invasions of Luzon (Philippines), Iwo Jima, and Okinawa. After the Japanese surrender, the USS *Ozark* was used to transport American ex-POWs from Japan back to the United States. Manuel remembers that many of these former prisoners gambled away much of their back pay before they arrived in San Francisco.

WHEN WE came back from Japan we had over a thousand American ex-prisoners on there. American repatriated prisoners of war. . . . They were all bloated, and a lot of them were sick. We left Japan on September eighth [1945]. We loaded them up and took off with them. We went to Guam, and we got there September twelfth. Then we took them ashore for examinations. They had to give them physical examinations. If they weren't too bad, we brought them back on the ship and we brought them to the States. The ones that were bad, they'd fly them back.

They had this pay coming for all the time that they were over there as prisoners. Three and four years, and they paid them aboard ship. You should have seen the crap games. Boy! Fifty-dollar bills, hundred-dollar bills. And one pile that had two or three thousand dollars in it. A lot of the guys lost all their money. Yes, a lot of those guys lost all their money before they got to the States over here. . . . They were so happy they were spending all their money in the crap games and card games. Blew a lot of money.

War's Aftermath: Postwar Images of Germany

GERMANY'S COLLAPSE in 1945 ushered in the postwar era in Europe. Unwilling to surrender even when defeat was obviously imminent, Hitler demanded that his armies fight on until the bitter end. And the end was bitter—by the time German forces capitulated in May 1945, the country had been economically and politically laid to waste. Germany would remain under joint Allied military occupation until 1949.

Military personnel shared their memories of the 1945–46 period in Germany. Some spoke of the destruction they encountered, especially in large cities; others of harboring angry feelings toward the civilian population. Many had contact with Germans: some perceived a hopelessness among those they met, others worked alongside them without issue. A number of servicemen were willing to speak about participating in the active black market or their involvement in prostitution, but most would do so, especially on the latter topic, only off the record.

✦   ✦   ✦

When the European war ended in May 1945, army first lieutenant and combat veteran Bill Devitt remained with an infantry unit on occupation duty in Germany. The tension and anger of battle did not immediately dissipate.

RIGHT AFTER the war ended, when the occupation duty started, we searched houses. I remember they were little cow towns, little farming towns, and we'd go through and search for weapons, unannounced searches when we were going to search for rifles and other kind of items. That was what we were looking for. Perhaps they thought there might be an uprising or something, I don't know.

At first [the American Military Government] had this policy that you weren't supposed to talk to Germans. Nonfraternization policy. We tried to enforce that. They finally did away with that. That was especially hard to keep a bunch of young American boys away from German girls, so they cut that out. I think probably the first few were cool toward us, but then it got somewhat better.

I think there were no Nazis in Germany when the war ended. One of the famous phrases was *Nicht Nazi,* "I'm not a Nazi." . . . It must have been full of them, or they wouldn't have fought so hard. [*laughs sarcastically*] As time went on I think we got along better. I never saw any arguments or that sort of thing.

I do remember our company ended up in a little town. I wanted to get an American flag up. I was mad at the Germans. . . . They were an advanced people in certain ways. How they could have tolerated such a system as they did? I do recall we were in this little town after the war was over, and I got an American flag. I suggested [to the company commander] that we make the Germans in this little cow town, as they walked by the flag, they would have to salute the American flag or something. He said no to it, and I think he was right. I'm sure I wasn't the only one who wondered at the Germans, who were mad at them. When people try to kill you, naturally you have some feeling about it. Not that those people in those towns were trying to kill me, but. . . . We got along all right. Little cow towns.

We lived in houses. Either we took over the houses and made the German people leave or . . . I was the company executive officer, and the company commander and I lived in the house, and maybe a couple other fellows, the other officers. We had five or six officers in the company. [We] lived in a lady's house, and we'd treat her well. She stayed in the house. She must have had a husband somewhere, but he was gone. Probably hadn't gotten back from the war. We treated her decently. I might have been more abrupt than a lot of people. I had a nagging anger about the Germans when I got home.

Following Germany's surrender, first lieutenant and combat veteran Gerald Heaney of the Army Rangers was reassigned to the Office of Military Government in Munich, Germany. Trained as a lawyer, he worked with others to rewrite the labor laws for the German state of Bavaria.

[IN JUNE 1945] I transferred to [U.S.] Military Government in Munich. I was there from June until October. One day this bulletin came through that said Military Government was looking for a labor relations officer for Bavaria. And then they listed the qualifications. Among the qualifications were a legal degree, with emphasis on labor relations. . . . So at that time, this was before V-J Day, and we didn't know whether the Rangers were going to be split up into cadres, whether they were going to go as a unit. If we had known that we were all going to go together [to the Pacific], I don't think I would have [applied for this position]. But when you didn't know what was going to happen. . . . [So I decided,] I'll make application and sure enough, it only took a few days and I got ordered to go to Munich. I stayed in Munich. It was pretty badly bombed.

In the Bavarian capital city, Gerald had daily contact with German civilians.

I worked with them, because one of my jobs was to rewrite the constitution for the labor movement. During Hitler's days they had these rules that characterized people. They had priority number one—that was if you were full-blooded German who was a member of the Nazi Party—and then down the line until if you were a Jew, you got nothing. So we had to rewrite all of that. I worked with the German civilians in rewriting that. It was satisfying, very satisfying. The most satisfying thing was that you had an opportunity to rewrite the labor laws, and to rewrite the constitution of the labor movement to eliminate the discrimination that had occurred in the past. Try to.

I was working with [German civilians] every day. Their attitude was, they didn't have any alternative but to say yes. But it was always, "If you think this is what we have to do." It was not, "We think this is the thing to do." It was, "You say it; we'll do it." [*pauses three seconds*] Yes.

Ken Jensvold (b. 1914) of the Army Air Corps flew his last combat mission in late April 1945 but remained at his base in the Netherlands until late that year. Germany was less than an hour's journey, and he used the opportunity to travel to parts of the country. What he saw shocked him.

I TRAVELED INTO Düsseldorf [a large city in western Germany], and the destruction was awful, everywhere. I mean, these once-thriving cities were pretty much ruined. The Rhine River goes through Düsseldorf, and these big long bridges going across, they were all shattered and in the river. The only way you could get across was these pontoon bridges, is what they were. I managed to pick up a few souvenirs, [*pauses three seconds*] but it wasn't really pleasant going through these places, because they were, like I say, such total destruction. . . . With me, and with those people I went with, we traveled to Germany mostly out of curiosity. We didn't have much of any reaction one way or another, except we knew there was an awful destruction. And we realized that, in all probability, [as bomber pilots] we had done some of this ourselves.

And kind of hopeless-looking people. . . . There were a lot of people that just kind of looked away from us, and others that wanted to be friendly. [*pauses three seconds*] It was just six of one, half a dozen of another. There were some of each.

Army nurse Martha Ryan in Hameln, Germany, spring 1945

I don't think [I ever felt unsafe], not in daylight. We kept together ourselves, as a group. [*pauses three seconds*] I once saw, I presume they were ex-German soldiers, they were still wearing jackboots and they looked pretty mean and rough. I wouldn't want to be out alone in the dark and meet one of them. Other than that, we never went anywhere after dark; we were always back in our quarters by dark.

Army infantryman Augustine Martinez waited in France until November 1945 before being shipped back to the United States. Soldiers were bored and more than ready to go home; some kept busy with black market activities.

A FTER WE GOT to France and that camp . . . we were doing nothing. Going crazy. We wanted to go home. Now it starts, the black market. Now we go to Paris. . . . [People were] buying soap, GI shoes, clothes, a lot of cigarettes, and cans of food and things like that. Like peaches, cans like that. You can sell all that stuff. You say, "Want any cigarettes?"

[We would get a] two-day pass. Like Saturday and Sunday. So we took all the cigarettes and everything we can sell to the black market. They come to you. There's corners. "Hey, you got cigarettes?" Some of them speak English. They pay with American money, with dollars. That was good money. I picked up a lot of money. I was young. What the hell. You have to take something home, you know. It was quite a bit of money. That was good for me.

Augustine also spoke openly about another topic, one almost all other ex-servicemen avoided or would only refer to when recorders were turned off: prostitution. According to Augustine, finding women in postwar France was not at all difficult, even if one was not looking.

There were women, yes. . . . Prostitutes, girlfriends, one way or the other. A lot of them got married over there, or they got a girlfriend. A lot of them like that. But they had prostitution, too. Just to sleep overnight with them. A lot of them [wanted] cigarettes, a lot for money. . . . They were all over the place. In the bars, you find them all over. All kinds of them. Some of them were half-naked there for you. They touch you, right there in the bar. But me, I keep my money safe and sound. Lay off that stuff. . . . I wasn't looking for that at all. No. Because I was scared of what you'd get. Guys got disease. . . . I don't monkey around. I just take my money and take off.

War's Aftermath: Postwar Images of Japan

LIKE GERMANY, Japan was militarily occupied after surrendering, albeit solely by American forces. Lasting until 1952, the occupation worked to rebuild the country's infrastructure and to feed the population—two enormous tasks. Everyone with memories of postwar Japan remarked on the physical destruction and the sometimes pathetic condition of the civilian population. The American bombing campaign of 1944–45 had reduced many of Japan's cities to ashes and left factories heavily damaged and the transportation system in ruins. U.S. submarines had sunk more than 1,300 vessels and almost completely destroyed the shipping industry. Food was in short supply, especially during the immediate postwar period, and imported foodstuffs were required to boost caloric intake above near-starvation levels.

There naturally was contact between occupier and occupied. Initially, cultural misunderstanding and racism produced trepidation about each side's intentions; some suspicion, even fear, was evident, and contact was minimal. But this situation did not endure. Some Japanese realized that the Americans were able and ready to supply many of their needs, and people sought each other out on various levels. At times this assistance took the form of employment, as American forces hired thousands of Japanese to perform various jobs at military and civilian facilities. In other cases this contact involved soldiers seeking girlfriends or the activities of black market buying and selling or prostitution. Finally, the recollections of a Japanese American woman who spent the war years in Japan supply an important alternative perspective.

◆ ◆ ◆

In November 1945, paratrooper Henry T. Capiz left the Philippines with his unit to serve on occupation duty in the northern Japanese city of Sendai. Henry would spend six months there, until April 1946.

I KIND OF looked forward to going to Japan. I didn't know what to expect. It was another new country, another adventure. Sendai was just leveled. B-29 bombers just did a number on that city. That was the headquarters of the 11th Airborne Division, and we would pick patrols to go into the central mainland. We were patrolling the area, to keep order. . . . We were armed. We were just patrolling. We worked closely with the Japanese police, the civilian authorities.

Once a month we'd draw a patrol duty. We'd go by train into a little town called Furukawa, which was inland [about thirty miles]. We were billeted in what used to be a grade school.

I did some traveling in Tokyo, in Yokohama. They had a real neat train system that somehow escaped the bombing. It was quite fast. We'd catch a train and we'd get on and head for Tokyo. There was a USO down there. The 1st Cavalry Division had a little hotel system down there where we could stay overnight. We would go around Tokyo shopping and all that kind of stuff.

Henry's negative images of the Japanese, formed during basic training and combat duty in the Philippines, changed when he came into close contact with local people. As he remembers it, relations between occupier and occupied were friendly.

It was like night and day. You couldn't believe it. It was their government and it was their army that we were fighting, not the people. They were just as nice as could be. I wandered around the back streets of Tokyo all the time, all by myself. Nobody bothered me or anything. It was not dangerous at all. It may have been other places that I didn't know about, but where I was I never experienced any danger or any hostility.

There was fraternization between GIs and the local civilian population. . . . Some of the guys had girlfriends, but there wasn't too much. Some of the older Japanese sort of frowned on their daughters going out with Americans. I never got to know any women at that time.

We never had any trouble at all with the Japanese. I learned to love the people. They'd welcome us into their homes, and we'd try to talk to them. They would nod. They'd give us sake. . . . I learned to love the people, and I learned to love the area.

Iron Range mineworker Angelo Legueri served during 1943–45 with an army engineer unit, first in Europe, then, after V-E Day, in the Philippines. His wartime
duty concluded with several months in Japan, building accommodations for U.S.
occupation troops. He remembers an encounter with an English-speaking Japanese civilian.

WE LANDED near the waterfront, in Yokohama. The Japanese, a
lot of their structures were made out of wood, their ware-
houses and things. They were all destroyed. They were blown apart
or burned. [American planes] dropped a lot of incendiary bombs on
them, and burned the place down.

I used to smoke a pipe. I was the only one in our outfit that
smoked a pipe, and in our rations there was always pipe tobacco. So
therefore I had a lot of pipe tobacco, a lot of cans of it piled up right
behind my bed.

This one guy [came in our camp one day]; he was a young guy, a
Japanese attorney. He spoke pretty good English. I would say he was
about my age. He came to me. He smoked a pipe, too, but he didn't
have any tobacco. . . . I didn't say anything, but I figured that he
wanted some. So then pretty soon he did ask me for some. I said, "No,
I want to use it." He didn't argue about it. He just talked for a minute
longer and then left. But he came back for three days, and each day
the same story.

I enjoyed talking with him. . . . We never talked about the war
and stuff like that, because some of them, like he, were embarrassed
at what they did. He knew what happened, and he didn't like to talk
about it. So we just talked about conditions. Talked about home, and
stuff like that. . . . He didn't like to talk about the war.

I knew if I gave him some tobacco he'd never come back. I had
him come back about three days. Every day he'd come back for some
tobacco. Finally I said I would give him some. I gave him some
tobacco, and he never came back.

Bill Sadler (b. 1926), an officer on a cargo ship in the Pacific, made several trips
to Japan after August 1945 and has distinct memories of both Tokyo, firebombed

by American planes, and Nagasaki, target of the second atomic bomb on 9 August 1945.

ONE OF THE first trips we made in there, we went into Yokosuka [a port city on Tokyo Bay]. Just by coincidence, we were tied up to the dock, within sight of the [battleship] *Missouri,* when the surrender was signed. We were in Tokyo Bay. I'd seen Europe by that time, but this was awesome. We went in through Yokohama, and we got up to Tokyo, [*pauses three seconds*] and it was just hard to describe. Everything was gone; everything combustible was gone. This was just from the firebombing. . . . There is no way to describe it. Like a great big dump that burned. Nothing identifiable anymore.

Then the next trip we went into Sasebo, Japan [on the southern island of Kyushu], and that's thirty miles away from Nagasaki. So I got permission from the captain to visit Nagasaki with a shore party. Seven of us went ashore. [*pauses three seconds*] They had a train that ran from Sasebo to Nagasaki, an old coal burner. It's only thirty miles, but it took three hours. One way, three hours. We go there and weren't able to go into the train terminal; we had to get off the train early, because the terminal was ruined. It was all blown up and burned. The water tanks had melted, the steel tanks had melted from the intensity of that [atomic] flash.

Clarence Leer was drafted into the U.S. Army in March 1945 and completed basic training just prior to the end of the Pacific war. In September he was among the first U.S. troops to arrive in Japan for occupation duty; he was stationed in Tokyo until September 1946. Clarence provides firsthand observations of Japan and the Japanese in the immediate postwar period.

WE GOT THERE to Yokohama at night for some reason. Got off the ship at night and went to what was called the Fourth Replacement Depot. That's where we were assigned where we were going to go and what we were going to do in Japan. . . . We were there for three or four days, and we slept in a tent at the replacement depot. Then we were ordered to get onto this train into Tokyo.

When we got to Tokyo we could see from the train the bombing that had taken place. Buildings were pretty mashed up, and the train depot was completely, it was just rubble. Rubble all over. It was fixed up enough so they could load people on the train. [Tokyo] was pretty bad, though. One thing that I noticed, they had electricity. . . . They lived in huts, and some of the huts that people lived in were made of whatever they could find. They built a shelter, but they always had a light bulb in there.

As a member of the occupation troops, Clarence had contact with the local population. At first he was apprehensive.

There were Japanese people around, but not very many. To begin with, for the first few weeks, the Japanese people seemed to be afraid of us. We noticed that. When we walked down the street, they would go on the other side of the street. . . . I think that lasted probably about three weeks at least. After that they kind of got a little more friendly.

Interactions with Japanese civilians remained limited.

In the building that we were in they hired some. The maintenance people were Japanese. The army had hired them, so we were in contact with them and we got to know them pretty well. [They spoke English] a little bit. But very little. So we had to use sign language and try to make ourselves understood if we wanted them to sweep the floor or something like that. A couple Japanese that worked in the building there, they became sort of friendly. We didn't really do anything together special, though. [I learned Japanese] a little bit. Say "good morning" and "good-bye" and "how are you." Things like that.

Clarence describes a world in which many activities were illegal but nevertheless tolerated.

To begin with we didn't have very much free time, but as time went on we got more free time. We would go out to the golf course, play a round of golf or something. Had little Japanese boys for caddies. . . . There was a day room in the building, too, that had a pool table and a ping-pong table. You could play cards.

Didn't go to Japanese restaurants. There weren't very many restaurants open while I was there. You could go in the shops and buy whatever. A lot of the guys would trade cigarettes. They would get free cigarettes from the army, and the Japanese were anxious to get them. [They wanted] American money and cigarettes. Couldn't sell them clothes, because they were army clothes. They would have taken it if they could have. It was kind of illegal, but nobody seemed to notice.

I didn't get involved in the black market very much, but there was one guy who was really involved in it. He traded cigarettes. One time I went down to some of the back streets in this place. . . . I was a little worried. He was getting money. They were just paying for it. . . . This area of town *and* what he was doing, too, [made me nervous].

Prostitution wasn't too evident, but . . . it happened. In fact a couple of guys that I know had Japanese girlfriends. I don't know if it was legal or not. It was tolerated.

Inducted into the army in 1945, Edwin Nakasone (left) was stationed at Fort Snelling near Minneapolis for training as a Japanese translator. He then served fifteen months in Japan as part of U.S. occupation forces. Devastation remained at the forefront, even in 1947: "Nothing but rubble all over. . . . Outside the rubble area many tin can shacks were built up. Going from Tokyo down to Yokohama, or down to the south, I could see factories that had been completely bombed, obliterated. Completely destroyed."

Minneapolis-born Anna Tanaka Murakami, who spent the war years in Japan with her aunt and uncle, shares a different perspective on relations between occupation troops and Japanese civilians.

AVOIDING THE [occupation troops] was common. And especially if you come from nice family, they don't want you to get contact with them. My aunt never let me go *talk* to them. . . . You are not supposed to talk to them, that's what they told us. But some people went to work for them, like those [Japanese women] who came back [to the United States] as war brides. That's why people that went to work in the GI [for the American occupation troops], they was desperate to get a job. So people kind of put them down, I mean they kind of looked down on them.

Like my father [who lived in Minnesota], he sent us a lot of things after the war, to Japan. Then people say, "Your father work in the Yankee; that's Yankee money he bought that with." This is *after* the war. . . . . They always kept saying "Yankee," that's the word I heard all the time. Here you would say "Yankee," but the Japanese word they said was a terrible name. Like here, you call black people the n-word.

Immediately after the war ended, the battleship USS *Iowa* made port in Japan, and Walt Radosevich and other marines stationed onboard went ashore. As Walt remembers, it was in many respects a surrealistic experience.

WE WERE ON the ship, and then we were assigned on land. Right when they said the war was over, there was one platoon of us that went in barracks on Japan, to a big city, to Yokosuka. We went to the mayor, confiscated all the guns they had and whatever the government wanted us to get from them.

This big [marine] Joe Lapore, he was six foot six, and those Japanese just couldn't believe it. They looked at him; they worshiped him. The kids hung on him because he was so damn big. They just couldn't get over it. He'd always, "Get out of here! Get out of here!" He'd lost a brother in the war there and wasn't too kind to the Japanese.

The way they lived—Tokyo was so bombed out. . . . It was just completely flattened out by our B-29 [bombers]. The main ginza downtown and everything. We got to go on liberty there—down in the heart of Tokyo, in the ginza—and we went down to a café, downstairs in this bombed-out building. And here an all-Japanese band is playing [the American jazz song] *Sentimental Journey* and that. I said, "What the hell is that?"

Then they had these geisha girls, they'd be there, and you could dance with them. They looked like dolls. Never changed the expression on their face. Beautiful little girls. The guys really, well, they had geisha houses—they were houses of prostitution—and guys would go there like flies. [Pay with] cigarettes, whatever. . . . For a carton of cigarettes you could be king.

There was a darker side to shore liberty. Like many Pacific veterans, Walt remembers being initially supportive of the "wonder weapons" dropped on Hiroshima and Nagasaki, because their use ended the war and assured he would not be part of any costly invasion. But his feelings eventually changed.

I was thankful it happened, until I saw Hiroshima and Nagasaki. We got to see it. . . . And the devastation. I thought, my god. [*pauses three seconds*] Well, maybe it was right, and maybe it wasn't. And then to see the people, how they were, I mean, little kids burned, women, men. Everyone begging for help, and we didn't. And to drop two of them in there, to get both [cities], you know, it was really . . . [*trails off, followed by three-second pause*]. Never again, we never should, anybody. . . . What good did it do to drop something like that, devastating everything? Who's going to fix it? How are you going to bring it back to life, where it was? You can't. . . . It was really, really . . . [*trails off, followed by three-second pause*]. After, I think, probably about a month and a half after, I thought, my god. War, war. Innocent people. What for?

The Postwar World at Home: Opportunities and Challenges

AND SO the war was over. Many American civilians and returning veterans finally had the chance to move on with their lives—or to start new ones. Yet these big changes did not, and could not, happen overnight. Simply transporting home the millions of service personnel stationed overseas in Europe and Asia took the remainder of 1945 and into 1946. But nationwide, a postwar frame of mind established itself almost immediately, driven by people's desire to leave behind the depression and war years as quickly as possible.

The postwar period in the United States is rightly seen as one of remarkable prosperity, with spectacular economic expansion, when the standard of living rose to new heights. Among many positives, one stands out: the Servicemen's Readjustment Act of 1944. Popularly known as the GI Bill of Rights, it provided unemployment benefits for demobilized soldiers, guaranteed loans for the purchase of a small business, farm, or home, and offered education benefits. For millions, the GI Bill opened the door to educational and technical training.

But the immediate postwar period was one of adjustment, too. Millions of servicemen and -women, freshly discharged, were searching for jobs and places to live. Many Americans were keen to acquire the consumer goods they had been denied during the war. But the transition to a peacetime economy took time: factories once again had to retool, and the construction industry switched to building homes. Especially in 1945–46, these factors meant continued shortages, high rents, and a difficult real-estate market.

Adjustments went beyond affording a new car or buying a new house. "Taking off the uniform," one European veteran said slowly over a cup of coffee, "was the easy part. Putting away what happened took a long time." He echoed the feelings of many others: the war may have ended in 1945, but for some it took years or even decades to truly know peace.

✦   ✦   ✦

Gerry Snyder (b. 1921) of Preston was discharged from the Army Air Corps in November 1945 and returned home to his wife and child. He began by looking for an automobile and a good set of tires, neither of which proved easy to find.

HAD TO buy an old car. They were practically junk because they couldn't fix them during the war. Everybody knew the guys were coming home, so they were getting rid of their junk. I got this old '36 Chevy; there was no spare tire or wheel on it. The tires were bald. I'd had a '36 before the war, and I had some tires that had blown out on me down at my mother's house, down in southeastern Minnesota. Anyway, I had to recycle these tires, put boots on them and stuff and use them for tires. I tried to get new ones, but you couldn't get them. One day they had in the paper, "sale on tires." I went around there, the place was—People waiting outside, people were waiting inside. I finally got *one* tire. That was it.

One time it took me three hours to get home because [the tire] had butyl inner tubes. I'd fix it, blow it up, go two blocks and it would blow on me again, and I'd fix it and go two blocks and it'd blow again. I finally stopped at a filling station. He had an old rubber tube that had ninety-nine patches on it. I don't know what, I think I gave him seventy-five cents for it or something, which was pretty good in those days, and put it in and then never had any trouble after that.

Farmer Ervin Borkenhagen was on a waiting list for a new 1946 automobile. He recalls how the local dealer in Truman added numerous "extras" to get around the price ceiling still in effect.

KNOW I put in for a car, and this was right after the war ended. Ford Motor Company, if you paid down $100 or $50, then you'd get your name in line for a car. So I put my money down for a car. That was for a '46 model. See, they didn't make them from '41 on until '46. I know I was on this list longer than some guys in [the town of] Truman, and I was watching to see how many cars would come in. I think they had about eight, ten cars come in Truman before I got mine. Supposedly I was supposed to get about the fifth one. They were a little foxy on a couple of them.

It was a '46 Ford. Moonbeam gray. I remember when we got the call that our car was there. They ended up giving me the car, that only cost $1,215 I remember, and they put everything on it they could. With seat covers and all, just to get the price up that high! . . . They had everything stuck on it they could, to raise the price up, because they could only charge so much. The dealers got more sometimes, but they got it under the table.

James Beck of Palisade was discharged from the army in July 1945 after five-and-a-half years of service in the artillery, two of them in North Africa and Italy. He and his wife, Velda, whom he married in 1944, arrived back in Minnesota late that summer with very little. Having only an eighth-grade education, Jim knew things would not be easy.

M Y INITIAL reaction to being out of the military was, how are we going to live? It was tough; there were still some jobs available in some factories when I got discharged, so I could have had employment for a while. But what skills did I have? I didn't have any money; I didn't even have any clothes, other than army clothes. Fortunately, one of the supply sergeants was from Albany, Minnesota, and we got to be good friends. When I was discharged he asked if I needed anything. . . . So I got, I think it was, fifteen sets of khaki pants and fifteen khaki shirts. And that is all I wore [for the next two years] and even after I went to work. Those khakis lasted for years. Little by little, as I got some money, I'd buy some civilian slacks and shirts and stuff.

After Jim decided to attend a trade school in Minneapolis, he and Velda rented an apartment in the city.

I don't recall anything that was unusually hard to adapt to or anything. Perhaps the fact that you couldn't go to the store and buy anything you wanted. The fact is, the little apartment we had, across the street was a little, tiny grocery store, so we'd get our groceries there. There were no boxes, no paper bags; you stacked them on your arm and carried them home! And it was hot in that upstairs apartment. Velda went all over Minneapolis trying to buy a fan, and they'd just laugh at her! "There is no such thing to be bought as a fan." You know, it's made out of metal. Things like that were annoying.

Army veteran and former POW Paul Peterson returned to the United States from Europe in 1945. While home in Minneapolis on leave, he was married on short notice. He remembers how shortages affected a wedding.

A LOT OF things were hard to come by in those years immediately after the war, because there just *weren't* things. When we got married in 1945 we had a big wedding. It was a tribute to my mother-

Lucinda Holst and husband Art on the farm at war's end

in-law, who organized and orchestrated this whole thing. Amazing the way she did that, because we had two weeks from the time we decided to get married to the day of the wedding—two weeks. She made all the bridesmaid's dresses. Further than that, they couldn't find the colors they wanted because that stuff wasn't available. She made the dresses and then dyed them. All of this in two weeks.

She gathered the ration stamps of friends and neighbors and so on in order to provide the food for the reception and the gas for our honeymoon. Stuff wasn't available. When it came to wedding presents, we wound up with a complete sterling silver set of flatware for twelve people, because there wasn't much you could buy. Again, there wasn't stuff available—you couldn't buy a toaster, or you couldn't buy these kinds of things. They were not ready yet on the market. When it came to buying civilian clothes, I had two suits tailored because you couldn't buy clothes off the rack.

Betty Myers Sarner was discharged from the WAVES in late 1945 and returned
home to St. Paul. By 1946 she was engaged to ex-marine Thorvald "Joe" Sarner.
They, too, faced challenges in the search for consumer goods and affordable
apartments, challenges shared with countless others.

A T THE TIME luckily my uncle worked at [a local appliance store],
a big place. We got a refrigerator and stuff from him. Those
things were hard to find, hard to get at the time.

Shirts, too, I know were real hard to get, for guys. I recall when
we got engaged—at the time I was working at the railroad—I would
go down to Cook's every week. It was a men's store that was kind of
nice. I'd go down there all the time and ask for some shirts, white
shirts, because that's all my husband wore at the time, was white
shirts. That Christmas I just deluged him with white shirts; he
couldn't believe how many I got, but I just bought them and saved
them. Clothing wasn't that easy to get.

And apartments were hard to get. Because I know when my husband and I got married [in 1947] we had to lease an apartment from
my brother. . . . It was my brother that was instrumental in telling us
we could lease his apartment—that's why we chose to get married at
that time. They weren't that easy to get, within our price range.

Navy veterans Pat and Orville Ethier, married in January 1945, were both discharged and back in St. Paul by the end of that year. Pat vividly recalls the
dreadful housing market the young couple faced.

T HERE WAS NO housing available; it was very difficult to find a
place to live. To try to find a place to rent was almost impossible.
We were able to sublease an apartment from a friend of my mother's.
We did that, but then immediately started to look for a house to
buy. . . . We felt we had enough money to buy a house if we could
find one.

You'd see an ad in the paper in the morning, and when we did find
the one that we did, the house was advertised in the morning paper.
There was a morning and evening paper, and this was in the morn-

ing paper, and I saw it. Orv came, and I said, "It's going to be open at four thirty, but we've got to get there before." We were the first ones there, and we went up to the attic to discuss whether or not we thought we should buy it.

We came back downstairs, and there were two more couples there looking at the house. Now we had already given the real-estate man earnest money, and he took it. Then this other fellow came up to him, but the real-estate man said, "I've already taken earnest money from this couple." He says to the real-estate agent, "What are you asking for the house?" "Five thousand dollars," he says. We had offered him $4,500. The man said, "Well, I need a house for my son, and I'll give you that in cash right now!" Of course our eyes pop out, you know, and the real-estate agent says, "No, I've already accepted this earnest money." Anyway, that was how it was. You had to be there ahead of the crowd to even *find* a house that would be anywhere *near* what you could afford to pay for it.

Pat and Orville Ethier on their wedding day, January 1945

With GI Bill educational benefits, young men (and some women) who had been destined for unskilled labor or factory work could now go to school and aspire to the middle class. More than seven million veterans received training or education, slightly more than two million at the college level. Many of those whose memories are part of this volume recognize how fortunate they were to have had this opportunity. Examples of lives changed by GI Bill benefits abound: these representative voices illustrate the impact.

While serving occupation duty in Japan, Clarence Leer of Abercrombie, North Dakota, thought about life after the military and whether he could afford to attend college.

WHEN I GOT out of the army [in December 1946], I tried to decide what I was going to do next. I always wanted to be a civil engineer for some reason, even when I was in high school. I was wondering about help for going to school, because I knew my folks couldn't afford to send me to college. I was wondering how I was going to do that. I'd have to get a job someplace. I had an aunt that lived in Fargo, and her husband had an automobile supply shop. I was thinking I could get a job there with him, and maybe I could make enough money to go to school.

Clarence feels that the GI Bill changed his life.

When I found out how much I could get from the GI Bill, I didn't need to work. This friend of mine had talked to me about it. He was going to go to school, and he wanted somebody to go with him. So we decided we'd go together. We made application to NDAC, North Dakota State Agricultural College [in Fargo].

There was housing made available. It was right on campus. It consisted of a series of Quonset huts. Military surplus, I suppose. They were small, but they were comfortable. It was very cheap.

I think without the benefits college would not have been possible. I would have been back on the farm.

Frank Valentini (b. 1919) of Chisholm, one of eleven children of Italian immigrant parents, left his hometown and a future in the iron ore mines to earn a teaching degree.

I STARTED St. Cloud Teachers College in September of 1946. I took all that time off after being discharged in October [1945]. I enjoyed myself for three or four months; then I went to work for the mining company. I worked in an open pit mine in the summer months. In the meantime I enrolled at St. Cloud.

I always wanted to become a teacher. I fell in love with my eighth-grade American history teacher. [*laughs*] I thought she was beautiful. She was a good teacher. She made history interesting to me. And I wanted to become a teacher. . . . When I first heard about the GI Bill through my brother, I said, "I'm going to do this. I'm going to be a teacher. I'm going to go to teachers college, and I'm going to be a teacher." . . . I never would have followed that route if the GI Bill hadn't been there.

Simply receiving GI Bill benefits did not guarantee success. There was pressure to succeed—and the risk of failure. By late 1945, Jim and Velda Beck had settled in Minneapolis, where Jim was starting a course at Dunwoody Institute, which offered technical training.

I WAS OUT of the service one week when I signed up at Dunwoody. I started school immediately. That was very valuable to me, that additional education I got that I had missed [while in the army].

They were strict at Dunwoody. The government was paying the ex-servicemen's tuition; at that time it was thirty-five dollars a month. If you got one failing mark, they called you into the office and warned you that the government won't tolerate that. If you got another failing mark, you were out. It was tough. They made you study. You couldn't take a chance on getting a couple of failing marks.

Within the months after I had signed up there—there was initially only a couple hundred—after a few months there was two thousand, and there was a waiting list of another two thousand that had signed up. Practically all of them were veterans; I didn't know anybody that wasn't.

Army veteran Tom Takeshi Oye returned from Europe in November 1945 to be reunited with his wife and infant son. Living with his wife's parents in Chicago, he had ambitious plans to use GI Bill benefits to complete his law degree. Though driven to succeed, he could not successfully juggle everything.

I KNEW I wanted to finish law school—that was set. How I would get that law degree wasn't quite set. I knew I had to find a job. I had that law school to worry about, so that meant that I couldn't go to work full-time, in a full-time situation. It wasn't too easy.

I went to Northwestern for two years, and it was physically too much for me. I was working, too, for the American Bar Association. It was part-time. I was going to school in the morning and going to work there about one o'clock. I lost a lot of weight. . . .

It was very difficult [to admit that I couldn't manage job and school and family]. At one point I realized I was just trying to do the impossible. So I quit school for a period of time and found a full-time job and went to law school at night. That was much easier. I finished up in 1953 at DePaul University, at a night school.

Postwar adjustment to civilian life was sometimes a struggle. The transition, depicted in the words of former service personnel, took many forms, including drifting, drinking, and seeking structure. Some described this period as a temporary phenomenon, something they were eventually able to overcome. For others, adjustment became a lifelong battle.

Ed Holtz (b. 1921) was born and raised in the southern Minnesota town of Waseca. He served in the Army Air Corps as a ground technician and spent almost two years in the Pacific. After discharge he attended Stout Institute in Wisconsin (now University of Wisconsin–Stout). He describes how the military way of life affected him.

IN THE MILITARY you were so used to being regimented, this business, and suddenly, I'm on my own. I can eat when I want to; I can go to bed when I want to; I can get up when I want to—wow. It took some doing. You'd think it would be wonderful, it *was* wonderful, but it was kind of scary. You got so you almost *depended* on someone to tell you what to do. [*laughs*] That gets to be kind of easy, too—you don't need to think.

Ken Jensvold of Montevideo, a pilot and officer in both the Royal Canadian Air Force and the U.S. Army Air Corps, served over five years in uniform and flew more than twenty-five combat missions in Europe during 1944–45. Readjustment to civilian life proved too great a shock: after a brief period he rejoined the service—as an enlisted man.

THE THING WAS, after I got out in 1945, I had been in the service a long time. I got out and got into civilian life, and I was totally lost. I had no idea which way I was going; I never thought about this when I *should* have been thinking about it all along. I just thought about what I'm doing now, and tomorrow—that was about it. I drifted and drifted and could *not* get squared away. . . .

I lived at home for a while, trying to get squared away, trying to think of what to do. . . . I'll have to admit, I really didn't think things through very well at this time. [*laughs*] I was coming down off a high, and that was difficult to get squared away, for me anyway. Others went right back into the civilian life and adapted quite quickly. But I couldn't.

After discharge I had thirty days to re-enlist as a master sergeant, if I wanted to. I used most of that thirty days and decided, I'm going to have to get back in again, because I don't know where else to go. So I did—I re-enlisted.

Red Cross worker Gertrude Esteros returned to the United States in 1945 after almost three years in the Pacific. Formerly a university instructor, she was uncertain about what to do next.

I WAS ADRIFT. I really wasn't sure what I wanted to do. . . . Do I want to teach at a university? Is this what I really want to do? That was when I came back, and the University of Minnesota asked me to be on the faculty. I said, if it's a temporary position, if I know that I can leave if I want, with very short notice, I'll take on a temporary position.

The very next summer, that first summer following, [in 1946,] a friend in the department . . . said to me at the end of the [spring] quarter, she said, "Gertrude, why don't we go to Guatemala?" I said, "What is there in Guatemala that's special? Why should we go to Guatemala?" She said they had absolutely magnificent weaving, some of the most wonderful weaving in the world. . . . We only got one-way tickets to Guatemala because we thought we might want to go on someplace farther. Go on to South America somewhere. We had a beautiful time in Guatemala, and we stayed there all summer.

You see, the very first summer back, there was the interest in just wandering. You'd think that I would want to stay put, but I didn't. I had trouble staying put.

Other service veterans do not recall the same sense of uncertainty. One example is submariner Dick Baumann, who served two years in the Pacific on

the USS *Greenling*. After being discharged from the navy in January 1946, he "raised hell" for a time before getting on with his life.

I WAS PRETTY WILD for a few weeks there with this friend of mine, Jack, who was on PT boats, when he got out of the navy. We had enlisted at the same time.

There was [a need to blow off steam]. Well, I hadn't seen Jack since we went into the navy in '42, and we just—we were still young, and still had a lot of life in us left—we raised a little hell for a while. And all the people were getting out.

Most of them drank for a week or maybe two weeks, to celebrate with their buddies that they went into the navy with. Just the idea of being out of uniform, and you could go and come when you wanted to, and nobody told you when to go to bed or what to eat.

We partied for a few weeks, and my father said, "Dick, don't you think you ought to get a job or go to school?" So I decided to go to school down in Chicago for two years. I got out of school and came back to Minnesota in 1948.

Army veteran Alan Woolworth echoes Dick Baumann's experience but personally required more time to work through the process.

M Y DISCHARGE was on December 3, 1945. I was given a one-way railroad ticket. We got into St. Paul—I had left from there almost three years earlier. We rode on this train. By that time there were just a few of us in the passenger car, maybe the caboose or something, on a little train going up to Watertown, South Dakota. They stopped, and I got off at a place about six miles north of my home. I called my parents, and my father and older brother came up and got me and another fella from the same county.

It was nice to see my dad again. He was very understanding, of course; he had had a lot of the same experiences himself in World War I. My mother was at home.

We went and visited relatives and friends. The old familiar scenes. We'd get together at cafés and drink beer nights and talk with each other. We had to catch up on things. . . . We all smoked. A lot of us drank more than we should probably. Kind of stuck together and gradually began filtering into civilian life again. I don't know, it took a long time. . . . I had a great advantage in having a job right away, in my father's contracting business. Being amongst relatives and friends, a lot of my peers. People I knew well.

Alan describes the wartime images that remained in his memory for years after his return from Europe.

I got married quite a few years later. My wife would get irritated at me if I heard a sudden loud noise or something, I'd react, for quite a few years. I would dream, or not dream, but just visualize one of those things, emotions, some of the tragic events. Of course, gradually it began fading into the background, and I deliberately kind of compartmentalized the things, pushed them into a recess in my mind. And in a sense, something like this [interview] is kind of a catharsis.

[7]

War's Legacy

Coming Back, Going Back, Reflecting Back

I N 1945, American society sped ahead after nearly four years of war. Prosperity and conformism became benchmarks of the 1950s, and difficult memories from the World War II years could drift into the past. After all, the U.S. mainland suffered no tangible destruction during the war, and its physical and psychological casualties remained largely out of the public eye.

Hollywood motion pictures provide an excellent window onto cultural values of the period. Films such as *Sands of Iwo Jima* (1949), starring John Wayne, and *To Hell and Back* (1955), featuring decorated combat veteran–turned–actor Audie Murphy, were high-grossing movies in their respective years. One reason for their success at the box office was that each presented World War II as a heroic and worthwhile crusade, demanding sacrifices but resulting in bloodless wounds and, the audience knew, assured victory. The troubling costs of seared landscapes and broken lives remained out of camera range. The myth of the Good War had taken hold, to be further developed through the mid-1960s in such Hollywood epics as *The Longest Day* (1962).

But, as the memories collected here make evident, individual lives are more complex than those of characters in an epic film. Veterans and civilians faced difficulties, some serious, but also found reasons to celebrate. As time passed and this generation aged, some veterans were seized by a desire to revisit those places where they had been soldiers; their motivations varied, as did their experiences upon returning to former battlefields. Finally, all members of this generation sought to put the war into perspective, to try to express what it meant—and what it still means.

Coming Back: Lifetimes of Adjustment

WHILE MEN AND WOMEN, veterans and civilians, faced an array of immediate postwar adjustments, the long-term realities could be equally as daunting. The war was over, but it was not something easily boxed up or forgotten—even though some attempted to do just that. For many combat veterans, images of war recurred in dreams or nightmares, inescapable and troubling episodes from war's reality. Disquieting adjustments for both civilians and military personnel could include a veteran's ongoing search for the answer as to why he was alive when those around him had been killed, a war widow's struggle to move on and make a new life, and a medically deferred man's lifelong guilt over not being able to serve. Such stories generated few if any headlines, were certainly not Hollywood fare, were easily overlooked as the war receded further and further into the past.

But not all was bleak: far from it. A distinct sense of excitement and opportunity came with war's end and discharge from service. Many described an energy, an impatience to move ahead; one veteran who spent three years in the Coast Guard summed up these shared feelings when he remarked, "there weren't enough hours in each day to get done all that I wanted to do." Businesses were started, money was made, careers put in motion. For couples, home life moved toward a sense of normalcy as men returned after long periods away. A St. Paul homemaker and mother put it simply: "We were both so happy to be back, you know, be together. . . . We were just living for that." One might suspect this account to be romanticized, but scores of recollections display a remarkable consistency; only the particulars change.

✦ ✦ ✦

Frederick Branham of Cloquet was an army infantryman with the 70th Infantry Division; he saw combat in France and Germany in 1945.

M Y WIFE says I left as an eighteen-year-old and came home a fifty-five-year-old. [*pauses three seconds*] That's pretty sobering, you know.

There isn't a day goes by that I don't think of my time in service, one facet or the other of it. I also think how fortunate I am. . . . I've grown more mellow, I guess; I don't fly off the handle like I used to. The first two years I was home must have been terrible for my wife, Dorothy, and my children. I didn't sleep well. I didn't function real well. I just, well, I just can't explain it.

At this point Dorothy joins the conversation.

We were sitting on the front porch of the house one day, just sitting and talking, and a car backfired down further on the highway. Everybody kind of looked to see what was going on, and when we turned back Fred was gone. We couldn't find him. We kept calling, "Fred, where are you? Where did you go? Fred?" [*pauses three seconds*] He had crawled under our truck and was laying there curled up.

Frederick pauses several seconds before responding.

That's something you don't get used to.

Navy torpedo bomber pilot Leon Frankel flew more than two dozen missions in the Pacific.

F OR SOMEONE who hadn't been out there it was difficult to explain, to tell the emotions and excitement. [After the service] I started the University [of Minnesota], and I started having nightmares. I'd fight every battle every night.

One of the most traumatic experiences I had was during an attack on Okinawa. We were all stretched out in tandem, flying one behind the other, and I was the second airplane in tandem, right behind the skipper. There was one fighter of ours in our squadron; he got out of position. He came flashing across and ran right into my skipper's airplane. Right in front of me. I looked up and just had time to react— we were that close. . . . There was a big explosion. [My skipper's] blue airplane, one wing was completely off. It was brown; the flames just peeled off all the paint. It was hanging like suspended in the air and was just heading right straight for the ground. I pulled back on the stick as hard as I could, and as I went past, and I could feel the heat from the two airplanes.

I used to have nightmares about that. That was the most traumatic thing, I think. Right in front of me—there it was. *Boom!* And it happened just, just in an instant. That would be a recurring theme all the time in my dreams. I would wake up. I remember my wife giving me a shot with her elbow when I might have yelled out or something in my sleep. That happened several times, for years. I still have them. Every once in a while I have the craziest dreams about flying and combat and various other things.

Gerald Heaney, an officer with the army's 2nd Rangers, landed on Omaha Beach on D-Day and was in combat through the end of the war.

I DIDN'T THINK about the war much until they started to have these unit reunions and to make these movies. And [the historian] Stephen Ambrose's books. Then I thought more about it in the last ten years than in the whole time preceding, than in the previous forty.

For the first year or two I would dream about artillery barrages, because laying in bed you would start dreaming about laying in the foxhole and having . . . [*trails off*]. That kept on for a year or two. Then it's only very rarely since then that I've had dreams. When I saw the film *Saving Private Ryan,* that night I had difficulty sleeping. It had serious impact, I guess. It made things worse than what they really were, and it was bad enough as it was.

Personal adjustments were required when some realized that war had changed them, making them unsure how to fit in or how to relate to others in their new-found civilian life. One example is Bob Michelsen, who spent May–August 1945 imprisoned in Japan after his B-29 bomber was shot down over Tokyo. In 1946, Bob was back in Minneapolis.

I THINK MOST OF what I had was a, a melancholy reaction. I wanted to fight. . . . I picked a few fights down on Lake Street [in Minneapolis], but that was with another soldier, and he and I were both in the same situation. Tommy Tommasco was his name. I said, "Tom, let's go out and beat the shit out of each other." And we did. Several times. My attitude was, I can't die, and nobody can hurt me. And I don't care how much you beat on me, you can *not* hurt me. That attitude was there for more than a year.

[At home] my father asked a few questions, but I never answered them. . . . He wanted to know if I was okay, did I have any deficiencies, and so forth. I think he approached it from that angle, and I said, "No, and don't worry about it." And that ended that conversation. And my mother never said a word; she said, "We are just so happy you're home." Never said a word. [*pauses five seconds*] Nor would I allow them to ask a question. I would not allow it. . . . Nobody knew. They knew I was a veteran, that's all.

I think that the days and the nights were different. During the day [I was in college and] I wanted to learn and accomplish something and decide what the future of my life would be. But at night, I would be lured back to that old army thing of discipline and attack and want to do destructive things. So there was a control thing; I had to control myself, especially when I was alone.

There was difficult sleeping if I tried to *think* of things. But during that period I was also able to disengage the mind, so to speak, and not think of anything. . . . [Dreams were not a problem,] not immediately. The dream parts of it came somewhat later, maybe a couple of years later. At first I just refused to think; not *refused,* I was *able* not to think of it. And many a night, when some of these things would start, I would just say, "no, no, stop it." And it would end.

[Later] I think I became concerned more about my own future, my wife and family. And these things don't end, you know. I mean, they don't end; you don't dream about them every night, they're more sporadic, but they don't end.

Paul Peterson was a prisoner of war in Germany during 1944–45. As Germany collapsed, many POW camps were evacuated and the prisoners force-marched away from the front; conditions were abysmal, and thousands died.

B Y THAT TIME the guy that I was walking with was Bert Doane, from Sioux Falls, South Dakota. I had liberated a blanket somewhere. It was just an awful German ersatz blanket, made with wood chips, I think. We slept in that. We stayed on the main deck in this brick factory [in the town of Duderstadt] because it was close to the latrine. Neither of us were in very good condition by that time, toward the end of the march. One morning I woke up and Bert didn't.

You know, everyone was sick. Nobody knew how sick, because we all looked the same. Everybody had lost weight. He just didn't make it. They took his clothes, boots. He was finally dead. He was buried in a mass grave. Later he was reburied in a military cemetery.

Paul clearly recalls a visit to Bert's parents.

I went to see his folks years later, in 1949. I was working at that time for Capitol Records, on the road as a salesman, and I spent a night in Sioux Falls. Just on a whim I called his folks' house and said I'd like to talk to them. I said that I had been with Bert the night he died. So I went out to their place to see them, and his mother wouldn't believe that he was dead. She was in denial. Absolute denial.

She was convinced that he had escaped and was up in the Swiss Alps and didn't know that the war was over. They had another son, a brother who was younger than Bert [and] who went into the service, and he found Bert's grave and took a picture of it and brought it back home, and she still was in denial.

It was unbelievable. I couldn't. . . . I realized I probably had made a mistake even trying to enter into that situation at all. His dad walked me to my car and said, he just shook his head and said, "I don't know what to do with her. She just won't believe that Bert is gone." The father had accepted it, but not the mother. I don't know if she ever did. . . .

I think talking about things helped me to maintain a relatively healthy perspective on what was going on. The options are, you don't talk about it to anybody, you shut up, and I never felt that was a good thing. I felt that the story needs to be told. It needs to be told for my sake, and it needs to be told for the sake of the German people. It needs to be told for the sake of the horrors of war. This is the kind of thing that happens to people.

I think I certainly have come to terms. When I first got out I had some dreams. . . . [About] the prison facilities, the sickness, the constant itching, from the lice. Knowing that you weren't clean. Then seeing the faces of people that, you know, are long since forgotten. The guards. . . . But I don't dream anymore. That's very rare. I dream about a lot of things these days, but I don't dream about the war.

Earl Nolte served in the Pacific; in 1944 he was twice wounded during island invasions, the second time badly. Returning home to Fairmont in 1945, Earl was a changed person faced with difficult situations.

IN THE HOSPITAL they tried to get us thinking positively, that you were going to be okay and some of these things. "Try to get it out of your mind; don't think about combat. Try to think about something else right away, so you don't dwell on that." Long term, though, I didn't dwell on being hit or anything.

After I was wounded I tried to explain, "What happened to me shouldn't have happened. I shouldn't have been hit. I should be able to do the things I've always wanted to do and stuff like that. Boy, I'm going to do some of these things I want to do."

[When I got back,] I had an attitude that somebody owes me something. That's just the way. For several months, maybe even years, it seemed to plague me. I wasn't concerned about saving money. I bought a lot. I bought a new car. Just my way of getting back what I had coming or something.

[At home with my parents,] it's not something we ever really talked about. I didn't like to talk about it. I never brought it up, and they didn't either. I don't know if it bothered them or not. It never showed. I think they both were just glad to put it behind them. I think just the idea that it's past, I'm okay. I'm getting okay, I'm going on ahead. Once in a while when [my brother] Roy and I were talking there would be some funny thing that I did in service, but nothing related to combat or anything like that.

The thing that hurt me was that my girlfriend thought she was going to be married to an invalid. She just changed right away when she saw me. That kind of hurt. She didn't stick with me. I think she wanted to dump me. . . . We did a lot of things together and had a lot of fun together, but things were just not the same. . . . She was always nice to me and everything like that, but I could never talk to her about getting married. She didn't want to talk about that. "Let's take our time."

Every once in a while I would have a reaction, just out of the blue, kind of where I'd hyperventilate. When I was with her, she had to deal with that. She was very good. She was very concerned and very comforting. I never found out what the heck caused that or why or anything. After a short time it would go away and I would be okay.

I was convinced that that was the girl I was going to marry, so I hung onto that. Prayed a lot about it. That was kind of my thing I was hanging onto. . . . We kept going together until 1953. I think she was probably hoping the same thing I was, that I'd change.

Frank Soboleski of International Falls was an army paratrooper; his unit was in heavy combat in Holland, Belgium, and Germany during 1944–45.

M Y INITIAL REACTION to being out of the military was, it was a letdown. You know, like you had just lost your best friend or something. Everything was so dull and quiet and monotonous. Civilian life, the way of life back in the U.S., it was so slow, and you just had to shift down. Such a slower pace of life, it was hard to adjust to.

My family had changed so much, I had a hard time adapting to them. Everybody was different. . . . My mother and father were old people by then. When I left he was full of vitality and she was— [breaks off]. It was just hard to adjust to it. . . .

Like a displaced person, I had a hard time fitting in. I tried [moving to other places]. Washington. And then Texas. [*pauses five seconds*] Kansas. I went and looked for a [boot camp] friend of mine in Kansas, and I couldn't find him. I came back up here [to International Falls] and went back to college, got a job in the mill [at Boise Cascade]. And that wasn't enough, so I started a construction firm with another partner. And between all the sports activities and the trapping and hunting and fishing, you kind of got that adrenaline slowed down, and you applied it to surviving, making money to buy things you needed to live.

The book and TV miniseries *Band of Brothers* brought everything flooding back. Frank is a surviving member of the unit featured in the book, Company E, 506th Regiment, 101st Airborne.

I never completely got over it. I still have it. It's always there. That's why, for fifty-seven years . . . [*trails off*]. I was real close to completely getting it out of my system, and then they came up with this. [*picks up* Band of Brothers *off table*] It started all over again.

I'd like to *forget* about it, see what tomorrow brings in this world. I don't *want* to live in that other one any more. [*increasingly irritated tone; tosses book back on table*] You never have to endure that anymore; why do I have to be reminded of it? As you grow older, that childish stuff, like anticipation, excitement, and that—I am seventy-six years old; I don't *need* that anymore.

I used to go down to the [local VFW post], and . . . they're just in their glory talking about it. They want to sit there by the hour and talk about it. They really enjoy it. . . . The blood, the broken arms, shooting the enemy, the expression on their faces when they threw a hand grenade, and they came out with their hands up and blood running down their . . . [*trails off*]. I don't want to talk about that. . . . I never could quite gear into that feeling or situation. I just didn't like it. I'd finish my drink and leave.

I met a few friends that I had known in school shortly after I returned with my discharge, and we would get together and go on hunting trips and fishing trips and that, but you weed them out. If they thrive and live on blood and guts and that, then you don't call them up anymore. A couple of them around there are like that. But at my age, they're all dead; they've passed on. [*pauses three seconds*] So I'm pretty much alone. As far as military comrades, I don't have any.

There were many kinds of readjustment—for the families of servicemen, for those who lost loved ones, even for some who had never left home. While these transitions did not involve recovery from combat, they, too, were painful to observe or endure. Gertrude Esteros, who served with the Red Cross in New Guinea and the Philippines, remembers the impact the Pacific war had on a family member.

THERE WERE PATIENTS who went psycho. They had reached the point where they could no longer face it, and they became cata-tonics. . . . They had just lived through too much. I had a cousin—I didn't see him overseas—he lived in Virginia, Minnesota. He was husky, six feet two, what I call a gentle soul. . . . He went through all the important campaigns of the Southwest Pacific—Guadalcanal and the works. He was a medic. His job was to help the wounded and bring in the wounded and the dead in front-line fighting. He had been through just too many campaigns. He never got a respite. . . . He never had a break.

He finally, as they said in those days, he went psycho. He just left it. He was out of it. Catatonic. Just out of it. He was hospitalized about eight months. He came out of it but was never quite the same. He came back to Virginia, Minnesota. His parents had died in the meantime, and he had no siblings. He was a decent sort. He inherited the house, and he had several roomers, and he established a little business, an upholstery business. I was one of the few people he even talked with, when I saw him afterwards. But he was never the same again.

In 1947, ex-WAVE Betty Myers married Joe Sarner, a Marine Corps veteran of island campaigns in the Pacific. They were together for over forty years;

nevertheless, he remained reluctant to talk to her about his experiences, and even as his wife, she hesitated to ask.

M Y HUSBAND, Joe, he and his friend went in the service together as young men. He went in at seventeen or eighteen, with his buddy Dick. They went through so much. He was in New Guinea [in 1943], Peleliu [in 1944], and Okinawa [in 1945]. He was overseas thirty-three months and [went through some tough times]. . . . But then you couldn't get him to talk about it. There's no one *likes* to talk about the war. He went through hell, but you could hardly . . . [*trails off*]. Afterwards, Dick and Joe remained very, very good friends. Every so often he went to his friend, Dick.

I didn't ask a lot of questions. . . . I wish I would have been more curious than I was. I guess at the time I knew a little bit of things. I knew what he had gone through, and I knew it wasn't easy, and I knew he didn't like talking about it too well. I guess at that time I was just so glad that he was home and he was mine, that's all. To this day I regret that I never made him talk about it. . . . I wish I would have. Very much so.

Vivian Linn McMorrow of Howard Lake felt the war's effect, too. Her first husband, Ralph Gland, was killed in action in France in 1944. She remarried in December 1944, but she divorced her navy husband, Tom McMorrow, just over a year later, in 1946.

A FTER THAT I stayed with the folks. My sister came home, too. She had a baby, and I had a baby. My sister went to work, and I stayed home and took care of the kids. She paid me for taking care of her little girl. Then the folks moved to a different house, and we moved with them.

Several years later, Vivian and Tom remarried, but Ralph Gland's memory remained with her.

Oh, I dreamt about him. I dreamt about him for twenty years. But in my dream he never acknowledged me. He would say, "No, I just don't remember you. I just don't remember you." He spoke, but he just couldn't place me, and he was an old man in my dreams. . . . Over and over and over I dreamt about him, but he never, he couldn't quite place me. But when I woke up, I was happy to have seen him.

Vivian explains how her husband, Tom, dealt with the situation.

The kids all knew I had been married before and that my husband had been killed, but Tom was quite possessive. He didn't want any mention of it. [All my pictures,] they were always put away. . . . Ralph was more an intruder into this life of me and my kids . . . so I put it away. It was a part of my life that I shut up and kept private and never let anybody else into it.

Don Marinkovich of Chisholm was classified 4-F in 1943; he spent the rest of the war earning good money as a mineworker on the Iron Range. As other of the town's young men went off to service, however, the guilt he felt was hard to shake.

WE FELT WE were performing a useful function, mining iron ore. But I *did* feel guilty. It was rough lots of times. [If someone said,] "Hey, you're lucky. You're not over there," I couldn't tell anybody how I felt. Couldn't tell anybody. Sure I was lucky—but only *after* the war I felt like that. I don't know, maybe I had more sense, more maturity. Geez, I was nuts, you know, the way I felt during the war, wishing I could go.

And what do you tell your kids when they ask you, "What did you do during the war, Dad?" This was another embarrassment. I kept thinking about that as my kids were growing up. Not that I heard much. I didn't poke my nose in there; I didn't want to know.

I was here. I made the big bucks. Nobody ever *said* it to me, but I kept *thinking* it. I never had any problems with it, never got any snide remarks about that. They say some people really got it. I've heard of instances, but not to me personally. [*pauses three seconds*] Maybe it was in my head more than anything.

For others, postwar memories were positive: some returning veterans were eager to act on dreams and move into new careers. Chisholm native Veda Ponikvar had her postwar plans worked out before being discharged from the navy in 1946—she wanted to get into journalism. In 1947, Veda founded the *Chisholm Free Press and Tribune;* she worked as writer, editor, and publisher of the newspaper for more than fifty years.

I WAS ANXIOUS to get back home because I knew that I wanted to start a newspaper. In the final months that I was in the service I ordered my equipment. I ordered a Linotype. I ordered an offset press. . . . I went into debt. Over my head. My father one time said, "You know, Veda, you owe more than you weigh." [*laughs*]

I invested everything that I had saved, and of course as military people we didn't get paid that much. But I had saved some money, and I couldn't see going out to enter a department store or dress shop and buying all kinds of clothes. I took the gold buttons off of my uniform and sewed navy blue ones on. So honestly, I wore my uniforms with the light blouses for at least two years.

Navy WAVE Veda Ponikvar, 1944

I put in a lot of hours per week. A lot. I would be on the job many, many times at six, seven o'clock in the morning, and you know with your council meetings, your school-board meetings, other organization meetings and events that were going on, there were lots of times when I wasn't in bed much before one o'clock in the morning. . . . What drove me was, I *had* to make a success of this. I had borrowed a lot of money, and I didn't have very much collateral, outside of this equipment, and that wasn't paid for! But [local banks] had faith in me, and they wanted to help. They were happy.

I was the publisher and editor. Always had an editorial, and I wrote most of the stories myself. . . . I think the paper was a success because of the involvement of myself and staff in the community in all of the things that were going on. Being a part of drives and projects that meant a great deal to the town, and just taking part in everything. I think that meant a great deal to the people.

An officer in the Coast Guard from 1943–46, Bill Sadler was always interested in radio and electronics. He adjusted quickly to life after the military and was driven to succeed. Bill's career path took him to an exciting new technology— television.

I DON'T THINK that I had any real emotional hangover when I first hit the street. [*laughs*] I had a pretty good idea I was going to go into electronics; I had already decided to do that; that hadn't changed. But when you don't really know when the war's going to end, you tend to not think ahead too far. You just don't know.

After I got [discharged and] checked into a place to live in San Francisco, I decided it was over. I wasn't going to worry about government or military any more. I felt I had done enough of that. I got a job as a radio service technician at a radio shop, and I worked there, I don't know, several months. My salary, by the way, was ninety-eight cents an hour. [*laughs*] I thought, "There's got to be something better than this I can do." [In my spare time] I actually built a station in the basement [of my apartment building] and put it on the air. I also had the privilege of being one of the first teachers of television out in San Francisco, with Samuel Gompers School. I was teaching basically electronic fundamentals but with an orientation to how they would be used in television.

I was pretty determined. As soon as I got my first job with the television station, I knew that was going to be it. I got to mixing with the broadcast group and the engineers and so on, so I was getting to be known pretty well as a television engineer in the city. It was kind of fun to become known in a profession that was growing like crazy. So I built KPIX, and then I went over and built KRON-TV San Francisco, almost literally built the building. Then in the early 1950s I got involved with Hubbard Broadcasting [here in the Twin Cities].

I was a pretty serious young man. But that's how you get to be director of engineering at NBC when you're twenty-five years old. You have to go at it and know you are going to get there. Hard work.

Delbert Kuehl remained an army chaplain until he resigned his commission in 1947 to move into full-time ministry work. This continued service was rewarding, but there were adjustments to make.

THE HARDEST THING about being a civilian again was, I didn't get military pay any more! [*laughs*] My wife, Delores, and I took this little church in Minneapolis, and I only got fifty dollars a month there. I started out in the service at a hundred and sixty-six dollars a month, but then I made captain, and I got over two hundred a month. We didn't have much income. So it was pretty hard financially, because I wanted to go on to school and do more. But we got by.

I took schooling. I took medical training, and I took a masters degree at the University [of Minnesota]. I did get the benefits of the GI Bill; I couldn't have done it without that.

Even as many former service personnel moved ahead with their civilian lives—marrying sweethearts, going to work, and starting families—they still recognized that their paths differed from those taken by other young men. For example, Les Osvold (b. 1921) of Cloquet, who proudly served two years in the Pacific and was at numerous island invasions, feels that wartime service put him at a certain disadvantage.

I MIGHT HAVE been a little better off today if I hadn't had to fight that war. Financially, mostly. The people at home there were working at good jobs. They were making good money, and they were able to build up their homes. Buy homes and build up their stake for later on, where most of us guys fought that war for about forty-five dollars a month.

And then all these guys that were working, I don't [know] what kind of wages they were getting, but they must have been making good money for the war effort. They were way ahead of us when it comes to financial. We didn't have any stake. I think my wife, Vivian, and I had three hundred dollars between us when we got married. And so when I came home, I just had to go to work. And that's what I did—I went to work. I worked hard and made as much money as possible, and I kept my wife at home and raised the kids. We built this house. Bought this property and built this house.

I'm not resentful of most people, but I think our government could have done a little better job of taking care of the veterans after the war. I think they could have done a lot better job.

For female veterans, like pilot Betty Wall Strohfus of Faribault, the adjustment was often back to a society that still dictated a prescribed role for women. After the Women Airforce Service Pilots program was disbanded in December 1944, Betty returned home to Minnesota before moving to Kansas City to complete an FAA course to qualify as an aircraft communicator.

I FIRST CAME BACK to Faribault. Then I went to Northwest Airlines [in Minneapolis] and showed them my credentials. They would have liked very much to have me, but no way could I go back to an office at that time. I couldn't. Then my friend and I heard about aircraft communications, so we went down to Kansas City and went to aircraft communications school.

Betty worked briefly in aircraft communications, but by 1947 she had moved back to Faribault, gotten married, and started a family. She had to adjust to different expectations—and wait decades for acknowledgment of her service.

I kind of went back in the woodwork, I think. I just went home and did my job as a mother and a wife. I kind of put it in the back of my mind because, even at that time, I was not even an official veteran. I tell you, we were not given recognition. We didn't get recognized as veterans until a resolution was passed in 1978.

I thought no one cared about what we did during the war. I had put all my things in the closet, in boxes, because I didn't see any reason to tell my story. Not until the 1990s did I really believe that people were interested in my story. I sat on my story. My kids said, "Momma flew the planes during the war, and daddy fixed them."

[*laughs*] That was their feeling, you know. "Sure my mom flew, but didn't a lot of the women?" They had no knowledge of what I *really* did during the war. When I gave a program at school, my kids said, "Gee, Mom, I never knew you did that." "Well," I said, "you never asked."

Two final selections accentuate the positive, providing a sense of looking to the future and enjoying what many referred to as a "normal life," without military service, separations, or worry about the fate of loved ones in combat situations.

Lavinia Stone Murray's husband, Jim, finally returned home to St. Paul in December 1945 after three years in the army. Lavinia is certain she emerged from the war years a different person, but one still ready to live her life.

I THINK MY experiences during the war made me more independent. I was used to going to work, getting up and going to work, but now I was making decisions and doing things, what I thought was right for myself and the baby. I think it made me grow up.

As for postwar adjustments, she noted that their three-year-old daughter had a few to make but that she herself was able to focus on the future.

It wasn't hard for me [to adjust to having Jim around the house again]. It was hard for the baby because she wasn't used to him being around and saying, "Uh-uh, don't do that" or "Leave that alone" or something like that. She wanted him to leave. She wanted him to go back to Ayabama, as she called it. So we just had to talk to her and explain to her that he was home to stay, that he wasn't going back. The war was over.

I was just so happy when it was over. That we could get together and live a normal life. . . . It wasn't really a hard adjustment to make. It was something we had been looking forward to. We were just living for that.

A sense of unbounded optimism is evident in this poster from the immediate postwar period

Doris Shea Strand and her husband, Errol, were finally reunited in early 1946 after his discharge from the Marine Corps. The war years had produced new experiences and trying times for them both; Doris remembers the postwar years as a time when things worked out and life was good.

HOUSING WAS *really* at a premium then [in 1946]. People would just fix up little attic corners and charge exorbitant rents for it. But we were fortunate—my Aunt Hannah and Uncle Jim had a home out at Mound [Minnesota], and the house was probably four or five years old at that time. They said, "If you'd like to have the house in Mound, you can have it for thirty-five dollars a month." Okay. So we were tickled. On the last week of May 1946, Errol and I moved out to Mound.

We lived there until 1948, when we bought a farm in Carver. But during this time we had done things like painting and upgrading the yard for the house. When we moved to the farm, then my aunt gave us an amount of money equal to the thirty-five dollars a month we had paid for those two years we had lived there to help us out to get started on our farming project. That was above and beyond.

I was a city slicker, so I wasn't used to farm life. [*laughs*] You know, I'd feed calves and take care of the general flunky type jobs. But I was converted. I didn't work [outside the home]. Our son David must have been about four or five when we moved to the farm.

After we moved to the farm I helped out with different little short-term jobs in Chaska. We just got busy with the Carver County Fair, Carver County Safety Commission, Carver 4-H. We were just busy. . . . We were so tickled that we were home and starting a life together.

Going Back: Veterans Return to Europe and Japan

JUST AS the postwar decades saw veterans stepping away from their war experiences, happy to focus on family, work, and leisure, the 1990s witnessed increasing numbers of these same men, now retired and near the end of their lives, desiring to return to the scenes of their youthful memories. The opening and closing images of Steven Spielberg's *Saving Private Ryan* (1998) come to mind: an elderly James Ryan journeys back to the beaches of Normandy to pay homage to those who saved him, who paid for the deed with their lives. In this way, he closes a chapter of his life. This sentiment is evident in those speaking here, too: their words are of emotion, of healing old wounds, of coming full circle. These men represent the nostalgia of old age come to life. But one veteran of the European war describes the high emotional price these visits demand, one he is not convinced was worth it.

The following six recollections show a broad range of emotion, some of it unexpected, that was an integral part of these veterans' journeys. Five returned to Europe—where the overwhelming majority of return trips have been made—and one to Japan, where he had a special experience, one that touched many lives.

✦   ✦   ✦

Lyle Pearson (b. 1921) grew up in St. Peter. He joined the Army Air Corps in 1943, and by July 1944 was pilot of a B-17 heavy bomber, flying missions from a base in Italy. On 29 December 1944, Lyle was flying his final scheduled combat mission when his plane was shot down over northern Italy; only six of ten crewmembers survived the crash. Lyle spent the final five months of the war as a POW in Germany. In 1998 he returned to the crash site, near the Italian village of San Andrea, a trip that helped to close a chapter in his life.

I DIDN'T WANT to go at first. My wife and I talked about it, and then I talked to Charlie Lyons, my gunner, and he said he would go. So we and our wives went.

I guess I wondered how I would relate to these people, to the Italians. But they were so nice. It was good. In fact, I remember, we were up in this big building having lunch, and somebody said, "Mr. Pearson, there's a [German World War II] Me-109 fighter pilot out here that would like to talk to you." I said, sure, I would talk to him. So I went out. I said, "You flew an Me-109?" "Yes," he said. I said, "You're the guys that scared me so bad I lost all my hair." "No, no, no," he said, "I wasn't over that section of Italy [where you were]." [laughs] We laughed and had a good chat.

Boy, that was great, too, to interact with the people. I kind of thought maybe they might be a little resentful of us, but they weren't. They were very good; they took care of us. They didn't have any gripes or complaints, [even though] they got bombed [during the war] by some of our bombers. There was a bridge down there that we bombed two or three times. They were very good to us. This guy that interviewed us [for local Italian TV], he asked us if we were coming back to occupy the country again. [laughs] It was great going back there and kind of getting closure to a bad incident in our lives.

Chaplain Delbert Kuehl's unit, the army's 82nd Airborne, was in heavy combat in late 1944 as the Allies drove German forces out of the Netherlands. Chaplain Kuehl returned fifty years later to the site where elements of the 82nd crossed

the Waal River under intense enemy fire, suffering very heavy casualties. He
remembers a grateful reception.

FIFTY YEARS after our jump into Holland, in 1994, they had an
anniversary celebration. I had a call from city hall in [the Dutch
city of] Nijmegen telling me, "You have to be here. We Dutch want
to show you how much we appreciate what you did. You're one of the
few that's still alive that crossed the [Waal] river." My wife and I did
go, and they treated us royally. I couldn't believe how gracious they
were in so many ways to us.

Across the river, where we crossed, they have a big beautiful
memorial there with all the names inscribed in granite of those who
died crossing the river. Schoolchildren go to this memorial every
year. I was standing at the memorial on this fiftieth anniversary, and
there was a big panorama picture about our crossing of the Waal. I
was looking at that, and a young Dutch man comes up to me and says,
"Have you heard about that?" "Yes, sir," I said, "I was one of those
who crossed it." He said, "You did?!" He took my name and address,
and sometime later back in the States I get a letter back signed by him
and all the children of his class, thanking me again for helping.

Walt Mainerich of Chisholm served in Europe with the army's 101st Airborne. On
D-Day, Walt's company dropped behind Utah Beach in the early morning hours.
He returned to France in 1994 for the fiftieth anniversary of the Allied invasion.
It was an emotional but satisfying trip.

WHEN MY WIFE and I went back to France in 1994, I was really
surprised how those people treated us, even those little kids.
Waving the American flag and everything. And they'd say, "*Merci,
merci.*" The older ones, you could see tears in their eyes, and they
touched you on the shoulder and gave you a hug. They were smiling
when they did that. So you know we did a good job. They still
thank us over there. . . . They still appreciate it. They thank you all
the time. They offer to help you, to take you where you want to go.

When we went back, we had that ceremony at Omaha Beach. The
cemetery at Colleville. That's where I saw that kid that got killed right

next to me at Normandy. Trevino. He was buried there. I broke down; I cried. I'm not ashamed to admit it. And there was another one there, he was killed when we were making that attack on Carentan. He popped his head over the hedgerow, and he got shot right between the eyes. From me to you away [*two feet*]. And a couple others. Another one a sniper got; his name was Wilson. Another one was Malley. I saw all three of those graves there at Colleville.

They had a big ceremony at the time. I grabbed one of those sheets of paper with names, and I was looking for where the graves were marked. I had a list of where all the Americans in my outfit were buried in France. I had them all marked down. I had to get the map from the cemetery to find out where the plots were. . . . I sat by that monument right in the middle of the cemetery, and I was trying to change the film in my camera, and I was crying. Some guy came, a young guy, and asked me what was wrong. "Can I help you?" "No," I said, "I went to see my buddies." And I wondered, sitting there, if anybody from their families ever came to see them.

First Lieutenant Gerald Heaney landed on D-Day with the army's 2nd Rangers and was in heavy combat later that year at Hürtgen Forest, on the Belgian-German border. Some of the fiercest fighting centered on a hill near the town of Bergstein, Germany. He returned to both sites fifty years later.

RETURNING IN 1994 was a good thing. Yes, it was a very good thing. We went back, and we went to Omaha Beach and Pointe du Hoc. The people of this little town of Grandcamp put on a big celebration for us, and there was a band, and then the president. We had a ceremony at Pointe du Hoc, and President Clinton was there. We were honored at that celebration, and we got a chance to see all these old friends of years gone by.

After that was over a number of us got on the bus, and we went back to the town of Bergstein, in Germany. It was remarkable, because you'd never know that the war had taken place. The pine forest had been decimated during the fighting; there was so much artillery it looked as though a big lawn mower had come over and cut the tops off of all the trees. Those pine trees had been replaced by others. . . . All the towns were rebuilt. You'd never know. There was nothing there that would indicate that there had ever been a war. Even this little town of Bergstein—no monuments, no nothing. [Where the actual battle had been,] it had been converted into a park.

So we went to the top of that hill. Now they've built an iron observation post, with stairs. We went to the top of that, and we saw for the first time how vital that hill was, how far you could see. . . . I had a bronze plaque made; it said, "In memory of the Second Ranger Battalion, who gave their lives in the Hürtgen Forest." . . . I got some special glue from 3M, and we put that sucker up.

Not all veterans found pleasant memories or closure with a trip back to a European battlefield. Frank Soboleski of International Falls, the paratrooper from the unit featured in *Band of Brothers*, tried for decades to erase that time from his memory. The appearance of the film made it even more difficult to forget. Initially resistant, Frank was convinced in 2001 to return to France with other members of his unit as a guest of sponsor HBO, a trip that brought little pleasure.

I ALMOST DIDN'T go to France [in 2001]. I only went because my three kids ganged up on me. . . . Most of the time it wasn't peaceful or humorous or a time of great joy or anything like that. Everything you looked at was a reminder of what was over there during the war. We went to Normandy [Beach] and saw those big bunkers where the Germans had those machine guns just at the right level to rake the people that were coming. We saw all the tools that were used over there, the tanks, the ships, the jeeps, everything else. And the flag, and the names of the people that were there.

When we were at [*pauses three seconds*] Normandy Beach, and everybody had those yellow jackets on [the ones given by HBO to each veteran being honored], it was such a somber situation. Wherever you looked, "killed in action." . . . Just miles and miles of graves. Some of them I knew. The units that were there, they were carved in rock, etched in stone. I didn't enjoy that. Those banged up trucks and tanks and bullet holes—I didn't need to be there. . . . You could live without going to see it.

Thousands of veterans have returned to the battlefields of Europe—far fewer have revisited Pacific battle sites, many of them little more than sandy dots (Tarawa, Wake Island), acres of ocean (Coral Sea, Midway), or barren wastelands (Iwo Jima, Peleliu). And in Japan itself there were no battlefields at all, as the war ended before the planned invasion of the home islands. But Japan was in the memory of one U.S. veteran, a bomber pilot during the ferocious American firebombing raids of 1945—raids far more destructive and deadly than the two atomic attacks, yet largely forgotten.

Art Tomes was born in 1920 and raised in Aurora, on the Iron Range. Commander of a B-29 Superfortress in the Army Air Corps and stationed on the Pacific island of Tinian in the Marianas, Art flew thirty-five bombing missions over Japan. In 1945, in an attempt to force Japan to surrender, the U.S. military launched scores of incendiary raids on Japanese cities, torching urban areas and killing hundreds of thousands of civilians. Art flew a number of such missions, including one in early July to the city of Himeji. In one night, large areas of the city were burned and more than a thousand people killed.

WE BOMBED Himeji on July third, firebombed it and destroyed about 75 percent of it. Burned it down. About one hundred B-29s participated in the raid. I was one of them.

After the war, Art was active in a veteran's organization, the 20th Air Force Association. In the early 1990s, a Japanese veteran navy pilot, Shigeo Imamura, then living and teaching in Himeji, contacted the group, searching for information about the raid that had destroyed the city. A member of the association's board of directors, Art began corresponding with Imamura, who had the idea of bringing together American veterans of the raid and residents of Himeji in a meeting of reconciliation.

We ended up with an invitation then to come over. . . . We took them up on it and went to Himeji in 1995. . . . I felt compelled to go, really. But I was a little bit leery about going, too. I wrote to [former Vice President Walter F.] Mondale, who was then the [U.S.] ambassador [to Japan]. He wrote a nice letter and kind of set my mind at ease. He wrote, "Please come." That was a year before we went. The next year I wrote him again. That resulted in our visit.

We were there in Himeji for about three days or so. The day we got there they entertained us at a great dinner, on the grounds of Himeji Castle . . . and then they had some sake and beer, so tongues got a little loosened. We had a long, long table; we were on one side and the Japanese were on the other side. We had great conversation. . . . Our trepidation was effectively put at rest.

Then the next day we participated in a ceremony at their Memorial to the War Dead, to all the people in Japan that had died in the war. We put some flowers that they'd supplied at the foot of the memorial. We had all their TV crews from Kobe and around the country there taking pictures of us. Then we went to the castle and had a walking tour through the castle, which was very interesting. . . .

That afternoon we had a meeting in the chamber of commerce room. It held about two hundred and fifty people there. It was open to the public, and people applied for a ticket to get in. TV cameramen and reporters were present.

Art had been asked by his hosts to deliver a speech. During our interview, he read excerpts from what he said that day in Himeji.

"Back in the year 1945, when war raged between our two nations, who among us would have ever imagined a meeting such as this, a meeting dedicated to peace? Among those of you who experienced the raid of July 3, 1945 . . . who could have imagined it? Among those of us in our B-29s overhead . . . who could have imagined it? The war, which had raged for so long . . . was still taking a costly toll, a toll of our lives and your lives. And the war had been going on for such a long time that it was hard to imagine what peace would be like. Peace had an unreal quality, like a distant unattainable dream.

"But peace came at last, and our two nations set upon a long road of reconciliation. Here we are, half a century later, looking back on a period of war that now has an almost unreal quality. Yet we know that the war occurred and exacted a cost to us all, that we must never forget. . . . My prayer today is . . . that our gathering here represents an important, positive step towards a fair and equitable peace that lasts. . . . I am very encouraged by the thought that this occasion is not merely a looking back on divisive events of the past but also a building of bonds of understanding that brighten the future."

We had a little mingling at the end of the meeting, where people would come up, and we answered questions. There were about five or six others of us Americans there, too; I wasn't alone. They had several people there interpreting, so you could carry on conversations. There was one gal, her arm was shot off or burned off in that raid. We met a few of these old Japanese soldiers that returned. And I remember one old guy particularly, when he came home to Himeji at the end of the war, his home was gone and burned. His parents were gone because of the bombing. Of course he harbored these feelings for all these years. But he said after meeting us and shaking hands it kind of settled everything down.

After we talked to them it just seemed to set everybody at ease. Myself, too. We found that people, all people, are pretty much the same. It was a positive meeting. . . . The whole thing was satisfying. . . .

I disliked the Japanese from the beginning to the end. I kept up the attitude a long time. . . . It took me fifty years, until I got back there again, to finally settle it.

Reflecting Back: What Was It All About?

As MEMBERS of the World War II generation reflect, more than fifty-five years later, on that long-distant chapter in their lives, what remains? When individuals were asked what the war was all about, what that period meant for them, some discussed their personal situation; others, seeing the war as larger than themselves, expanded their focus to a societal perspective. But virtually all observed distinct "before" and "after" phases when considering these years, recognizing change regardless of the form it may have taken.

✦   ✦   ✦

Perceived proximity to danger affected how service personnel saw their experiences and how they talked about them. Wilbert Bartlett spent 1943–46 in the army, primarily at a training facility in North Carolina and on postwar duty in France. Stationed far from combat zones, he recognized that his war experience was a different one, but a transformative one nonetheless.

THE WAR WAS somewhere else. I was doing things because of the war, but it wasn't affecting me personally at all. So I didn't really have any kind of feeling that I was really in the war, even though I was in the service. How many times did I have to dodge bullets and do those kind of things? It didn't really affect me like it probably would have if I had been overseas in a combat zone or something. I just found the war, where I was, just another job to do while the war was going on.

I guess one of the important things that it changed was the idea that there are a whole lot of different people in the world than you, than your type of people. You see people of different races. You see

Wilbert Bartlett on leave in Switzerland, 1946

different countries that you probably would never see again otherwise. I think it expanded my horizons, so to speak, a little bit more than I would have if there hadn't been a war. I wouldn't have gone to the places that I had, to Greensboro, North Carolina, or France for sure. I wouldn't have been in either one of them. I would have been in areas around my state.

Many women and men acknowledged the various ways their experiences during 1941–45 changed not only them as individuals but also the course of their lives.

Gertrude Esteros, a University of Minnesota faculty member, served almost three years in the South Pacific with the Red Cross. Her war experiences changed her both professionally and personally.

IT WAS something that had to be done. . . . We were doing things that we really didn't think anybody should have to do. I learned then what a horrid waste war is. It's the worst possible way to solve your problems. But also, I learned that human beings can do things that are superhuman. You can't imagine what people are capable of doing. Both good and bad.

I think of the sacrifices that people made for other people. They'll put themselves into absolute harm's way to save somebody. Somebody else who isn't a family member, even. They will do it. They *will* do it. On the other hand, you see the bad things that we did. We were destroying environments. We were destroying other human beings. We were destroying people. Terrible. That's *against* everything that our values, most of us, grew up with.

I might have been as internationally involved as I was even without the war. But the war made me aware of us as part of the total globe, of the whole world. That was the biggest thing. I set out to incorporate that into my teaching. I could do that. I did some art history teaching, and I realized that the students knew only Western culture. They didn't know the rest of the world. I made that a requirement, that we learn about the Middle East and Far East. We learned something about that, and we could learn that history through the arts.

Don Stephenson of Spring Valley is a Marine Corps veteran of the Pacific, including Okinawa in 1945. He can identify some—but not all—of the ways the war had an impact on him.

I HAVE THOUGHT for several years about how the war changed my life, and, using hindsight, I have to believe I was affected more than I realized at the time. Exactly how, I do not know. You would have to ask others who knew me before the war and then analyze me now. I do feel that all of those two-plus years did change me—for the better or the worse, I do not know. Sometimes I feel I shouldn't dwell on it, but it's difficult not to do so.

Specifically, before the war started I had no direction; I had no idea where I was going, absolutely no idea. I didn't have the first inkling about life or what was going to happen. There were no thoughts of college; I had no idea I was going to be able to go to college. Not many in my hometown did go to college. This gave a direction, motivated me.

I learned the value of education. I still do; I really haven't stopped learning. If I wasn't well educated, I have no idea where I'd be now. I'd probably be digging ditches down around my hometown. [*laughs*] And there aren't many ditches down there.

Some women and men considered the larger perspective when asked what the war was all about; among their number was Air Corps veteran Clarke Chambers.

I WAS A PART of my generation, immersed. . . . I was right in the center of it. I shared that experience with my generation. It was an enormously important thing . . . [an] experience of sharing with a generation. And you see, it's a whole *generation,* it's a whole *country* that did that. So many men and women, sixteen million people of my generation went through this experience. And it's nothing since then like that.

I think people respond to the crisis and the needs, maybe; my generation certainly did. To romanticize that and sentimentalize it, though . . . [*trails off*]. I think we were a "pretty good" generation.

I thought, boy, if I were doing this project and writing a book, I'd call it *The Pretty Good Generation*.

But Clarke, who spent many years as a historian at the University of Minnesota, realizes his war experience had an impact on his personal life and career as well.

I was going to be an historian; I knew that at age twelve. I didn't know what it was, but I knew that's what I was going to do. [*laughs*] I think to be a good historian one has to be open. Obviously we don't know how those folks lived in the past; that's a hard assignment. One has to be open to variety, to different systems, to different values. It's a bigger world. And because I was exposed to that bigger world at age twenty-one to twenty-four, it made me an entirely different historian. I became a social historian, a historian of those people in America who never amounted to much—widows, orphans, recent immigrants, the mentally ill, the physically handicapped—and how a society takes care of the least and the aged.

I think I was on my way [to being a historian], but certainly [my experience during the war] accelerated it. And it was an epic experience. And if you're going to be an historian, that's a pretty neat piece.

Navy WAVE Pat Cavanagh Ethier also recognizes the larger picture, and she sees that the war helped broaden her horizons.

WELL, THE war changed everybody's outlook on life. Like I said, I was in school at St. Catherine's [before I enlisted], and I felt, what's the point? There must be something better that I can be doing to hasten the end of the war. Certainly that was your biggest goal, for it all to be over. It disrupted and changed everybody's life. You weren't able to plan for the future, anything in the future, and we never had any conception that it was going to last as long as it did—you never thought *four years*! You couldn't conceive of that.

Had I not joined the navy, would I have ever gone away from St. Paul? I don't know. You know, would I have *ever* gone away, gone some place else? I don't know what the outcome would have been without the war; that really changed things. I guess it was such a big part of our lives, you just never conceived of it ever having been any different because that was it, that was the way it was.

Tom Takeshi Oye, in combat with the U.S. Army in Italy and France in 1944–45, was another who looked beyond his personal situation when considering the changes produced by the war. He believes the most important thing to keep in mind is the effect war can have on human beings.

I REALIZED THAT war is just pure hell, and if you're not careful it can change you from a human being to something other than a human being. You have to be careful, because you're in there doing things that ordinary society does not condone, and that's killing people, and you've got to be sure that you're focused on the purpose of your being there. If you just let your animal instincts take over, you become something far less than human.

And also, very, very acutely I realized that war fought upon your land is just pure hell. I saw this in France, where we were in the battlefield and digging trenches to keep ourselves from being shelled and so forth. Here out in the field, unprotected, are the farmhands harvesting their crops, because that's what they're living on. War on one's land is devastating.

Anna Tanaka Murakami, in Japan during the entire war and enduring bombings and severe shortages, offers a very different perspective on what the war was all about.

I DON'T SUFFER with anything. I mean, even if some trouble happens, I survive. That's why sometimes I get disgusted that the American people complain so much. I feel like, you should go through the war once, and then you don't complain! I did have a German girlfriend, and she felt the same way—American people complain about little things, you know, and we don't do that. We had it bad, and nothing bothers us. If something happens to us, then we say, "Tomorrow will be a better day." That's the way we feel. I can't understand so many people complains for little things. I tell them, I tell my kids, little things shouldn't bother you.

For returning army veteran Alan Woolworth, there was a perceptible change in the small South Dakota town where he grew up—and in the people who lived there.

IN GENERAL, my life changed so much when I got back home. I entered college quite soon, and I spent the next five years or more trying to get along through that. Most of those older men [I had known in service] went back to jobs and their girlfriends or were married.

My hometown of Clear Lake, South Dakota, became much more of a part of the larger world. We had radio and of course newsreels, newspapers, and communication like that. They shagged people like me out of that small town and the surrounding countryside and put us on the broad stage of the world at large. They were in the Marines, in the Navy, the Air Corps, or they were in the Army like I was, and went to all kinds of odd places, Guadalcanal and what have you.

Our outlooks changed so much after you've seen a lot of the much larger world. Our whole lives were changed. It was a much different world that we came back to. A prosperous one, with all kinds of options and opportunities.

Further Reading

FOR BACKGROUND knowledge and reading specific to various themes, these reference works provide a good first step. In addition to signed entries, numerous statistics, and many maps, individual articles are followed by suggestions for further reading.

Dear, I. C. B., general ed. *The Oxford Companion to World War II*. New York: Oxford University Press, 1995.

Sandler, Stanley, ed. *World War II in the Pacific: An Encyclopedia*. New York: Garland Publishing, 2001.

Zabecki, David T., ed. *World War II in Europe: An Encyclopedia*. New York: Garland Publishing, 1999.

THE FOLLOWING WORKS provide overviews of the global conflict and the war's impacts on American society:

O'Neill, William L. *A Democracy at War: America's Fight at Home and Abroad in World War II*. Cambridge, MA: Harvard University Press, 1995.

Overy, Richard. *Why the Allies Won*. New York: Norton, 1995.

Parker, R. A. C. *The Second World War: A Short History*. New York: Oxford University Press, 1997.

Purdue, A. W. *The Second World War*. New York: St. Martin's, 1999.

van der Vat, Dan. *The Pacific Campaign: The U.S.–Japanese Naval War, 1941–1945*. New York: Simon & Schuster, 1991.

Winkler, Allan. *Home Front U.S.A.: America during World War II*. Arlington Heights, IL: Harlan Davidson, 2000.

HERE ARE HELPFUL starting points for major themes addressed in this book:

Basinger, Jeanine. *The World War II Combat Film: Anatomy of a Genre.* 1986.
Reprint, Middletown, CT: Wesleyan University Press, 2003.

Buchanan, A. Russell. *Black Americans in World War II.* Santa Barbara, CA:
Clio Books, 1977.

Daniels, Roger. *Prisoners Without Trial: Japanese Americans in World War II.*
New York: Hill and Wang, 1993.

Doherty, Thomas. *Projections of War: Hollywood, American Culture, and World
War II.* 1993. Rev. ed., New York: Columbia University Press, 1999.

Dower, John. *Embracing Defeat: Japan in the Wake of World War II.* New York:
W. W. Norton and Co., 1999.

————. *War Without Mercy: Race and Power in the Pacific War.* New York:
Pantheon, 1986.

Frank, Richard B. *Downfall: The End of the Imperial Japanese Empire.* New York:
Random House, 1999.

Holm, Jeanne. *Women in the Military: An Unfinished Revolution.* Novato, CA:
Presidio Press, 1993.

Hynes, Samuel. *The Soldiers' Tale: Bearing Witness to Modern War.* New York:
Penguin, 1997.

"Posters of the Second World War." Kittleson Collection. Minneapolis Public
Library. http://www.mplib.org/wpdb/index.asp?.

Werrell, Kenneth P. *Blankets of Fire: U.S. Bombers over Japan During World War
II.* Washington, DC: Smithsonian Institution Press, 1996.

AMONG THE MANY oral history sources on Americans and World War II, these
stand out:

American Folklife Center. "Veterans History Project." Library of Congress.
http://www.loc.gov/folklife/vets/vets-home.html.

Hoopes, Roy. *Americans Remember the Home Front: An Oral Narrative of the World
War II Years in America.* New York: Berkley Books, 2002.

"The Institute on World War II and the Human Experience." Florida State University. http://www.fsu.edu/~ww2/.

Terkel, Studs. *"The Good War": An Oral History of World War II.* 1984. Reprint,
New York: The New Press, 1997.

MANY U.S. SERVICE VETERANS have published memoirs of their wartime experiences. These works are among the best, well written and revealing:

Fahey, James J. *Pacific War Diary, 1942–1945: The Secret Diary of an American
Soldier.* 1963. Reprint, New York: Mariner Books, 2003.

Hynes, Samuel. *Flights of Passage: Recollections of a World War II Aviator.* 1988.
Reprint, New York: Penguin, 2003.

Irwin, John P. *Another River, Another Town: A Teenage Tank Gunner Comes of Age
in Combat, 1945.* New York: Random House, 2002.

Jernigan, E. J. *Tin Can Man.* Clearwater, FL: Vandamere Press, 1993.

Kernan, Alvin. *Crossing the Line: A Bluejacket's World War II Odyssey.* Annapolis,
MD: Naval Institute Press, 1994.

Kotlowitz, Robert. *Before Their Time: A Memoir.* New York: Knopf, 1998.

Sledge, E. B. *With the Old Breed: At Peleliu and Okinawa.* 1981. Reprint, New
York: Oxford University Press, 1990.

List of Interviewees

THE FOLLOWING 135 women and men, civilians and service veterans, were interviewed for this book, March 2001–October 2003.

Toshio Abe, Manuel Aguirre, Bill Amundson, Margaret Amundson, Elmer L. Andersen, Doug Anderson, Frances Arcement, Norman Arcement, Wilbert Bartlett, Dick Baumann, James Beck, Velda Beck, John Behlen, Aileen Boggs, Roy Melvin Boggs, Ervin Borkenhagen, Frederick Branham, Lois Breitbarth, Edmund Broberg, Maybelle Ortenblatt Broberg, Ardice Brower, Lawrence Brown, Catherine Brueggeman, Evelyn Bruss, Henry Buczynski, Henry Capiz, Marie Cavanagh, Clarke Chambers, Mary Clardy, Bill Devitt, Reynold Dittrich, Bob Drannen, Phyllis Dunstone, Gertrude Esteros, Orville Ethier, Pat Cavanagh Ethier, Ken Firnstahl, Leon Frankel, Elaine Bunde Gerber, Warren Gerber, Florence Glasner, Joe Gomer, Jacob Gondeck, James Griffin, Harry Gurrola, Ed Haider, Keith Hansen, Gerald Heaney, Stan Hill, Herman Hinrichs, Lucinda Holst, Ed Holtz, Ken Jensvold, Carl Johnson, Gloria Johnson, Beatrice Kellgren, James G. Kirk, Jr., Karl Klein, Al Kopp, Aileen Krusell, Warner Krusell, Delbert Kuehl, Walter Larson, Agnes Bjorke Leer, Clarence Leer, Angelo Legueri, Dorothy Legueri, Fritjof Lokensgard, Norty Lund, Vivian McMorrow, Aline MacNevan, Walt Mainerich, Donald Marinkovich, Jo Anne Marshall, Lester Marshall, Augustine Martinez, Waldo Meier, Dick Mertz, Robert Michelsen, Fred Miller, Anna Tanaka Murakami, Lavinia Murray, Georgia Myking, Lawrence Myking, Edwin Nakasone, Heloise Neal, Sam Nenadich, Earl Nolte, Mildreth Nelson Olson, Osmund Olson, Bernt Opsal, Les Osvold, Tom Oye, Lyle Pasket, Lyle Pearson, Art Pejsa, Paul Peterson, Alice Pieper, Veda Ponikvar, Albert H. Quie, Walt Radosevich, Maurice Raether, Russell Reetz, Martha Ryan, William Sadler, Bert Sandberg, Betty Sarner, Louis Sass, Bert Schauer, Otto Schmaltz, Lottie Shultz, Gladys Skaarnes,

Bob Snow, Gerald Snyder, Lois Snyder, Frank Soboleski, Ed Sovik, Priscilla Starn, Martin Steinbach, Don Stephenson, Doris Strand, Larry Strand, Betty Wall Strohfus, Janabelle Taylor, Art Tomes, Herb Treichel, Ted Troolin, Frank Valentini, Guadalupe Velasquez, Martin O. Weddington, Orville Westby, Alan Woolworth, Emmett Yanez, Nick Zobenica

Index